REFLE...
F...
DAILY P...

ADVENT **2024** TO
EVE OF ADVENT **2025**

JUSTINE ALLAIN CHAPMAN
KATE BRUCE
TOM CLAMMER
STEVEN CROFT
MAGGI DAWN
LUIGI GIOIA
PAULA GOODER
MALCOLM GUITE
LIZ HOARE
JOHN INGE
MICHAEL IPGRAVE
GRAHAM JAMES
LIBBY LANE
JAN MCFARLANE
MARK OAKLEY
JOHN PERUMBALATH
JOHN PRITCHARD
SARAH ROWLAND JONES
BROTHER SAMUEL SSF
CATHERINE WILLIAMS

With Holy Week and Easter Reflections
by DAVID FORD

Church House Publishing
Church House
Great Smith Street
London SW1P 3AZ

ISBN 978 1 78140 457 7

Published 2024 by Church House Publishing
Copyright © The Archbishops' Council 2024

The opinions expressed in this book are those of the
authors and do not necessarily reflect the official policy of
the General Synod or The Archbishops' Council of the
Church of England.

Liturgical and commissioning editor: Peter Moger
Designed and typeset by Hugh Hillyard-Parker
Printed and bound by CPI Group (UK) Ltd, Croydon CR0 4YY

What do you think of *Reflections for Daily Prayer*?

We'd love to hear from you – simply email us at

publishing@churchofengland.org

or write to us at

Church House Publishing, Church House,
Great Smith Street, London SW1P 3AZ.

Visit **www.dailyprayer.org.uk** for more
information on the *Reflections* series, ordering
and subscriptions.

Contents

Table of contributors

About the authors

Justine Allain Chapman served as a parish priest and in theological education specializing in mission and pastoral care. She is currently Archdeacon of Boston in the Diocese of Lincoln committed to the wellbeing of clergy, congregations and churches. Her most recent book, *The Resilient Disciple*, is for Lent.

Kate Bruce is a serving RAF Chaplain. She writes in the area of homiletics and has published a number of books and articles in this field. Recent volumes are *Out of the Shadows: Preaching the Women on the Bible,* Vols 1 and 2 (SCM, 2021, 2024), written with Liz Shercliff. She offers day conferences in preaching around the country, leads retreats and preaches regularly in a variety of contexts. She is a Visiting Fellow at St John's College, Durham.

Tom Clammer served as a parish priest in two contexts in Gloucestershire before becoming Canon Precentor of Salisbury Cathedral. Since 2019 he has worked freelance as a theological educator and spiritual director. He is a Brother of the Anglican Order of Cistercians.

Steven Croft is Bishop of Oxford. He was previously Bishop of Sheffield and team leader of *Fresh Expressions*. He is the author of a number of books including *The Gift of Leadership* and *Pilgrim Journeys*.

Maggi Dawn is Professor of Theology at Durham University and Diocesan Theologian in Rhode Island, USA. She specializes in reading theology through the lens of literature, art and music. She is a priest in the Episcopal Church (USA).

David F. Ford OBE is Regius Professor of Divinity Emeritus in the University of Cambridge, a Fellow of Selwyn College and a Reader in the Church of England. He is co-chair of the Rose Castle Foundation and the author of *The Gospel of John. A Theological Commentary* and (with Ashley Coxworth) of *Glorification and the Life of Faith*.

Luigi Gioia is the Theologian in Residence at Saint Thomas Church Fifth Avenue, New York City, and Research Associate at the Von Hügel Institute at the University of Cambridge (UK). He is the author of *Say It to God: In Search of Prayer*, the Archbishop of Canterbury's Lent Book 2018 (Bloomsbury, 2017) and *The Wisdom of St Benedict: Monastic Spirituality and the Life of the Church* (Canterbury Press, 2021). His books have been translated into six languages.

Paula Gooder is Chancellor of St Paul's Cathedral, London. She is a writer and lecturer in biblical studies, author of a number of books including *Women of Holy Week; Journalling the Psalms; The Parables* and *Phoebe: A Story*, and a co-author of the *Pilgrim* course. She is also a Licensed Lay Minister (Reader) in the Church of England.

Malcolm Guite is a life fellow of Girton College, Cambridge, a poet and author of *What do Christians Believe?; Faith, Hope and Poetry; Sounding the Seasons: Seventy Sonnets for the Christian Year; The Singing Bowl; Word in the Wilderness; Mariner: A voyage with Samuel Taylor Coleridge*, and *David's Crown: Sounding The Psalms*. He also writes the 'Poet's Corner' column for *The Church Times*.

Having spent the last 16 years teaching in theological education in Oxford, **Liz Hoare** has recently returned to her roots in North Yorkshire. She works part-time at St Bede's Pastoral Centre in York, teaching and offering spiritual direction and wrote *Using the Bible in Spiritual Direction* (SPCK, 2014). She is ordained and has a doctorate in Church History. She has also written on women spiritual writers and is currently working on a book about contentment.

John Inge became the 113th Bishop of Worcester in 2007. Prior to that he had been chaplain of Harrow School, a parish priest on inner-city Tyneside, a Canon of Ely and Bishop of Huntingdon. Trained as a scientist, his academic interest is now in the theology of place.

Michael Ipgrave is Bishop of Lichfield and has previously ministered in Rutland, Japan, Leicester and South London. He has a particular interest in ecumenical, Christian–Jewish and interfaith issues.

Graham James was Bishop of Norwich for almost 20 years until his retirement in 2019. Since then he has chaired the Paterson Inquiry, an independent inquiry for the Government on patient safety in the NHS and private healthcare, and now serves on the Human Fertilization and Embryology Authority. Earlier in his ministry he was Bishop of St Germans in his native Cornwall where he has returned to live, and is an honorary assistant bishop in the Diocese of Truro.

Libby Lane has been, since 2019, the Bishop of Derby. In 2015, she was consecrated as the Church of England's first woman bishop, serving as Bishop of Stockport in the Diocese of Chester. She is a Lord Spiritual with particular care for children and young people, especially Young Offenders, and is lead Bishop for Sport.

Jan McFarlane is Interim Dean of Lichfield and Assistant Bishop in the Diocese of Lichfield. She has served as Bishop of Repton, Archdeacon of Norwich, Director of Communications, Chaplain to the Bishop of Norwich, Chaplain of Ely Cathedral and Curate in the Stafford Team Ministry.

Mark Oakley is Dean of Southwark. Prior to this he was Dean and Fellow of St John's College, Cambridge. He is also Honorary Canon Theologian of Wakefield Cathedral in the Diocese of Leeds. He is the author of *The Collage of God* (2001), *The Splash of Words: Believing in Poetry* (2016) and *My Sour Sweet Days: George Herbert and the Journey of the Soul* (2019) as well as articles and reviews, usually in the areas of faith, poetry, human rights and literature. He is a Fellow of King's College London, where he is also Visiting Lecturer in the department of Theology and Religious Studies.

John Perumbalath is the Bishop of Liverpool, having previously been Archdeacon of Barking and Bishop of Bradwell. He has served as a theological educator and parish priest in the dioceses of Calcutta (Church of North India) and Rochester. He regularly guest lectures in the fields of faith and social engagement and in biblical studies.

John Pritchard was Bishop of Oxford from 2007 to 2014. Prior to that he was Bishop of Jarrow, Archdeacon of Canterbury and Warden of Cranmer Hall, Durham. His only ambition was to be a vicar, which he was in Taunton for eight happy years. He enjoys armchair sport, walking, reading, music, theatre and recovering.

Sarah Rowland Jones was a mathematician, then a British diplomat with postings in Jordan and Hungary, before ordination in the Church in Wales. After eleven years as researcher to successive Archbishops of Cape Town, she returned to Wales, and is now the Dean of St Davids. She serves on international Anglican think tanks, broadcasts regularly and writes on spirituality, public theology and ecumenism.

David Runcorn is a writer, speaker, spiritual director and theological teacher. He lives in Devon.

Rachel Treweek is the Bishop of Gloucester and the first female diocesan bishop in England. She served in two parishes in London and was Archdeacon of Northolt and later Hackney. Prior to ordination she was a speech and language therapist and is a trained practitioner in conflict transformation.

Catherine Williams is a Spiritual Director and Writer. She contributes to various spirituality resources and is the lead voice on the Church of England's Daily Prayer App. She is licensed to the Bishop of Norwich as a Public Preacher and is passionate about poetry, music, theatre and butterfly conservation.

About *Reflections for Daily Prayer*

Based on the *Common Worship Lectionary* readings for Morning Prayer, these daily reflections are designed to refresh and inspire times of personal prayer. The aim is to provide rich, contemporary and engaging insights into Scripture.

Each page lists the Lectionary readings for the day, with the main psalms for that day highlighted in **bold**. The collect of the day – either the *Common Worship* collect or the shorter additional collect – is also included.

For those using this book in conjunction with a service of Morning Prayer, the following conventions apply: a psalm printed in parentheses is omitted if it has been used as the opening canticle at that office; a psalm marked with an asterisk may be shortened if desired.

A short reflection is provided on either the Old or New Testament reading. Popular writers, experienced ministers, biblical scholars and theologians all contribute to this series, bringing with them their own emphases, enthusiasms and approaches to biblical interpretation.

Regular users of Morning Prayer and *Time to Pray* (from *Common Worship: Daily Prayer*) and anyone who follows the Lectionary for their regular Bible reading will benefit from the rich variety of traditions represented in these stimulating and accessible pieces.

This volume also includes both a simple form of *Common Worship* Morning Prayer (see inside front and back covers) and a short form of Night Prayer – also known as Compline – (see pp.326–7), particularly for the benefit of those readers who are new to the habit of the Daily Office or for any reader while travelling.

Building daily prayer into daily life

In our morning routines, there are many tasks we do without giving much thought to them, and others that we do with careful attention. Daily prayer and Bible reading is a strange mixture of these. These are disciplines (and gifts) that we as Christians should have in our daily pattern, but they are not tasks to be ticked off. Rather they are a key component of our developing relationship with God. In them is *life* – for the fruits of this time are to be lived out by us – and to be most fruitful, the task requires both purpose and letting go.

In saying a daily office of prayer, we make the deliberate decision to say 'yes' to spending time with God – the God who is always with us. In prayer and attentive reading of the Scriptures, there is both a conscious entering into God's presence and a 'letting go' of all we strive to control: both are our acknowledgement that it is God who is God.

> ... come into his presence with singing.
>
> Know that the Lord is God.
> It is he that has made us, and we are his;
> we are his people, and the sheep of his pasture.
>
> Enter his gates with thanksgiving ...
>
> (Psalm 100, a traditional Canticle at Morning Prayer)

If we want a relationship with someone to deepen and grow, we need to spend time with that person. It can be no surprise that the same is true between us and God.

In our daily routines, I suspect that most of us intentionally look in the mirror; occasionally we might see beyond the surface of our external reflection and catch a glimpse of who we truly are. For me, a regular pattern of daily prayer and Bible reading is like a hard look in a clean mirror: it gives a clear reflection of myself, my life and the world in which I live. But it is more than that, for in it I can also see the reflection of God who is most clearly revealed in Jesus Christ and present with us now in the Holy Spirit.

This commitment to daily prayer is about our relationship with the God who is love. St Paul, in his great passage about love, speaks of now seeing 'in a mirror, dimly' but one day seeing face to face: 'Now I know only in part; then I will know fully, even as I have been fully known' (1 Corinthians 13.12). Our daily prayer is part of that seeing in a mirror dimly, and it is also part of our deep yearning for an ever-clearer vision of our God. As we read Scripture, the past and the future converge in the present moment. We hear words from long ago – some of which can appear strange and confusing – and yet, the Holy Spirit is living and active in the present. In this place of relationship and revelation, we open ourselves to the possibility of being changed, of being reshaped in a way that is good for us and all creation.

It is important that the words of prayer and Scripture should penetrate deep within rather than be a mere veneer. A quiet location is therefore a helpful starting point. For some, domestic circumstances or daily schedule make that difficult, but it is never impossible to become more fully present to God. The depths of our being can still be accessed no matter the world's clamour and activity. An awareness of this is all part of our journey from a false sense of control to a place of letting go, to a place where there is an opportunity for transformation.

Sometimes in our attention to Scripture, there will be connection with places of joy or pain; we might be encouraged or provoked or both. As we look and see and encounter God more deeply, there will be thanksgiving and repentance; the cries of our heart will surface as we acknowledge our needs and desires for ourselves and the world. The liturgy of Morning Prayer gives this voice and space.

I find it helpful to begin Morning Prayer by lighting a candle. This marks my sense of purpose and my acknowledgement of Christ's presence with me. It is also a silent prayer for illumination as I prepare to be attentive to what I see in the mirror, both of myself and of God. Amid the revelation of Scripture and the cries of my heart, the constancy of the tiny flame bears witness to the hope and light of Christ in all that is and will be.

When the candle is extinguished, I try to be still as I watch the smoke disappear. For me, it is symbolic of my prayers merging with the day. I know that my prayer and the reading of Scripture are not the smoke and mirrors of delusion. Rather, they are about encounter and discovery as I seek to venture into the day to love and serve the Lord as a disciple of Jesus Christ.

+ Rachel Treweek

Monday 2 December

Psalms **50**, 54 *or* **1**, 2, 3
Isaiah 42.18-end
Revelation 19

Revelation 19

*'Salvation and glory and power belong to our God,
for his judgements are true and just' (vv.1,2)*

Salvation and glory have not always sat together wholly comfortably in the Christian tradition. Although the mighty acts of God and his tremendous power have been the focus at different points in the Church's life and still are in parts of the Church today, others have drawn attention to the vulnerability of a God who was prepared to die a hideous and shameful death on a cross. Truth and justice were achieved but at a terrible cost.

Jesus was raised from the dead by the power of God, but first he emptied himself of all glory and became obedient to the point of death, as Philippians 2 describes. Christian art has focused sometimes on the glory of the resurrection, sometimes on the cruel suffering of the figure nailed to the cross. Revelation portrays this paradox beautifully, in portraying Jesus as a lion and a lamb, almost in the same breath. The context of chapter 19 is worship and the mood one of noisy, exuberant praise, for truth and justice are always worth celebrating with a Hallelujah. What is being celebrated here is no less than the defeat of evil and all its associates.

As the Advent cry goes up once again this week, keep hold of this hope amidst all the untruths and injustices around us.

COLLECT

Almighty God,
give us grace to cast away the works of darkness
and to put on the armour of light,
now in the time of this mortal life,
in which your Son Jesus Christ came to us in great humility;
that on the last day,
when he shall come again in his glorious majesty
    to judge the living and the dead,
we may rise to the life immortal;
through him who is alive and reigns with you,
in the unity of the Holy Spirit,
one God, now and for ever.

10 | *Reflection by* **Liz Hoare**

Psalms **80**, 82 *or* **5**, 6 (8)   **Tuesday 3 December**
Isaiah 43.1-13
Revelation 20

Revelation 20

'... another book was opened, the book of life' (v.12)

When a book is opened, it yields its treasures within, and what could
be more wonderful than a book filled with life itself? The previous
sentence sounds an ominous note: 'books were opened'. It sounds
like a final reckoning as we stand before the head teacher at the end
of the year or sit with the bank manager who has been examining
our accounts. The judgement theme is prominent in Revelation from
the beginning, where John has his vision of the Son of Man weighing
in the balance the seven churches and commending or reprimanding
their behaviour, depending on their faithfulness.

Advent also focuses our attention on judgement, for it is the second
coming at least as much as the first that lies at its heart. The image
of God as judge has put fear into people's hearts, as medieval doom
paintings still seen in some churches testify, but Advent tells us that
the King is coming to right every wrong, and therefore we have
nothing to fear from his judgement. Indeed, Christians have longed
for God to come again to banish the darkness and act on behalf of
all those who have suffered injustice. The book of life symbolizes the
goodness of God who is on the side of light and life for all creation.

Almighty God,
as your kingdom dawns,
turn us from the darkness of sin to the
light of holiness,
that we may be ready to meet you
in our Lord and Saviour, Jesus Christ.

COLLECT

Wednesday 4 December

Revelation 21.1-8

*'And the one who was seated on the throne said,
"See, I am making all things new."' (v.5)*

Where the translation here has 'See', older versions of the Bible use the word 'Behold', which is more suggestive of an invitation to look, look again, and keep looking until we see what we are meant to see. To behold is to look with wonder, with close attention, and with all our powers of observation.

There has been much destruction in the course of John's visions throughout Revelation: scorched earth, barren wastes, and lakes of fire. Now at last, we are invited to watch as a new heaven and a new earth are presented to us. As we do so, we are given a glimpse of beauty and wholeness beyond our wildest imaginings. The writer seems to be stretching language to its limits with the lavish imagery used to describe this new creation, and no wonder, for God himself is at its very heart.

It is like a bride adorned for her husband; it is a place that knows no sorrow, no death and nothing harmful or out of place will be found there. That this is more than just a fantasy rests on the source of all the newness: the creator and redeemer of all things. This is no fairytale; it is the Christian's true hope. It is what our disenchanted world so desperately needs to behold.

COLLECT	Almighty God,
	give us grace to cast away the works of darkness
	and to put on the armour of light,
	now in the time of this mortal life,
	in which your Son Jesus Christ came to us in great humility;
	that on the last day,
	when he shall come again in his glorious majesty
	to judge the living and the dead,
	we may rise to the life immortal;
	through him who is alive and reigns with you,
	in the unity of the Holy Spirit,
	one God, now and for ever.

Reflection by **Liz Hoare**

Psalms **42**, 43 *or* 14, **15**, 16
Isaiah 44.1-8
Revelation 21.9-21

Thursday 5 December

Revelation 21.9-21

'... the holy city Jerusalem coming down out of heaven from God'
(v.10)

In the Hebrew Scriptures, when the prophets looked forward to a nation restored and in right relationship with God, they focused on the city of Jerusalem, rebuilt with the temple at its centre, a sign that God had returned to dwell with his people. The prophet, Ezekiel, for example, described in graphic detail the way the glory of the Lord departed from Jerusalem and much later how it returned in great splendour (Ezekiel 43.1-5).

In John's vision of the new Jerusalem, however, there is no temple, nor is the city a new version of the old earthly one. The new Jerusalem comes down out of heaven and God is everywhere present within it. This is a central part of God making all things new with heaven and earth now joined together forever. This is what Paul meant when he wrote to the Ephesians of the gathering up of all things in him, things in heaven and things on earth (Ephesians 1.10). As John goes on to describe the dimensions of the new Jerusalem, he makes it clear that God's presence fills its every measure and shines out of every stone.

How might this vision of a world remade encourage us in our worship and witness during this Advent?

Almighty God,
as your kingdom dawns,
turn us from the darkness of sin to the
light of holiness,
that we may be ready to meet you
in our Lord and Saviour, Jesus Christ.

COLLECT

Friday 6 December

Revelation 21.22 – 22.5

'Its gates will never be shut by day – and there will be no night there' (21.25)

It was many years ago, but I can still recall the shock of seeing for the first time a gated house enclosed behind a fenced compound with a locked entrance. It seemed so forbidding and unfriendly to my young eyes and still does now. Open gates signal an invitation to enter and to find a warm welcome waiting. The picture painted here of the new Jerusalem is inviting indeed, with layer upon layer of rich imagery following rapidly one after another.

Much of the imagery recalls the way the Gospel of John refers to Jesus: light that guides, living water flowing crystal clear, leaves that heal and the Lamb himself. Such beautiful imagery is deployed here to present a world full of goodness and beauty, a world that welcomes all who desire to see the face of the Lamb. Three times John refers to the fact that the new Jerusalem will be a place full of light (21.23, 25; 22.5) for the God who created the light of the sun and stars will now himself be the all-pervasive light, shining with radiant beauty.

At last the encouraging words in John's Gospel that the darkness does not overcome the light have become a full and final reality. Advent is here to remind us to watch and wait for the coming of the light in the sure hope that it will come.

COLLECT

Almighty God,
give us grace to cast away the works of darkness
and to put on the armour of light,
now in the time of this mortal life,
in which your Son Jesus Christ came to us in great humility;
that on the last day,
when he shall come again in his glorious majesty
    to judge the living and the dead,
we may rise to the life immortal;
through him who is alive and reigns with you,
in the unity of the Holy Spirit,
one God, now and for ever.

Reflection by **Liz Hoare**

Saturday 7 December

Revelation 22.6-end

'See, I am coming soon' (v.12)

When I put 'Back soon' on my study door it is an invitation containing a promise to wait, because it will not be long before I return. I hope any visitors know that they can trust me to keep my promise. There are two promises made in today's reading: one by the author who testifies to having heard and seen all these things (v.8), and the other is by the Lord Jesus himself, the Alpha and Omega, the first and the last, the beginning and the end. The one who makes the promise that he is coming soon is the one who is 'trustworthy and true' (v.6).

Just as the light referred to in yesterday's reading fills everything with glory, so the Lord Jesus encompasses everything and gathers all things into himself. The Spirit and the bride are to be joined together for ever, heaven and earth are to be united, and everyone who longs for this day to come will be included.

This passage includes some of the imagery that makes up the Great 'O' antiphons traditionally chanted before and after the *Magnificat* at evening prayer from 17 to 23 December. As the intensity of Advent increases, the imagery of the root of David and the bright morning star stirs our hearts to yearn for God's coming.

Maranatha, is the great cry of Advent. Amen, come Lord Jesus.

Almighty God,
as your kingdom dawns,
turn us from the darkness of sin to the
light of holiness,
that we may be ready to meet you
in our Lord and Saviour, Jesus Christ.

COLLECT

Reflection by **Liz Hoare**

Monday 9 December

Psalm **44** *or* 27, **30**
Isaiah 45.14-end
1 Thessalonians 1

1 Thessalonians 1

*'... you received the word with joy, inspired by the Holy Spirit,
so that you became an example' (vv.6-7)*

1 Thessalonians is among the earliest documents of the New Testament to be written and the church at Thessalonica was possibly only a few months old when it received Paul's letter. Here was something new, a radical experiment in living that was intended to form a community of followers of Jesus Christ in the midst of an alien and often hostile culture.

Reading it today with this in mind sheds fresh light on Paul's priorities in addressing them. The grace and peace with which he greets them lead to thanksgiving for these brothers and sisters, closely coupled with words of affirmation and encouragement. Paul has confidence in this small group of believers, because he can testify to the power of the Holy Spirit in them. As a result, they have become an example to all.

It seems that it was their joy in believing that was particularly striking, a quality that keeps appearing in this letter. How true is this of the fellowship of believers to which we belong? Is our joy genuine? Is it evident at all? True joy, the kind that is inspired by the Holy Spirit, stems from lives that have been given a new perspective through being infused with God's own being. The Advent hope helps us to hold fast to this perspective, whatever else is happening around us.

COLLECT

O Lord, raise up, we pray, your power
and come among us,
and with great might succour us;
that whereas, through our sins and wickedness
we are grievously hindered
in running the race that is set before us,
your bountiful grace and mercy
may speedily help and deliver us;
through Jesus Christ our Lord.

| *Reflection by* **Liz Hoare**

Tuesday 10 December

1 Thessalonians 2.1-12

'... we are determined to share with you not only the Gospel of God, but also our own selves' (v.8)

Paul came to Thessalonica from Philippi, where he had been beaten and imprisoned (Acts 16), only to find more opposition and hostility. A small group, including 'leading women', became believers, nevertheless, and Paul regards these people almost as his children, and himself as their nurse, gently tending their souls. There seems to have been a special bond with the Thessalonians and Paul is determined to bare his heart and share his life with them.

He had only a short time with them, and he and his companions gave everything they had to serve them in Christlike ways. He refused to burden them with providing for his needs, but carefully set a good example of Christlike behaviour and taught them about the Lord Jesus, 'urging, encouraging and pleading with them' (v.12).

Thinking back on people who have influenced you most, what was it about them that drew you to pay close attention? For me it was people who took the risk of sharing themselves in ways that did not impose their story onto mine but invited me to see how Christ was with them in bad times as well as good. They may not all have been very eloquent teachers, but their lives spoke volumes and drew me in.

Almighty God,
purify our hearts and minds,
that when your Son Jesus Christ comes again as
judge and saviour
we may be ready to receive him,
who is our Lord and our God.

COLLECT

Reflection by **Liz Hoare** | 17

Wednesday 11 December

1 Thessalonians 2.13-end

'For we wanted to come to you ... but Satan blocked our way'
(v.18)

It's easy to imagine that someone like Paul would always pray in the power of the Spirit and that his prayers would be heard. Surely he prayed earnestly to find a way to visit the Thessalonians who were his 'glory and joy' and about whom he was so anxious. In this letter, we can almost hear the yearning he felt for his children in the faith.

How was it, then, that Satan 'blocked his way' and prevented him from visiting? Paul had been forced to leave Thessalonica by night to escape his opponents who pursued him to the next town (Acts 17). He longed to see them again, but it was not to be. Wondering whether his work had been in vain, he sent Timothy to visit and was reassured by his report of the faith and love present among them, along with their desire to see Paul again (cf 3.6).

Like Paul, we might make plans that seem godly and wise, only to find that things turn out differently. God is not thwarted, but sometimes it is only in retrospect that we can see where he has been at work. Perhaps we can identify with Paul waiting for news also. As we journey through the season of watching and waiting and pay attention to events, both immediate to us and beyond, let that sense of yearning turn us to pray with expectant longing for God's kingdom to come.

COLLECT

O Lord, raise up, we pray, your power
and come among us,
and with great might succour us;
that whereas, through our sins and wickedness
we are grievously hindered
in running the race that is set before us,
your bountiful grace and mercy
may speedily help and deliver us;
through Jesus Christ our Lord.

| *Reflection by* **Liz Hoare**

Psalms 53, **54**, 60 *or* **37***
Isaiah 48.1-11
1 Thessalonians 3

Thursday 12 December

1 Thessalonians 3

'... may the Lord make you increase and abound in love for one another, and for all, just as we abound in love for you' (v.12)

Paul's anxiety for his new converts, whom he had known in person for only a few weeks, shows us someone who needed connection and relationship with those to whom he preached the gospel. He was not the kind of evangelist who sowed the seed and moved on without concern for his hearers. His letter to them shows that he considered the little church at Thessalonica as family and such was the joy that Timothy's good report of them brought him, that it sustained him through a period of distress and persecution (v.7). Filled with joy, it made Paul thankful and even more eager to make a return visit. Meanwhile his letter to them turned into prayer to their Father in heaven, asking for growth in love, strength and purity, so as to be ready to stand before God in confidence.

I have found it helpful when someone who understands and cares for me not only tells me that they have prayed for me, but what they have prayed. Is there someone who needs to hear not only that we have prayed for them in this Advent time of preparation, but the kind of graces we have asked God to grant them – such as courage or peace. We might not be able to visit them, but we can build on Paul's example and pray for spiritual graces that will help them to grow in love too.

Almighty God,
purify our hearts and minds,
that when your Son Jesus Christ comes again as
judge and saviour
we may be ready to receive him,
who is our Lord and our God.

COLLECT

Friday 13 December

Psalms 85, **86** *or* 31
Isaiah 48.12-end
1 Thessalonians 4.1-12

1 Thessalonians 4.1-12

'... aspire to live quietly, to mind your own affairs, and to work with your hands, as we directed you' (v.11)

Paul both prays and spells out some instructions to encourage the Thessalonians to keep growing. He could not give them a Gospel to read or a set of New Testament letters, but he had no qualms about reminding them what he had taught them and how he had been an example to them. He preached an embodied spirituality, wherein our bodies are accorded dignity, and we have regard for the physical and spiritual wellbeing of our brothers and sisters.

Aspiring to 'live quietly' in today's anxious world could be understood as 'stay calm' and as we shall see, the Thessalonians had a particular need to avoid panic in the face of the future. Minding our own affairs also has resonances for a world that seems to require an opinion on everything, preferably one made as public as possible. The instruction to work with our hands has a poignancy in a world where some people are unable to work, and others are prepared to take huge risks to find employment to support their families. It seems that some of the Thessalonians had downed tools to await the second coming and Paul is eager to correct their misunderstanding in this regard.

Overall, in other words, keep on being faithful. Which of Paul's instructions strikes you most this Advent season?

COLLECT

O Lord, raise up, we pray, your power
and come among us,
and with great might succour us;
that whereas, through our sins and wickedness
we are grievously hindered
in running the race that is set before us,
your bountiful grace and mercy
may speedily help and deliver us;
through Jesus Christ our Lord.

| *Reflection by* **Liz Hoare**

Psalm **145** *or* 41, **42**, 43
Isaiah 49.1-13
1 Thessalonians 4.13-end

Saturday 14 December

1 Thessalonians 4.13-end

'We do not want you to be uninformed ... about those who have died' (v.13)

Have you ever sung the rousing Advent hymn 'Lo he comes with clouds, descending?' and wondered what all the imagery means? Christians have frequently tied themselves in knots concerning the second coming and the Thessalonians had likewise become confused about what to expect. Like all the early Christians, they were looking forward to the Lord's imminent return, but to their growing dismay, some of their number were dying and there was no sign of it taking place. Would they miss out and not be part of God's new creation? Paul addresses the issue head on, but – perhaps to their disappointment and to ours – he obviously could not provide exact details of what it would be like. What he does say is that grief is normal, but they do not need to grieve with no hope, for the departed are still part of God's future. They too will meet the Lord when he comes and 'so we will be with the Lord for ever' (v.17).

Today's Old Testament reading from Isaiah 49 uses rich metaphorical language to help us imagine God's future, but we are nowhere given a blueprint of exactly what that will be like or when it will take place. The two essential truths to give us hope for Advent and beyond are that the Lord will come and his followers will be with him for ever.

Almighty God,
purify our hearts and minds,
that when your Son Jesus Christ comes again as
judge and saviour
we may be ready to receive him,
who is our Lord and our God.

COLLECT

Reflection by **Liz Hoare** | 21

Monday 16 December

Psalm **40** *or* **44**
Isaiah 49.14-25
1 Thessalonians 5.1-11

1 Thessalonians 5.1-11

'... encourage one another' (v.11)

The Thessalonians, to whom Paul writes, believed that the end of their lives was imminent. The Day of the Lord, and the end of all things, would not be long delayed. They looked forward eagerly. It was hope, not fear, that drove them.

Paul, though, has both a warning and a word of encouragement. The Day of the Lord would come unexpectedly, 'like a thief in the night'. Hence disciples of Christ were not to waste time calculating when the end would come. (Not all Christians have taken note of his advice down the centuries.) Their salvation in Christ was assured. Despite the tragic state of the world with its wars and famines, there was nothing to fear.

Encouragement is Paul's watchword. He wants the Thessalonians to live entirely in the present moment. That's what matters because they already have Christ with them.

Living entirely with Christ in the present moment is a challenge in a disturbed and warlike world. It's why we still need to encourage one another. A wise old priest once told me that his ministry in his final years was one of encouragement. He was determined not to despair at the state of the world, but to find something positive to commend in people around him, including those who were hard to love. Whom will we encourage today, as part of living fully in the present moment?

C	O Lord Jesus Christ,
O	who at your first coming sent your messenger
L	to prepare your way before you:
L	grant that the ministers and stewards of your mysteries
E	may likewise so prepare and make ready your way
C	by turning the hearts of the disobedient to the wisdom of the just,
T	that at your second coming to judge the world

O Lord Jesus Christ,
who at your first coming sent your messenger
to prepare your way before you:
grant that the ministers and stewards of your mysteries
may likewise so prepare and make ready your way
by turning the hearts of the disobedient to the wisdom of the just,
that at your second coming to judge the world
we may be found an acceptable people in your sight;
for you are alive and reign with the Father
in the unity of the Holy Spirit,
one God, now and for ever.

Reflection by **Graham James**

Psalms **70**, 74 *or* **48**, 52
Isaiah 50
1 Thessalonians 5.12-end

Tuesday 17 December

1 Thessalonians 5.12-end
'Beloved, pray for us' (v.25)

Paul concludes his letter with a series of aphorisms instructing the Thessalonians how to behave: '… encourage the faint-hearted, help the weak, be patient with all … rejoice always, pray without ceasing …' Then, before he signs off, Paul asks the Christians in Thessalonica to pray for him. The confident teacher becomes the one seeking prayerful support.

I recall vividly making my confession for the first time when I was 14. It was an expected part of our confirmation preparation. I was nervous and rather embarrassed. But I've never forgotten the moment when the priest said as we concluded, 'Go in peace; your sin is put away; and pray for me, a sinner.'

Suddenly I realized we were in this together as fellow disciples. This was a different relationship from the one I had at school with my headmaster. He sought nothing from me. He hardly knew me. Until then, I think my image of God was of a distant headmaster, and it was in that spirit I approached my first confession so nervously. Those words of the priest, used by every confessor, gave me a new perspective. Both the priest and I were sinners drawn together on a journey of discipleship, encouraging each other, and above all praying for each other.

Whom will you ask to pray for you today? What impact do you think it may have?

God for whom we watch and wait,
you sent John the Baptist to prepare the way of your Son:
give us courage to speak the truth,
to hunger for justice,
and to suffer for the cause of right,
with Jesus Christ our Lord.

COLLECT

Wednesday 18 December

2 Thessalonians 1

'Paul, Silvanus and Timothy ...' (v.1)

The ascription with which this letter (and the previous one to the Thessalonians) begins is easily overlooked. Paul does not write simply on his own behalf but includes Silvanus and Timothy too. It's a corporate enterprise. When we refer to these letters simply as Paul's, we may forget he does not write in his own name alone.

Timothy is included at the beginning of no fewer than six of Paul's letters. Alongside 1 and 2 Thessalonians, the others are 2 Corinthians, Philippians, Colossians and Philemon. 1 Corinthians comes from Paul and Sosthenes. Uniquely Paul begins his letter to the Galatians by saying it comes from him 'and all the members of God's family who are with me'. Paul is not exercising an individualistic, lone ranger ministry. Who knows just how much these other missionaries contributed to Paul's thinking?

This second letter to the Thessalonians is short and covers the same themes as the first. Some passages are almost identical. According to Acts 18, Paul and Silvanus (also known as Silas) were together for about 18 months in Corinth, so it's likely these letters were written from that location. This second letter may quickly follow the first after reports come through that false teachers were leading the Thessalonian believers astray, and misinterpreting what that first letter said. It was time for some plain speaking from friends. That takes some courage. And it's best done together.

COLLECT

O Lord Jesus Christ,
who at your first coming sent your messenger
to prepare your way before you:
grant that the ministers and stewards of your mysteries
may likewise so prepare and make ready your way
by turning the hearts of the disobedient to the wisdom of the just,
that at your second coming to judge the world
we may be found an acceptable people in your sight;
for you are alive and reign with the Father
in the unity of the Holy Spirit,
one God, now and for ever.

Reflection by **Graham James**

Thursday 19 December

2 Thessalonians 2

'Let no one deceive you ...' (v.3)

Deception is rife in our world. Online financial scams are commonplace. Some deceivers play a longer game, drawing someone into an intimate relationship before relieving them of property and money. Until the deception is revealed, those being deceived frequently believe they possess a firm hold on reality. It can make their friends despair.

If Paul sounds desperate to make his point here, it's because he is arguing with those who refuse to admit their deception. And what is it about? Some Thessalonians believe that the day of the Lord has already come. The signs of that day, e.g. the gift of tongues or miraculous healings, are being mistaken for the day itself, when Jesus comes to complete all things in the final act of history. Perhaps this false belief has led some to give up work or, worse, to believe they have a new moral liberty. Paul reminds them of his teaching about the day of the Lord ('I told you these things when I was still with you'.) He's taught them that a day of judgement must precede the day of the Lord, and it has not yet happened.

Advent reminds us that the Church has lived for two thousand years in an in-between time. Christ has come. He is risen. But God in Christ has not done with us yet. Advent, this time of waiting upon God for his kingdom to come, is a period to build our defences against spiritual scammers.

God for whom we watch and wait,
you sent John the Baptist to prepare the way of your Son:
give us courage to speak the truth,
to hunger for justice,
and to suffer for the cause of right,
with Jesus Christ our Lord.

COLLECT

Friday 20 December

2 Thessalonians 3

'... some of you are living in idleness' (v.11)

Paul had a high doctrine of work. Some members of the Thessalonian Church had given up their day jobs and were waiting for the cataclysmic end of all things, when they would be with the Lord for ever. This combination of spiritual presumption and laziness was guaranteed to touch a raw nerve in Paul. He engages in a tirade against idleness.

Paul reminds his friends that he supported his ministry entirely by the work of his hands. As a tentmaker, he had skills that could be deployed swiftly anywhere. He and his colleagues paid their way ('we did not eat anyone's bread without paying for it'). If we detect defensiveness here, it's probably because there were preachers and teachers in Thessalonica who prided themselves on being paid by the Church, and who may have been living rather well as a result. Paul saw his self-supporting ministry as a sign of the authenticity of the gospel of free and undeserved grace. He did not proclaim Christ to make a living.

As the Church grew, it came to need clergy who gave their entire time to ministry. But whenever the rewards have become too high, corruption has always set in. Paul would not be surprised. In this early letter of Paul's we see why we should thank God for a great revival of self-supporting Christian ministries in our own age, a reminder in themselves of the gospel of free and undeserved grace.

COLLECT

O Lord Jesus Christ,
who at your first coming sent your messenger
to prepare your way before you:
grant that the ministers and stewards of your mysteries
may likewise so prepare and make ready your way
by turning the hearts of the disobedient to the wisdom of the just,
that at your second coming to judge the world
we may be found an acceptable people in your sight;
for you are alive and reign with the Father
in the unity of the Holy Spirit,
one God, now and for ever.

Reflection by **Graham James**

Saturday 21 December

Jude

'... there will be scoffers' (v.18)

This brief letter is full of puzzles. It's not even a letter as such but a general warning to the whole Christian community. Jude says he is the brother of James, most likely the Lord's brother, who became the leader of the Church in Jerusalem. Jude (Judas) is mentioned in Matthew 13.55 and Mark 6.3. He urges his readers to 'remember the predictions of the apostles', as if they are no longer alive. So if it's Jude's work, he wrote it when already old. It was a latecomer for inclusion in the New Testament, perhaps because it cites non-biblical sources such as the Book of Enoch and the Assumption of Moses, a work now largely lost that contained secret sayings of Moses to Joshua.

There is serious internal turmoil in the Church. We don't know what it's about, but 'scoffers' threaten its unity. They live licentiously, 'reject authority' and cause division. The faithful are led astray. Believers live in spiritual peril.

The images and language used in Jude may seem a long way from the Church today. Yet go online and you'll find plenty of scoffing at the authorities within the Church, and many 'grumblers and malcontents ... bombastic in speech, flattering to their own advantage'. It's a prevalent spiritual disease, not confined just to the internet, and can easily draw us into its web. Are we guarding against it as Jude would have us do?

God for whom we watch and wait,
you sent John the Baptist to prepare the way of your Son:
give us courage to speak the truth,
to hunger for justice,
and to suffer for the cause of right,
with Jesus Christ our Lord.

COLLECT

Monday 23 December

Psalms 128, 129, **130**, 131
Isaiah 52.13 – end of 53
2 Peter 1.1-15

2 Peter 1.1-15

'... my death will come soon' (v.14)

The Second Letter of Peter is presented as a farewell discourse given by Peter before he died, a common enough form of Jewish writing. The Church is already well established, perhaps more so than one would have expected in Peter's own lifetime. That's why many scholars doubt whether it was written by the apostle in the form it now takes. It's not mentioned by any Christian writer before the third century AD, though may well preserve elements of his teaching faithfully.

As Peter was the first bishop of Rome, he is frequently identified with the Church at its most institutional. Indeed, the Roman Catholic Church is sometimes described as 'the barque of Peter', with the fisherman-apostle navigating the Church through stormy seas. The Swiss theologian Hans von Balthasar characterized Peter in the Gospels as representing the 'Church of office', the highly organized and authoritative teaching Church, active in defence of her doctrine and faith. In that sense this letter belongs firmly in the Petrine tradition. Peter warns against false prophets and teachers, and is very direct in his language. He is defending the Church resolutely, but in today's passage there is deep affection and kindliness too. Those to whom he writes are invited 'to support your faith with goodness ... and godliness with mutual affection, and mutual affection with love'. These are not the words of an overbearing ecclesiastical autocrat but of a kindly pastor, perhaps one who knows he has made a mistake or two in his own discipleship.

COLLECT

God our redeemer,
who prepared the Blessed Virgin Mary
to be the mother of your Son:
grant that, as she looked for his coming as our saviour,
so we may be ready to greet him
when he comes again as our judge;
who is alive and reigns with you,
in the unity of the Holy Spirit,
one God, now and for ever.

| *Reflection by* **Graham James**

Psalms **45**, 113
Isaiah 54
2 Peter 1.16 – 2.3

Tuesday 24 December
Christmas Eve

2 Peter 1.16 – 2.3

'... we did not follow cleverly devised myths' (v.16)

Most dictionaries have two definitions of the word 'myth'. A myth can be a false idea, even if widely believed. Or it may be a traditional story explaining some deeper truth, frequently involving supernatural beings. Every feature of the story may not hold together, but it is the deeper meaning that is the truth. Fairy tales are clearly not true in the literal sense, but they do teach us that appearances can be deceptive, for example. At this season when Father Christmas, the story of the nativity and pantomimes jostle for our attention, it's important to understand the distinction between the two meanings of myth. In this passage the writer is warning believers against false teaching while defending the veracity of 'the coming of our Lord Jesus Christ' since 'we had been eyewitnesses of his majesty'.

We are not told the content of these 'cleverly devised myths' that worry the writer so much. It sounds as if they may minimize the importance of Jesus. Although there's no mention of the birth narratives, one wonders whether the humility displayed within them is being used within the Church inappropriately. Would God put himself in such danger?

In our own age Christmas has become the most popular of all Christian festivals. We are drawn to the idea that God comes to earth in the defenceless form of a human child, relying on human love and care even to survive. This is no 'cleverly designed myth' but the truth come down from above.

Almighty God,
you make us glad with the yearly remembrance
of the birth of your Son Jesus Christ:
grant that, as we joyfully receive him as our redeemer,
so we may with sure confidence behold him
when he shall come to be our judge;
who is alive and reigns with you,
in the unity of the Holy Spirit,
one God, now and for ever.

COLLECT

Reflection by **Graham James** | 29

Wednesday 25 December
Christmas Day

Psalms **110**, 117
Isaiah 62.1-5
Matthew 1.18-end

Matthew 1.18-25

'Joseph … do not be afraid' (v.20)

The angel's first words to Joseph are 'Do not be afraid', the same words that Mary heard when the angel tells her that she will give birth to Jesus (Luke 1.30). The shepherds in the fields are also told 'Do not be afraid' (Luke 2.10).

There are plenty of reasons for fear in the Christmas story. What young woman already engaged to be married (but who had never slept with her fiancé) would not be fearful on discovering she was pregnant? What young man would not be fearful and angry too upon discovering his fiancée was pregnant when he knew he was not the father? What couple wouldn't be afraid if away from home with nowhere to stay when the birth of their child was imminent? Shepherds were good at minding their own business, so getting into matters beyond their comprehension was bound to terrify. In a country with a tyrant like King Herod around, everyone lived in some measure of fear.

'Do not be afraid.' The angel's words are addressed to us too. We live in a world full of fear, where war, conflict and climate change disrupt and ruin countless lives. Today we recall that Jesus was born in occupied territory with a violent puppet king in charge. This risky birth in a dangerous place is about God living among us in our troubles, not arriving after our problems have been solved. 'Do not be afraid.' God is with us.

C O L L E C T

Almighty God,
you have given us your only-begotten Son
to take our nature upon him
and as at this time to be born of a pure virgin:
grant that we, who have been born again
and made your children by adoption and grace,
may daily be renewed by your Holy Spirit;
through Jesus Christ our Lord.

Reflection by **Graham James**

Psalms **13**, 31.1-8, 150
Jeremiah 26.12-15
Acts 6

Thursday 26 December

Stephen, deacon, first martyr

Acts 6

'... together with Philip, Prochorus, Nicanor, Timon, Parmenas, and Nicolaus, a proselyte of Antioch' (v.5)

If Stephen gets a bit overlooked because his feast follows Christmas Day, let us spare a thought for those chosen with him 'to wait at tables', a task that the twelve apostles were keen to delegate. The seven deacons are all named. Nicolaus is noted as 'a proselyte of Antioch', a Gentile convert to Judaism who had become a follower of Christ. This is the first time someone not born a Jew was given an office in the Christian Church. This happened about three or four years after Pentecost when the Church was still in its infancy.

The seven deacons are appointed because there is conflict in the Church. There's no attempt to disguise this. The Greek-speaking widows think they are losing out to the Hebrews in the daily distribution of food. It's a time-consuming task, and the apostles think they will be neglecting their preaching and teaching ministry if they have to sort it out themselves. Hence the appointment of seven deacons.

But a ministry of service itself speaks volumes and, in Stephen's case, he is clearly not inhibited from preaching with power and persuasion. Philip too becomes an evangelist as well as a deacon, baptizing the Ethiopian eunuch (Acts 8). The seven turn out not to have any sort of lesser ministry. The apostles discover afresh how God honours service. We may have something to learn here about the role of deacons and all who serve in the Church today.

Gracious Father,
who gave the first martyr Stephen
grace to pray for those who took up stones against him:
grant that in all our sufferings for the truth
we may learn to love even our enemies
and to seek forgiveness for those who desire our hurt,
looking up to heaven to him who was crucified for us,
Jesus Christ, our mediator and advocate.

COLLECT

Friday 27 December

John, Apostle and Evangelist

Psalms **21**, 147.13-end
Exodus 33.12-end
I John 2.1-11

1 John 2.1-11

'... an old commandment you have had from the beginning' (v.7)

By the time the first letter of John was written, enough years have passed for Jesus' instruction to his disciples to 'love one another as I have loved you' (John 13.34) to become 'an old commandment'. Yet it's being disregarded. Some believers seem to claim they walk in the light of Christ 'while hating a brother or sister'. The writer of this letter is plain that this is impossible.

A century or more later, Tertullian (c.160–220 AD), a prominent theologian in Carthage, noted that pagans were jealous of the way Christians treated each other with such exceptional love. 'See how they love one another' was what Tertullian heard them say.

Would people look at our Christian communities today and be amazed by the way we love each other? Or would we be more likely to hear 'see how these Christians love one another' spoken ironically. We may be less divided about the nature of God or the doctrine of the Holy Trinity than the earliest theologians were, but we demonize one another more easily over ethical issues or the nature of authority within the Church.

If the way we, as Christians, live with each other fails to accord with the commandment of Jesus to 'love one another', then we have forgotten what caused the faith to spread so widely. Do we read this passage from the first letter of John as an historical document, or one that addresses us personally? It speaks volumes to today's Church.

COLLECT

Merciful Lord,
cast your bright beams of light upon the Church:
that, being enlightened by the teaching
of your blessed apostle and evangelist Saint John,
we may so walk in the light of your truth
that we may at last attain to the light of everlasting life;
through Jesus Christ your incarnate Son our Lord.

| *Reflection by* **Graham James**

Psalms **36**, 146
Baruch 4.21-27
or Genesis 37.13-20
Matthew 18.1-10

Saturday 28 December
The Holy Innocents

Matthew 18.1-10

'Whoever becomes humble like this child ...' (v.4)

Many years ago a well-known parliamentary figure wrote a book with the title *Humility*. It was rumoured that he went into a famous London bookshop and asked why they were not displaying copies prominently in the window. Writing about humility clearly has its dangers.

Jesus includes humility among the qualities needed in those who will 'enter the kingdom of heaven'. He chooses to illustrate his teaching by calling a child to stand among him and his disciples. He then says that anyone becoming 'humble like this child' will be the greatest in the heavenly kingdom.

Parents and teachers will testify that not all children are naturally endowed with humility. Even very young children may be show-offs. It was not humility as an interior disposition, but the humble status of a child within society at the time that was at the heart of Jesus' teaching. The question 'who is the greatest?' was about status. Children had little of it.

Today we remember the holy innocents killed by Herod in pursuit of the child Jesus. Children are frequently killed in wars and the power games of dictators. On this day we are reminded of the low status and disposability of children throughout much of history, and in the world today. It's their humility, low status and vulnerability that show us the entry requirements for the kingdom of heaven.

COLLECT

Heavenly Father,
whose children suffered at the hands of Herod,
though they had done no wrong:
by the suffering of your Son
and by the innocence of our lives
frustrate all evil designs
and establish your reign of justice and peace;
through Jesus Christ our Lord.

Reflection by **Graham James**   33

Monday 30 December

John 1.19-28

'I am not worthy ...' (v.27)

John the Baptist's testimony is grounded in his humility. We know that great crowds flocked to see him from Jerusalem and Judea. John is at the centre of a significant revival across all sections of society. Yet the Gospel emphasizes above everything else his humility. His first words are clear: 'I am not the Messiah.' But John goes on to confess that he is neither Elijah nor the prophet who was to come. When pressed, he chooses the most self-effacing of the Old Testament prophets, the one who calls himself simply a voice crying in the wilderness, the unnamed prophet of Isaiah 40–55.

John baptizes with the humblest of materials – water – in contrast with the one who is to come. We hear none of the Baptist's radical social teaching here: he simply points us to Jesus. John is not worthy to untie the thong of his sandal.

Humility comes from the Latin *humus*, soil. John is close to the people whom he serves, rooted and grounded in the ordinary life of his communities. This humility is our best guide as we look back over the last year. We too need to be clear who we are, and also who we are not. We too need to remember that we bear witness to one who is greater than we will ever be. We are not worthy ...

COLLECT

Almighty God,
who wonderfully created us in your own image
and yet more wonderfully restored us
through your Son Jesus Christ:
grant that, as he came to share in our humanity,
so we may share the life of his divinity;
who is alive and reigns with you,
in the unity of the Holy Spirit,
one God, now and for ever.

Reflection by **Steven Croft**

Psalms 102
Isaiah 59.15b-end
John 1.29-34

Tuesday 31 December

John 1.29-34

'... the Lamb of God' (v.29)

There is a strange and fragile vulnerability in this first image John the Baptist chooses for Jesus. We are overfamiliar with his words for we say or sing them in every Eucharist. But, in the first majestic chapter of John's Gospel, this is the second major name for Jesus the Christ after the Word of God, the Logos. The Baptist's phrase is repeated in verse 36. The fourth Gospel is building our understanding of Jesus Christ, our Christology, and this notion of the lamb is a cornerstone.

There are resonances with the passover lamb, of course, and a look ahead to John's account of the passion and to Jesus' death on the night of the passover, remembering the deliverance of the Israelites from slavery in Egypt. There are resonances too with Isaiah 53.7: 'like a lamb that is led to the slaughter'. The Baptist has already quoted the voice of Isaiah 40–55 in 1.23.

We see in this one name the seriousness and the scope of God's mission to the world: Jesus has come to take away the sin of the world. But the only way that this mission is accomplished is embedded in this same name. Jesus, the Lamb of God, will offer his life to take away our sins. The Son of God has come, anointed by the Spirit in his baptism, and the purpose of his coming is to give his life. How will we respond?

God in Trinity,
eternal unity of perfect love:
gather the nations to be one family,
and draw us into your holy life
through the birth of Emmanuel,
our Lord Jesus Christ.

COLLECT

Wednesday 1 January

Naming and Circumcision of Jesus

Psalms **103**, 150
Genesis 17.1-13
Romans 2.17-end

Romans 2.17-end

'... real circumcision is a matter of the heart' (v.29)

The page of the year turns and with it the gift of a new beginning: a clean sheet to begin a new chapter. We make our resolutions whether trivial or profound. We remember on this day the naming and circumcision of Jesus and with it our own naming and our own baptism. The name Jesus is given to Mary by Gabriel (Luke 1.31); and to Joseph by the angel of the Lord (Matthew 1.21). It means, of course, Saviour: the one who rescues us from sin and death and restores us to new life here and in the resurrection.

Baptism is a richer and deeper symbol than circumcision. In Christ there is neither Jew nor Greek, slave nor free, male nor female (Galatians 3.28). Whoever we are, baptism is the universal sign and symbol of our salvation. We remember on this New Year's Day that we have been washed and made new in Christ. We remember that we have died with Christ and have been raised with him to new and eternal life. We return to the very centre of our faith, confessing our sins and weaknesses and seeking afresh God's grace for this new year.

Tomorrow or the next day or the one after that, we know that some of the resolutions will be broken; there will be stains and blots on the page. But our baptism and salvation will be new and fresh and real each day. Thanks be to God.

COLLECT

Almighty God,
whose blessed Son was circumcised
in obedience to the law for our sake
and given the Name that is above every name:
give us grace faithfully to bear his Name,
to worship him in the freedom of the Spirit,
and to proclaim him as the Saviour of the world;
who is alive and reigns with you,
in the unity of the Holy Spirit,
one God, now and for ever.

| *Reflection by* **Steven Croft**

Psalm 18.1-30
Isaiah 60.1-12
John 1.35-42

Thursday 2 January

John 1.35-42

'What are you looking for?' (v.38)

The first words spoken by Jesus in the fourth Gospel are not parable or teaching or command but a question: 'What are you looking for?' The Word of God, the Lamb of God, begins a personal conversation, an exploration, designed to build a friendship and a community of friends.

You might want to imagine yourself in this conversation as you stand at the beginning of the year, perhaps on the first working day of the year with 364 days still stretching before you. Imagine yourself walking behind Jesus by the banks of the Jordan near Bethany. Jesus turns and begins the conversation. What are your hopes and fears for this year? What is it that you need? Where will you find joy and fulfilment? What are you looking for?

The two disciples answer with a question of their own: 'Where are you staying?' The words translated as stay, rest, dwell and abide are all the same root word in John. This will be a key concept in the Gospel: 'Those who abide in me and I in them bear much fruit' (15.5).

The disciples' question is answered with the most beautiful of invitations: 'Come and see!' Again, the Gospel intends us to hear the words addressed personally to the reader – to you and to me today. An invitation to come deeper, to rest and abide, to discover all that we are seeking.

Almighty God,
who wonderfully created us in your own image
and yet more wonderfully restored us
through your Son Jesus Christ:
grant that, as he came to share in our humanity,
so we may share the life of his divinity;
who is alive and reigns with you,
in the unity of the Holy Spirit,
one God, now and for ever.

COLLECT

Reflection by **Steven Croft** | 37

Friday 3 January

Psalms **127**, 128, 131
Isaiah 60.13-end
John 1.43-end

John 1.43-end

'He found Philip ...' (v.43)

Most talks and reflections on this passage focus on Nathanael's journey from rejection to faith with echoes of Jacob's dream in Genesis 28. We almost pass over Philip. But pause for a moment on this one phrase: Jesus found Philip. Jesus has come looking for him and found him. When Jesus finds Philip, he issues his distinctive invitation, which we hear in each of the Gospels and we will hear again addressed to Peter and the beloved disciple in the very final chapter (21.19, 22), 'Follow me.'

Jesus finds Philip. His encounters with the disciples were not random, chance meetings. Nor were they engineered by mutual friends – though friendship plays its part. Jesus is himself looking for individuals, by name. Jesus comes to find us. Jesus comes to call us.

The beginning of a new year is a good moment for each of us to reflect on our own calling, centred on the truth that Jesus has found us and issues this once in a lifetime and everyday invitation, 'Follow me.' It is more than an invitation to walk behind Jesus. It's an invitation to set Christ and Christ's call as the pattern of our lives; to grow deeper in friendship with Jesus each year of our lives; to be willing to leave everything for the sake of knowing Christ and to search out and follow our own calling, our vocation, to the end of our lives.

COLLECT

Almighty God,
who wonderfully created us in your own image
and yet more wonderfully restored us
through your Son Jesus Christ:
grant that, as he came to share in our humanity,
so we may share the life of his divinity;
who is alive and reigns with you,
in the unity of the Holy Spirit,
one God, now and for ever.

Reflection by **Steven Croft**

Psalm **89.1-37**
Isaiah 61
John 2.1-12

Saturday 4 January

John 2.1-12
'... the first of his signs' (v.11)

The miracle at Cana looks forward in several ways. John calls Jesus' miracles signs, encouraging deep and continuous reflection on the meaning of each. The signs point beyond themselves to deeper truths about Christ and his identity, often matched in the 'I am' sayings scattered through the text. The changing of water into wine is the first sign, looking forward to the rest that build to the resurrection of Lazarus in the eleventh chapter.

There is no 'I am' saying here: instead we must look forward to the last of these sayings in chapter 15: 'I am the vine, you are the branches'. The first of the signs and this final 'I am' saying bracket each of the others. Together they point to the wine of the Eucharist. The fourth Gospel contains no words of institution for Holy Communion. Instead we have this miracle, Christ the true vine, the feeding of the five thousand and Jesus the bread of life. The wine is a sign both of the suffering of Christ in the passion and the joy of resurrection and the new wine of the kingdom.

The wedding miracle looks forward to the life of the Church, the Bride of Christ, again to both suffering and joy and to the great banquet at the end of the ages, the wedding feast of the Lamb. The steward's words are echoed as we give thanks to God for the blessings we have known: 'you have kept the good wine until now.'

God in Trinity,
eternal unity of perfect love:
gather the nations to be one family,
and draw us into your holy life
through the birth of Emmanuel,
our Lord Jesus Christ.

COLLECT

Reflection by **Steven Croft**   39

Monday 6 January

Epiphany

Jeremiah 31.7-13

'I will let them walk by brooks of water ...' (v.9)

Jeremiah's vision is remarkable. The prophet has seen the depravity of the chosen people, the destruction of Jerusalem and the desolation of exile. Yet he will not let go of hope. He is still able to see a day when God's people will again be gathered, when exiles will return from the north and the farthest parts of the earth. The Lord himself will lead and guide them like a shepherd, by streams of water and on straight paths. The prosperity of the land will be restored: 'their life shall become a watered garden and they shall never languish again'. Their mourning will be turned to joy.

This is an extraordinary vision on which the later prophets will build. But Jeremiah can still see only a part, a fraction, of the picture. For God's vision fulfilled in Christ is to draw together not one nation but every nation into the chosen people of God. The light of Christ is to shine out to all the nations. God's grace will lead every people home as a loving shepherd, beside brooks of water.

This is the vision caught by Matthew in the story of the magi from the East (2.1). This is the vision caught by Luke in Simeon's song: 'A light for revelation to the Gentiles and the glory of your people Israel.' This is the vision of Epiphany. The light of Christ draws all the people of the earth to living water.

COLLECT | O God,
who by the leading of a star
manifested your only Son to the peoples of the earth:
mercifully grant that we,
who know you now by faith,
may at last behold your glory face to face;
through Jesus Christ our Lord.

| *Reflection by* **Steven Croft**

Psalms **99**, 147.1-12 *or* **73**
Isaiah 63.7-end
1 John 3

Tuesday 7 January

1 John 3

'... that we should love one another' (v.11)

1 John is more like poetry than prose. Themes familiar from the Gospels are packed together like sardines. There is more than enough in a single chapter for a whole series of reflections. But one concept above all the others is the recurring theme.

There are a dozen references to love in this chapter. This love is generous, undeserved and faithful. This love is rooted in the love God bears for us in calling us to be his children (v.1). This love is to be our way of life, our daily bread (v.14). Our love rests on the truth that Jesus lay down his life for us and so we are called to lay down our lives for one another: love is costly and sacrificial (v.16). The love we practice is to be observant and practical and open handed (v.17).

In our wordy Church and even more wordy society we need to be reminded that love is not about what we say but about our actions (v.18). We can love only because we abide in Christ and Christ abides in us by his Spirit.

We can hear in the repetition and encouragement one of the life lessons of the author: this love is not easily learned or practised. Love is not always the hallmark of the Church. This is the very reason for the letter. 1 John pleads with us to love and to love better. Are we listening? How will that shape our lives this day?

Creator of the heavens,
who led the Magi by a star
to worship the Christ-child:
guide and sustain us,
that we may find our journey's end
in Jesus Christ our Lord.

COLLECT

Reflection by **Steven Croft** | 41

Wednesday 8 January

1 John 4.7-end

'Beloved, let us love one another' (v.7)

Loving other people can be very, very difficult. Loving family and friends is hard enough. But we are called to love the Church, the body of Christ; our neighbours (including those who are not like us); even our enemies. We are called to love not as an exchange, a transaction in which there is giving and receiving, but to love even when that love is not returned.

Why should we do this? John does not try to argue that those we are called to love are loveable or worthy of love. John knows, most probably, that humanity can be petty and spiteful, jealous and proud, both in the Church and the wider world (just like you and me).

So our motivation for love when love is hard does not rest in trying harder to like people and find the good in them. Our motivation for love rests instead in what God is like. We are to love because God loves. We are to love because love is divine. We are to love because we have discovered that we are loved – and that love is transforming our own lives. The more we struggle to love others, the more deeply John invites us to understand God's love for us: 'he sent his Son to be the atoning sacrifice for our sins' (v.10).

The answer to the question of how to love the unlovable is always to turn towards the God of love.

COLLECT

O God,
who by the leading of a star
manifested your only Son to the peoples of the earth:
mercifully grant that we,
who know you now by faith,
may at last behold your glory face to face;
through Jesus Christ our Lord.

| *Reflection by* **Steven Croft**

Thursday 9 January

1 John 5.1-12

'And this is the victory that conquers the world, our faith' (v.4)

The word 'victory' stands out in a passage otherwise full of rich, familiar vocabulary from Johannine writings. This is the only occurrence of the abstract term in the New Testament. The language takes us to the sense of struggle, even of battle, at the heart of the Christian experience and connects us with the Pauline language of athletics or boxing or of the army. A life of love is not an easy life but one lived against the grain of the world. The keeping of God's commandments involves demands and hard choices; it means resisting temptation. Life even in the Church is not always straightforward but can be costly.

In all this we are called – in the language of the baptism service – to fight valiantly against 'the world, the flesh and the devil'. In each of these conflicts the key to victory is neither personal virtue nor good deeds, but faith: both the content of what we believe and our trusting in that content. The act of saying the creed with other Christians Sunday by Sunday is a way of re-centring our lives, of drawing down the resources for the struggle in the week to come, of reminding one another of the truths we hold.

This is why 1 John follows this promise with testimony: the reasons we can trust in Jesus: the witness of the Spirit, the water and the blood. As another year unfolds, bind these testimonies closer into your heart for the struggles to come.

Creator of the heavens,
who led the Magi by a star
to worship the Christ-child:
guide and sustain us,
that we may find our journey's end
in Jesus Christ our Lord.

COLLECT

Friday 10 January

Psalms 97, **149** *or* **55**
Isaiah 65.17-end
1 John 5.13-end

1 John 5.13-end

'And this is the boldness we have in him ...' (v.14)

There are many kinds of courage in the Christian life. 1 John ends with a call to a particular boldness: to dare to make requests of God in prayer. Prayer is more than simply asking for things for ourselves or for others. But there is an aspect of prayer that is foregrounded here. We should not be afraid to ask or be neglectful of our intercessions.

John's letter counsels us first to be bold in our intercessions: not to be content with the way things are, to contend in prayer. Second, we are to ask according to God's will: this requires both thought and rigour in our prayer for others and presumes that our prayers will be specific. Third, we are to pray especially for those whose sin is not 'mortal' (literally unto death) – perhaps especially those who are drifting from the centre of their faith, those to whom this letter is written. The implication is that our prayers and our love will then be translated into practical action and care.

The beginning of a new year is an excellent time to review the way in which we pray for others regularly and systematically: family and friends; those in particular need; those for whom we are responsible in our workplace or ministry; those who have wandered from the faith. May our petitions for healing and salvation and blessing be above everything else bold and courageous in the presence of the Lord who loves to hear our prayers.

COLLECT

O God,
who by the leading of a star
manifested your only Son to the peoples of the earth:
mercifully grant that we,
who know you now by faith,
may at last behold your glory face to face;
through Jesus Christ our Lord.

Reflection by **Steven Croft**

Psalms 98, **150** *or* **76**, 79
Isaiah 66.1-11
2 John

Saturday 11 January

2 John

'I would rather not use paper and ink' (v.12)

Winston Churchill once ended a letter with an apology: 'I'm sorry this is such a long letter: I didn't have time to write a short one.' It's harder to say all that needs to be said succinctly. But brevity is also a gift, helping us distil the most important truths in memorable ways. Here, once again, the writer offers the central and lasting message of the Johannine writings: the new commandment is 'let us love one another'.

This short letter also offers us a clear model of how to communicate as Christians: the more we are able to meet in person, the better. The Church in recent years has lived through lockdowns and learned to meet and even to worship remotely through the gift of technology. Meeting patterns have changed in consequence. 2 John is clear that while paper and ink are good, meeting face to face is better. Verse 12 looks forward to speaking 'face to face' – literally 'mouth to mouth'. As twenty-first-century Christians we would surely say the same of meeting remotely. For those who celebrate the fullness of our humanity, there can be no substitute for worship, care and community that is built up through regular and personal contact.

And the purpose of that meeting and of our fellowship is 'that our joy may be complete'. With personal contact there is the satisfaction of interaction; smiles and laughter, tears and signs of affection, the fullness of our humanity leading to the fullness of joy.

Creator of the heavens,
who led the Magi by a star
to worship the Christ-child:
guide and sustain us,
that we may find our journey's end
in Jesus Christ our Lord.

COLLECT

Reflection by **Steven Croft** | 45

Monday 13 January

Amos 1

'The Words of Amos ... which he saw concerning Israel' (v.1)

One of the complexities of reading the prophets is untangling the voices within the text. Are all the words that follow quite literally 'what God said'? Or does Amos take what he 'saw' and put it into his own words?

In the fourth century, St Augustine warned his readers not to read the Bible 'literally'. And ever since then, people have debated what it means for the scriptures to be 'inspired'. In 1824, Samuel Taylor Coleridge wrote that inspiration does not mean every word is literally given by God; rather, that every stage in bringing God's 'word' to the page has an element of inspiration – not only writing, but editing, compiling and translating, each of which also contains an element of interpretation. And he noted that reading is also an act of interpretation and that reading can also be inspired by God.

In Amos, we will read that God seems, by turns, to be just and merciful, but also furious and wrathful; that he is bent on harsh punishment, and yet also willing to change his mind. It's important to remember that we are listening to Amos' words, which have been edited and translated, and that the truth that lies within them needs to be teased out from the surface impressions.

COLLECT

Eternal Father,
who at the baptism of Jesus
revealed him to be your Son,
anointing him with the Holy Spirit:
grant to us, who are born again by water and the Spirit,
that we may be faithful to our calling as your adopted children;
through Jesus Christ our Lord.

| *Reflection by* **Maggi Dawn**

Psalms 8, **9** *or* 87, **89**.1-18
Amos 2
1 Corinthians 1.18-end

Tuesday 14 January

Amos 2

'... they have been led astray by the same lies' (v.4)

Today's reading continues to name the crimes Israel's neighbours have committed against them, and the punishment that God will inflict on them. You can imagine, as Amos delivered his prophecy to Israel, that his audience would shout 'Amen' every time their enemies were denounced – the more passionate, perhaps, because their neighbours included former allies: Damascus! Edom! Ammon! Moab! – and the noisy shouts of approval rise as the crowd agrees with each of Amos' diatribes.

But then there is a shocked silence as Amos directs God's anger towards them. God, it seems, is not 'on their side' as such, but on the side of righteousness and justice. And notably, Amos makes no distinction between social injustice – selling people to slavery, sexual abuse, getting ahead by trampling on other people – and religious sins, such as forcing the Nazirites to break their own religious code, or silencing their prophets.

Amos is renowned as the prophet of social justice, but for him, social and religious life are so closely intertwined that it is impossible to separate them. He is as incensed by those who disrespect their own religious rules as by human rights abuses. Amos wants his hearers to understand that religious observance and social justice are of a piece; one is incomplete without the other, and in so doing, he foreshadows Jesus' summary of the law: 'love the Lord your God ... and your neighbour as yourself'.

Heavenly Father,
at the Jordan you revealed Jesus as your Son:
may we recognize him as our Lord
and know ourselves to be your beloved children;
through Jesus Christ our Saviour.

COLLECT

Reflection by **Maggi Dawn**   47

Wednesday 15 January

Amos 3

*'You only have I known of all the families of the earth;
therefore I will punish you ...' (v.2)*

Yesterday we saw Amos aiming his fury as much at his own people as their enemies. In today's reading he seems to suggest that God's anger is even *more* stirred against his own people, but not because God sets higher standards or different rules for his own people. God's expectations of justice and right living are the same for everyone. Rather it is because God made a relationship of covenant and faithfulness with his own people that it is doubly shocking when they pay scant regard to God's words.

The language of destruction and punishment is difficult to square with the idea of a God of love and forgiveness. But Amos' God is not a brutal power-monger issuing commands to his subjects. The point is precisely that God is neither a despot nor a 'sugar-daddy'; but that the people can flourish only if they invest in the covenant relationship of love and mutuality with God. God wants to 'walk together' with his people, and – rather touchingly – to share confidences with them. This is not a God who abuses power, but who wants to give power to his people – if only they will walk with him. It is not pique or vengeance on God's part that threatens destruction, but people's refusal to engage in the relationship God offers.

COLLECT

Eternal Father,
who at the baptism of Jesus
revealed him to be your Son,
anointing him with the Holy Spirit:
grant to us, who are born again by water and the Spirit,
that we may be faithful to our calling as your adopted children;
through Jesus Christ our Lord.

Reflection by **Maggi Dawn**

Psalms **21**, 24 *or* 90, **92** **Thursday 16 January**
Amos 4
I Corinthians 3

Amos 4

'... yet you did not return to me' (v.6)

Yet again, Amos recites a litany of disasters that have befallen God's people, but this time, the message is inverted. Amos views their misfortunes not as a punishment, but as a wake-up call. They were observing their daily religious rituals, but while they continued to do nothing about those who were oppressed, or poor, or crushed by injustice, all the meaning was leached out of their worship. Praising God and doing good cannot be separated.

Prophets don't predict the future so much as they read the signs of the times. Amos lists events that occurred in the past: minor calamities that were costly, or frustrating, or inconvenient, but not ultimately destructive. And he frames these events, not as retribution or repercussion, but as warnings. According to Amos, God was not punishing his people, but trying to stop them in their tracks and get their attention before something really bad happened.

Sometimes it's difficult to understand why bad things happen to good people. And, especially when things are very bad indeed, it would be deeply unhealthy to suppose that God 'made it happen'. The underlying truth to this part of Amos' message, then, is that when bad things happen, rather than backing away and wondering whether God is not loving after all, we need to run towards God, and not in the opposite direction.

Heavenly Father,
at the Jordan you revealed Jesus as your Son:
may we recognize him as our Lord
and know ourselves to be your beloved children;
through Jesus Christ our Saviour.

COLLECT

Friday 17 January

Psalms **67**, 72 *or* **88** (95)
Amos 5.1-17
1 Corinthians 4

Amos 5.1-17

'Seek the Lord and live' (v.6)

Amos attributes a full range of emotions to God; after the anger, frustration, patience and angst of earlier chapters, we now see God's heartbreak. When things go wrong for us, far from being pleased, or vindictive, or satisfied, God laments over us. Amos repeats his message that the people need to seek God, but not merely in order to avoid calamity. What God wants is for them to *live*, not merely in the sense of avoiding death, but – as Irenaeus, Bishop of Lyons would describe in the second century – being 'fully alive'.

Where do we look for help when we are in trouble? Amos warns against seeking help only from sources that are temporary or unstable; from friends who may be unfaithful, or from material sources that may vanish. The only way to be fully alive is to look for the spiritual help that only God can give. This means seeking God, both through religious practices and by pursuing justice and right living.

Getting God's help in trouble, though, is not easy. Seeking the Lord is not always a matter of instant joy, relief and comfort – it may also involve lament. God laments, and we will too. But we should not fear sorrow, if it is part of the work of mending, reconciliation and healing that in the end leads us into life.

COLLECT

Eternal Father,
who at the baptism of Jesus
revealed him to be your Son,
anointing him with the Holy Spirit:
grant to us, who are born again by water and the Spirit,
that we may be faithful to our calling as your adopted children;
through Jesus Christ our Lord.

| *Reflection by* **Maggi Dawn**

Psalms 29, **33** *or* 96, **97**, 100
Amos 5.18-end
1 Corinthians 5

Saturday 18 January

Amos 5.18-end

*'... let justice roll down like waters, and righteousness
like an ever-flowing stream' (v.24)*

These words are often attributed directly to Dr Martin Luther King Jr, without noting their source in the Bible. Dr King chose this quotation, which was reputedly his favourite Bible verse, for his iconic 'I have a dream' speech on the steps of the Lincoln Memorial in 1963. Since then his words have often been quoted to summon up an image of how the world could be – *should* be. Yet Dr King knew his Bible better than most of those who quote him, and he knew very well that Amos' words were not merely inspirational; they were a dire warning of the judgement that would rain down on a nation that failed to grasp such a call to justice.

To treat King's words as a neat soundbite is to miss the tenor of the whole of Amos' message, which he undoubtedly had in mind. Like Amos, he saw that religious observances are a mockery of God if they are divorced from justice and righteousness. And it is a mistake to assume that the imagery of a mighty river of justice is merely something to celebrate; in places where human rights are ignored, people are trampled underfoot, and even the most religious of people catastrophically fail to 'love their neighbour', a river of justice could be a fearsome thing, a torrent that will sweep away injustice.

Heavenly Father,
at the Jordan you revealed Jesus as your Son:
may we recognize him as our Lord
and know ourselves to be your beloved children;
through Jesus Christ our Saviour.

COLLECT

Reflection by **Maggi Dawn** | 51

Monday 20 January

Psalms 145, **146** *or* **98**, 99, 101
Amos 6
1 Corinthians 6.1-11

Amos 6

'Alas for those who are at ease ... and for those who feel secure'
(v.1)

Today's reading shines a spotlight on two dangers in our spiritual life. One is slipping into a sense of superiority. It is too easy to believe that finding truth in God somehow puts us in a safe position, with a perspective on life that is morally or spiritually commendable. But Amos warns us not to let the fact that we are God's people fool us into thinking we are better than others.

The other danger is adopting a complacency that shields us from reality. There is a fine line between depending on the safety of God's love, and treating it as an insulation against the harsher aspects of life. It is notable that the Psalms are full of reassurances that God is faithful, kind, and will defend us. But those reassurances usually occur in the context of lament (e.g. Psalms 27, 90), where the psalmists were in deep trouble and even life-threatening situations. This was not comfort, it was defiant faith and hope-against-hope.

Like the psalmists, Amos calls on God's people not to treat their religion as a comfort blanket, or a bubble of safety; he calls them (and perhaps us) to stay awake and recognize that true prayers will not only bring us close to God, but will give us a clear view of reality, even when that is not comfortable viewing.

COLLECT

Almighty God,
in Christ you make all things new:
transform the poverty of our nature by the riches of your grace,
and in the renewal of our lives
make known your heavenly glory;
through Jesus Christ our Lord.

| *Reflection by* **Maggi Dawn**

Psalms **132**, 147.1-12 *or* **106*** (*or* 103)   **Tuesday 21 January**
Amos 7
1 Corinthians 6.12-end

Amos 7

'The Lord relented concerning this; "It shall not be," said the Lord'
(v.3)

Can mere mortals really make God change his mind? Amos is not the only biblical figure to have argued with God. But this conversation is not focused so much on who wins the argument, as on the fact that dialogue is taking place at all! As St Paul noted centuries later (1 Corinthians 3.1-2), God does not seek unthinking obedience from his people, but an engaged relationship that leads to people becoming fully developed, mentally and spiritually.

God would be our equal, not our creator, if he needed our friendship to make him complete. God does not seek us out because he is lonely, but because relationship is God's very essence. The nature of love is to give; the dynamic of God is a relationship of three-in-one, communing within the Godhead from eternity to eternity, and the mutability of God is based in this orientation towards relationship. For God to 'change his mind' does not suggest that God was wrong or needed human input to correct his view. Rather it is that God's creation – and us within it – depends upon relationship to function. It's when we engage with God that the world begins to right itself. Amos could see that his people were on the verge of bringing disaster upon themselves; but the solution lay not so much in persuading God to avert punishment, but in restoring the human–divine relationship.

COLLECT

Eternal Lord,
our beginning and our end:
bring us with the whole creation
to your glory, hidden through past ages
and made known
in Jesus Christ our Lord.

Reflection by **Maggi Dawn**   53

Wednesday 22 January

Psalms **81**, 147.13-end
or 110, **111**, 112
Amos 8
I Corinthians 7.1-24

Amos 8

*'I will make the sun go down at noon, and darken the earth
in broad daylight' (v.9)*

Amos is almost at the end of his outpourings, and this penultimate chapter reads, I think, as the bleakest point in his prophecy. He has delivered God's warning shots to wake the people up, and warnings of worse to come, and pleadings with tears, yet still there is yet no change, no response. The kingdom was divided, and religious life was at a low ebb, but economically speaking, life was good – they were absorbed in buying and selling and getting material goods, so much so that even fellow human beings have become commodities. So Amos returns to talk to God. What will happen next? It's not good: the end has come, joy will turn to sorrow, and deaths will multiply. So once more he speaks out, his message more urgent than ever. The sun, says Amos, will go down in the daytime, and day will turn to night.

Amos could hardly have imagined that some eight hundred years later, the sun would go down in the middle of the afternoon, as a man died on a cross, and the light of the world was extinguished. But, as the writer Thomas Fuller first said in 1650, and songwriters and poets have repeated ever after, the darkest hour is just before the dawn.

(Spoiler alert: don't despair! – there will be a glimmer of hope in tomorrow's reading.)

COLLECT

Almighty God,
in Christ you make all things new:
transform the poverty of our nature by the riches of your grace,
and in the renewal of our lives
make known your heavenly glory;
through Jesus Christ our Lord.

Reflection by **Maggi Dawn**

Psalms **76**, 148 *or* 113, **115**
Amos 9
1 Corinthians 7.25-end

Thursday 23 January

Amos 9

'I will restore the fortunes of my people Israel' (v.14)

After eight chapters quite unrelenting in their bleak predictions, it is a relief to come to a point of hope. God has already said that it's all over, that he will not return, that death and destruction will follow, and this chapter continues to predict misfortune and sorrow on a pretty grand scale. Bad things will happen, except, except, except....

'I will not completely destroy,' says God. God will shake things up to the very foundations, but the house will not fall down. There will be a reckoning, but there will be a restoration. And after all the grim and frightening words, there is a glimmer of hope in the final verses. This time is fearful, but another time will come.

And when that time comes, Amos does not imagine God wiping the slate clean and starting over. Rather, God will repair, rebuild and recreate. This idea is in keeping with other apocalyptic biblical judgements. Noah's flood was not an obliteration, not just a washing-away of the world, but a 'rewinding' of the processes of creation in order to restart something that had gone bad. And Amos, too, sees that when the time comes, something new will be built out of the rubble of the old.

Eternal Lord,
our beginning and our end:
bring us with the whole creation
to your glory, hidden through past ages
and made known
in Jesus Christ our Lord.

COLLECT

Reflection by **Maggi Dawn** | 55

Friday 24 January

Psalms **27**, 149 *or* **139**
Hosea 1.1 – 2.1
1 Corinthians 8

Hosea 1.1 – 2.1

'Say to your brother, Ammi, and to your sister, Ruhamah' (2.1)

This story is so shocking that it is hard to know quite how to begin. The whole purpose of Hosea's marriage is to hold up his wife as an example of everything that is wrong with the world, and to give their children vicious names that represent God's judgement. There is no physical violence, but the level of shame and verbal abuse meted out to Gomer is shocking enough to place this chapter with what the theologian Phyllis Trible called 'Texts of Terror' in her book of the same name. Trible's approach was neither to explain away the horror of such stories by giving them a 'redemptive twist', nor to suggest they be excised from the scriptures, but to sit with them long enough to see why they are there at all.

Contemplating this chapter for some hours, I find a shaft of light in the way it plays with names. It opens with the names of kings who represent a nation divided by a civil war, but closes with the promise that Jezreel's name (meaning 'scattered') will be celebrated when the kingdom is reunited. The final verse we read sits isolated between the two chapters. It does not contribute anything to the plot. But its significance is the removal of 'Lo-' from the names. Lo-ruhamah (merciless) becomes Ruhamah (pitied one), and Lo-ammi (not my people) becomes Ammi (my people). This one slightly disjointed verse, then, is like a crack of light in an otherwise mystifyingly dark narrative of shame and rejection.

COLLECT

Almighty God,
in Christ you make all things new:
transform the poverty of our nature by the riches of your grace,
and in the renewal of our lives
make known your heavenly glory;
through Jesus Christ our Lord.

| *Reflection by* **Maggi Dawn**

Psalms 66, 147.13-end
Ezekiel 3.22-end
Philippians 3.1-14

Saturday 25 January

Conversion of Paul

Ezekiel 3.22-end

'I will make your tongue cling to the roof of your mouth' (v.26)

Paul, from his conversion onwards, was acutely aware that words are not disembodied, but related to all our senses. Jesus was the Word made flesh, and God's word continues to be embodied in our lives. Ezekiel tells a similar story. The bodies of angels (10.12), dry bones (37.1-14), and the contrast between speech and silence, all witness to God's words impacting our physical and material lives. 'I will speak with you,' says God, and so silences Ezekiel. The translator and reformer Miles Coverdale coined the phrase 'my tongue cleave to the roof of my mouth' (Psalm 137.6, *BCP*): such a poetic description of being speechless that Shakespeare used it in Richard II (Act 5, Scene 3) to express that among the most punishing aspects of exile was being sent somewhere where one cannot speak the language, and is effectively silenced and isolated.

Paul's conversion led to a period of quiet isolation; he stopped talking, and listened to God. Zechariah was memorably silenced by God. In his case, it was not a punishment, but so that the priestly blessing he would have delivered on the Temple steps (Luke 1.22) was deferred and spoken by Christ at his ascension (Luke 24.50), highlighting the priestly nature of Christ's ministry. Ezekiel's silence is also not a punishment, but a pause in transmission. Don't speak too soon, God seems to be saying. When the time is right, I'll give you the words.

Perhaps today, where opinion is increasingly polarized through the over-use of social media soundbites, we might consider God's call to intersperse speech with times of silence.

Almighty God,
who caused the light of the gospel
to shine throughout the world
through the preaching of your servant Saint Paul:
grant that we who celebrate his wonderful conversion
may follow him in bearing witness to your truth;
through Jesus Christ our Lord.

COLLECT

Reflection by **Maggi Dawn**   57

Monday 27 January

Psalms 40, **108** *or* 123, 124, 125, **126**
Hosea 2.18 – end of 3
1 Corinthians 9.15-end

Hosea 2.18 – end of 3

'I will have pity on Lo-ruhamah' (2.23)

Even in an age of 'no fault' divorces, marriage breakdown is traumatic for all involved. Even more so in ancient Israel, when a wife could be summarily repudiated by a husband at whim, damaging the sense of identity of spouse and children alike.

Hosea and Gomer's marital relationship is complex and contested; it is unclear whether the language used is factual or metaphorical. But to name a daughter *Lo-ruhamah*, 'Not pitied', and a son *Lo-ammi*, 'Not my people', is clearly to set destabilizing denial at the heart of the identity their names convey.

The negation, though, is cancelled as the Lord affirms that *Lo-ruhamah* will be pitied, *Lo-ammi* will be his people. This affirms the mutuality of relationship that runs through the Hebrew scriptures: Israel is 'his people'; the Lord is 'their God'. But the affirmation comes only after disruption, denial and repentance. This bond is not a biological given but a deliberately restored and reconstituted relationship. God's people must be invited by his mercy; they cannot claim their identity as of right.

If this is true of the chosen Israel, how much more so of us who are gathered from the nations. The First Letter of Peter reminds a group of early Christians: 'Once you were not a people, but now you are God's people; once you had not received mercy, but now you have received mercy' (1 Peter 2.10). All that we are comes of God's mercy alone.

	Almighty God,
COLLECT	whose Son revealed in signs and miracles
	the wonder of your saving presence:
	renew your people with your heavenly grace,
	and in all our weakness
	sustain us by your mighty power;
	through Jesus Christ our Lord.

Reflection by **Michael Ipgrave**

Psalms 34, **36** *or* **132**, 133
Hosea 4.1-16
I Corinthians 10.1-13

Tuesday 28 January

Hosea 4.1-16

'... it shall be like people, like priest' (v.9)

Two things are clear from this bad-tempered passage. First, the prophet has a low estimation of his fellow Israelites' behaviour. He fires a salvo denouncing their personal morality, social structures, ecological standards and religious practice.

Second, he emphasizes the complicity of priests and people in this lamentable situation. The priests have failed to give true guidance; but neither are the people blameless. In a sense, each deserves the other, and each bears an equal burden of guilt. For those who read this as religious ministers, it can be profoundly dispiriting to absorb Hosea's fierce rhetoric as we will naturally apply his trenchant condemnations to ourselves.

However, the prophet is addressing a whole society, not merely a religious organization. The opening of this chapter makes clear that his message is for all 'the inhabitants of the land'. Within his society, priests were the principal influencers to whom people looked for guidance and teaching, and they had failed together with those whom they were influencing.

Depressing as Hosea's picture of his times is, we can surely recognize similar dysfunction of a similar order in our own society. We then too must ask, how adequate are our sources of public influence to shape better patterns of behaviour? Rather than beat ourselves up over our ministerial failings – though, inevitably, we fall short in many ways – we need to discern how, with and for our people, we can be wholesome examples and patterns for the common good.

God of all mercy,
your Son proclaimed good news to the poor,
release to the captives,
and freedom to the oppressed:
anoint us with your Holy Spirit
and set all your people free
to praise you in Christ our Lord.

COLLECT

Reflection by **Michael Ipgrave** | 59

Wednesday 29 January

Psalms 45, **46** *or* **119.153-end**
Hosea 5.1-7
I Corinthians 10.14 – 11.1

Hosea 5.1-7

'Their deeds do not permit them' (v.4)

Amid Hosea's repeated denunciations of his compatriots' behaviour, he briefly recognizes that their acts might not entirely be the result of wilful choice: 'Their deeds do not permit them to return to their God,' he observes. The Hebrew means something like: 'do not give them what they need to be able to return', acknowledging that behaviour is not always a decision we can freely take. Previous behaviours can have consequences that remove the freedom of choice that goes with accountability.

What Hosea fleetingly concedes is a reality experienced by many of us that can govern our behaviour from early days. I am haunted by words I once saw written in a ten-year-old's school book: 'I want to be good, to start all over again. But it's too late now too late for me.' Everything in me wanted to cry out, 'No, it's not too late! You can always start again, especially when you're only ten!' But I know that child was on to something – our patterns of behaviour set constraints from which we need to be rescued.

This awareness is most fully developed in Paul's reflections on the depressing regularity with which 'I do not do the good I want, but the evil I do not want' (Romans 7.20). But that passage ends with heartfelt thanksgiving for God's grace which can and does come to his aid through Jesus.

Lord, show me that you can deliver me from the chains of my behaviour.

C O L L E C T	Almighty God, whose Son revealed in signs and miracles the wonder of your saving presence: renew your people with your heavenly grace, and in all our weakness sustain us by your mighty power; through Jesus Christ our Lord.

| *Reflection by* **Michael Ipgrave**

Psalms **47**, 48 *or* **143**, 146
Hosea 5.8 – 6.6
1 Corinthians 11.2-16

Thursday 30 January

Hosea 5.8 – 6.6

'... on the third day he will raise us up' (6.2)

It is almost inevitable that Christians, formed by the experience of the paschal mystery, should read the Israelites' expectation 'On the third day he will raise us up' as a foretelling of the resurrection. Given their conviction that Jesus embodied the fulfilment of Israel's story, it is not surprising that early Christian commentators like Jerome interpreted Hosea's words thus. Indeed, it might well be this verse that Paul had in mind when declaring that the Lord's resurrection on the third day was 'according to the scriptures' (1 Corinthians 15.4).

Of course, there are many problems with this reading of the passage – not least that these verses (6.1–3) appear nothing more than the ungrounded and light-hearted optimism of the Israelites, which in the following verses is rebuffed by God in his reproof of their shallowness and his renewed threats of punishment. Perhaps 'the third day', like the 'two days' that precede it, is simply a measure of the short attention span for which Hosea criticizes his contemporaries.

However, despite the stringency of the prophet's denunciations, Hosea is not a book without hope, and the hidden God who 'returns to his place' is also the God who turns again to his people in love (11.8). Perhaps our forebears were not wrong to see in the ancient expectation of 'the third day' a claim on the deathless mercy of God that would be fulfilled by the risen Lord.

God of all mercy,
your Son proclaimed good news to the poor,
release to the captives,
and freedom to the oppressed:
anoint us with your Holy Spirit
and set all your people free
to praise you in Christ our Lord.

COLLECT

Reflection by **Michael Ipgrave** | 61

Friday 31 January

Psalms 61, **65** *or* 142, **144**
Hosea 6.7 – 7.2
1 Corinthians 11.17-end

Hosea 6.7 – 7.2

'... they murder on the road to Shechem' (6.9)

Perhaps the most chilling evil we can experience happens in places that are supposed to be safe, and at the hands of people we are supposed to be able to trust. There is a particular sense of betrayal in such circumstances that intensifies the pain and revulsion we feel.

This provides the background to Hosea's striking allegation that the priests of his day are murdering 'on the road to Shechem'. Shechem, at the heart of the northern kingdom of Israel, had been designated by Joshua a 'city of refuge', a place of sanctuary for those who feared for their safety. Moreover, it is likely that the priesthood was itself charged with maintaining the safety of that sanctuary inviolate.

The priests, though, were doing the exact opposite: taking the lives of the vulnerable people seeking their protection. It is understandable that the prophet should refer to this as 'a monstrous crime'. The failure to safeguard those who have a claim on our protection, and worse still the deliberant exploitation of their vulnerability, is perhaps the most shocking and harrowing exposure of evil that any community can face. That horror is compounded when the community is one founded on faith, particularly faith in the One who speaks repeatedly of the need to honour the weak, the vulnerable and the 'little ones'.

Hosea's words plumb the depths of depravity, and speak incisively to today's Church, calling us to lament and repent.

COLLECT

Almighty God,
whose Son revealed in signs and miracles
the wonder of your saving presence:
renew your people with your heavenly grace,
and in all our weakness
sustain us by your mighty power;
through Jesus Christ our Lord.

| *Reflection by* **Michael Ipgrave**

Psalms **68** *or* **147**
Hosea 8
1 Corinthians 12.1-11

Saturday 1 February

Hosea 8
'... it is not God' (v.6)

'It's not God!' – three words, whether in Hebrew or English, that state succinctly what an idol is, and that remove it from the category of that which should be worshipped.

Hosea has in mind the 'calf of Samaria', a cultic object that probably corresponded to the cherubim in the worship of the northern kingdom of Israel, which, according to the theology of the southern kingdom of Judah, protected the presence of the Lord in the Temple. That being so, it might well be that a northern Israelite might agree with the principles of the prophet's statement about idols, while feeling resentment at the suggestion that they did not themselves appreciate the creaturely status of the calf. Some of them might have seen that object as a vehicle to symbolize and attend to the divine presence, like the cherubim. In other words, they may have heard Hosea's disparaging remark as a deliberate and polemicized Judaean misunderstanding.

However, the prophetic critique, addressed to us, reaches beyond material objects. In essence, an idol is anything that we put where the living God alone belongs. Such idols, created by ourselves, can equally be intangible yet very powerful objectives that we hold dear – e.g. wealth, security, success, celebrity, or even a reputation for goodness or for holiness. As William Cowper wrote:

'The dearest idol I have known,
Whate'er that idol be,
Help me to tear it from thy throne,
And worship only thee.'

God of all mercy,
your Son proclaimed good news to the poor,
release to the captives,
and freedom to the oppressed:
anoint us with your Holy Spirit
and set all your people free
to praise you in Christ our Lord.

COLLECT

Monday 3 February

Psalms 1, 2, 3
Azariah *and* Song 1-27
or Malachi 1.1, 6-end
John 13.1-11

Malachi 1.1, 6-end

'... a pure offering' (v.11)

From the earliest Christian centuries, the reference to a pure sacrifice offered in every place, has been seen as pointing to the Christian Eucharist. Sometimes this universal and 'unbloody' offering has been positively contrasted with the Jewish sacrificial system, confined to one altar in Jerusalem, and involving the slaughter of animals.

There is no need for disparaging Jewish practice, though. Malachi's criticisms were directed against those who deliberately withheld the best of what they had from the worship of God; his message speaks as clearly to us as it did to his contemporaries. We do not need to imagine ourselves better than the Jewish worshippers of his time to recognize that we also usually fail to offer the best of ourselves and what we have in God's service.

Even at the Eucharist, our 'sacrifice of praise and thanksgiving', our devotion is so often perfunctory, our commitment half-hearted, our self-offering at best partial. Yet our faith is that our offering, though inadequate and impure from a human point of view, is accepted by God because he receives it united to the sacrifice of his Son to whom we belong. In William Bright's words:

'Look, Father, look on his anointed face,
and only look on us as found in him.
Look not on our misusings of thy grace,
our prayer so languid, and our faith so dim;
for lo, between our sins and their reward
we set the passion of thy Son our Lord.'

COLLECT

Almighty God,
by whose grace alone we are accepted
and called to your service:
strengthen us by your Holy Spirit
and make us worthy of our calling;
through Jesus Christ our Lord.

| *Reflection by* **Michael Ipgrave**

Psalms **5**, 6 (8)
Song 28-end *or* Malachi 2.1-16
John 13.12-20

Tuesday 4 February

Malachi 2.1-16

'... my covenant with Levi' (v.4)

Malachi has a particular interest in priests and Levites – it's not clear whether he distinguishes between the two. He refers to God's 'covenant with Levi', something not unambiguously attested elsewhere in scripture; and it has been suggested that Malachi himself was from a priestly or Levitical family.

Perhaps that is why his strictures against priests are so vitriolic. His emphasis is particularly on the teaching ministry rather than the offering of sacrifice; but whatever the roles, priests do seem to be distinguished from the rest of God's people and held to a higher standard of behaviour.

Christian priests are also expected to hold to high standards of behaviour. The whole people of God (the laity) are called to holiness, and those who are ordained have a particular responsibility to bear public witness by their lives to the meaning of discipleship.

When I was ordained priest according to the Book of Common Prayer, the bishop laid great emphasis on 'the horrible punishment' that will ensue in the event of priestly failure or negligence. Common Worship liturgy, less dramatically but with equal challenge, reminds ordinands that 'it is to Christ that you will render account'. Whether a covenant with Levi is in force or not, those who are ordained priests are accountable in a particularly direct way to God and to God's people.

COLLECT

God of our salvation,
help us to turn away from those habits
which harm our bodies and poison our minds
and to choose again your gift of life,
revealed to us in Jesus Christ our Lord.

Wednesday 5 February

Psalm 119.1-32
Susannah 1-27
or Malachi 2.17 – 3.12
John 13.21-30

Malachi 2.17 – 3.12

'... he will purify' (3.3)

For me, it's practically impossible to separate this verse, from the spiritual elation that stems from the music of the great chorus in Handel's Messiah.

It's easy to forget that Malachi is speaking of the refiner's fire, which separates dross from pure metal. For those in the furnace, the experience is anything but enjoyable. Purification is painful, costly, terrifying.

When we are going through a time of personal testing and recasting, even though we may sense that the end result will be for our good, we may well know anxiety, fear, even agony. Such experiences in this life can be a way in which we grow in self-awareness, and in sanctification if we recognize them as part of the divine purpose for us. Malachi's warning is that it is necessary to be purified before one can come into the presence of God's pure holiness.

This verse has supported belief in purgatory, which has come, in popular usage, simply to mean pain and suffering. But its core meaning is a stage of purification and preparation on our journey towards God. Whatever happens after death, we can expect times in this life when we will experience that process.

Lord, give me strength to enter your purifying fire, knowing that it is your love that has devised this for me.

COLLECT

Almighty God,
by whose grace alone we are accepted
    and called to your service:
strengthen us by your Holy Spirit
and make us worthy of our calling;
through Jesus Christ our Lord.

Reflection by **Michael Ipgrave**

Psalms 14, **15**, 16
Susannah 28–end
or Malachi 3.13 – end of 4
John 13.31–end

Thursday 6 February

Malachi 3.13 – end of 4

'... the sun of righteousness shall rise' (4.2)

In our bibles, though not in the Hebrew scriptures, Malachi is the final book of the Old Testament. It's therefore unsurprising that this prophecy from Malachi's final chapter has been taken by Christians to point to a fulfilment in the New Testament. Jesus himself, according to Matthew, identified John the Baptist as 'Elijah who was to come' in preparation for the day of the Lord. As for Jesus, he was understood by early Christians to be the rising sun (v.2) – an image deeply woven into liturgy and hymnody:

> Hail the heaven-born Prince of Peace,
> Hail the Sun of Righteousness!
> Light and life to all He brings,
> Risen with healing in his wings!

Wesley's description fits the northern hemisphere climate, where sunlight is welcomed as gentle, restorative and enlivening, unlike the fierce, blistering and desiccating threat it can be in the Middle East.

We must be guarded in our use of themes from Hebrew Scripture to express Christian meaning. Some Christian quarrying of Old Testament proof texts in the past has been misguided and disrespectful. Nevertheless, Malachi's expectant prophecy is essentially open-ended; there is no reason why we shouldn't pray daily for its realization in our own lives. To quote Wesley again:

> Sun of righteousness, arise,
> Triumph o'er the shades of night;
> Day-spring from on high be near;
> Day star in my heart appear!

> God of our salvation,
> help us to turn away from those habits
> which harm our bodies and poison our minds
> and to choose again your gift of life,
> revealed to us in Jesus Christ our Lord.

COLLECT

Reflection by **Michael Ipgrave**   67

Friday 7 February

Psalms 17, **19**
Bel and the Dragon *or* Nahum 1
John 14.1-14

Nahum 1

'... a jealous and avenging God' (v.1)

Even the great reformer John Calvin was not renowned for his emollient language, commented on the vehemence and boldness of the prophet's opening words. Throughout the book, statements of God's fierce anger are directed against Nineveh and the Assyrians; unusually for prophetic literature, at no point are Nahum's messages of denunciation addressed to God's own people. Indeed, Nahum's name means 'comforter', and towards the end of this chapter God promises through him an end of affliction for Judah and the peaceful celebration of its feasts.

How should we incorporate such intense polemic into our own prayer life? Depending on chronological setting, there are two ways of reading Nahum, depending on its relation to historical actuality. One sees it as an account of the fall of Nineveh, which has already taken place. In that case, Nahum's exultant denunciation of the fallen Assyrians feels like vengeful nationalism, and may best be relegated to the status of historical record.

We can, though, read it as a promise of future deliverance for Judah, threatened by the dominant power of the region, whose brutality had already suppressed several neighbouring nations. We then hear Nahum's oracle as a protest against the injustice that still mars our world, and of hope for the establishment of God's kingdom. The nations are indeed still 'divided and torn apart by the ravages of sin', and still we pray that they may be made subject to God's gentle and just rule.

COLLECT

Almighty God,
by whose grace alone we are accepted
    and called to your service:
strengthen us by your Holy Spirit
and make us worthy of our calling;
through Jesus Christ our Lord.

| *Reflection by* **Michael Ipgrave**

Psalms 20, 21, **23**
Prayer of Manasseh *or* Obadiah
John 14.15-end

Saturday 8 February

Obadiah

'I will destroy the wise out of Edom' (v.8)

Obadiah is the shortest book of the Hebrew Scriptures, and among the most obscure. We know little about Obadiah, nor the period in which he lived. It is clear, though, that his message was directed against the kingdom of Edom: accusing the Edomites of abandoning their Judaean neighbours in their day of disaster. This behaviour was even more reprehensible because of the kinship that should have bound the two peoples – a kinship traceable back to the conflicted yet intimate relationship of the twin brothers Esau and Jacob.

Elsewhere, Edom is identified as a place where wisdom is known and practised; Obadiah prophesies God's destruction of this wisdom. We probably should not interpret wisdom in modern terms as a reference to Edom's 'soft power' as a culture or nation. It is possible that the origins of the Edomites' reputation for wisdom lay in their metallurgical skills; their military capacity, reliant on this, does not seem to be in question here. Nevertheless, there seems to be culpability in the combination of cleverness with betrayal. This is the basis for their condemnation: those blessed with greater ability are held more blameworthy.

In a world marked by sin and violence, which reaches its crisis in the betrayal and crucifixion of the Lord of glory, Paul told the Corinthians that God had made the world's wisdom into nothing, 'so that your faith might rest not on human wisdom but on the power of God' (1 Corinthians 2.5).

COLLECT

God of our salvation,
help us to turn away from those habits
which harm our bodies and poison our minds
and to choose again your gift of life,
revealed to us in Jesus Christ our Lord.

Reflection by **Michael Ipgrave** | 69

Monday 10 February

Psalms 27, **30**
Joel 1.1-14
John 15.1-11

Joel 1.1-14

'The fields are devastated, the ground mourns ...' (v.10)

Joel's is a short prophecy, and we shall read the whole of it over the course of this week. Agricultural imagery permeates the text, particularly in this opening section. The scene is of the devastation caused by locusts that leads to the loss of the harvest, and although we can interpret this section metaphorically, it is clear that for Joel, and the communities described here, this is a natural disaster of a catastrophic nature.

Joel's words are a reminder to us of the delicate and essential balance between humanity and the natural world. When the crops fail, people starve. Farming communities perhaps experience the fragility of our ecosystem most keenly, but all of us rely on the fruit of the earth. The call to repentance at the end of this reading, a text to which the Church has turned on Ash Wednesday since early days, reminds us that we must acknowledge our own complicity in the failure of harvests and the barrenness of the earth. As we reflect on the need for proper repentance and commit ourselves to a responsible stewardship of the world's resources, we can take heart from the opening verse of today's reading: that the 'word of the Lord' still comes to his waiting people.

COLLECT

O God,
you know us to be set
in the midst of so many and great dangers,
that by reason of the frailty of our nature
we cannot always stand upright:
grant to us such strength and protection
as may support us in all dangers
and carry us through all temptations;
through Jesus Christ our Lord.

| *Reflection by* **Tom Clammer**

Psalms 32, **36**
Joel 1.15-end
John 15.12-17

Tuesday 11 February

Joel 1.15-end
'For the day of the Lord is near' (v.15)

The 'day of the Lord' is a phrase familiar to us from Old Testament prophecy, and it is likely that Joel is consciously referencing Isaiah, Ezekiel, Malachi and others when he uses this phrase here. As prophetic voices have reminded the community from earliest times, often serving as the 'grit in the oyster', we must have an eye both to the present and the future. We are living in a place between the promises of God and their fulfilment, and what is certain is that we will be called to account for the way in which we honour and nurture that which God has given us. Complacency is not an option, and indeed it can be disastrous.

Striking in today's passage is the way in which Joel describes 'how the animals groan', and 'the wild animals cry to [God]'. St Paul, centuries later, will take up a similar message when he writes that, 'the whole creation has been groaning in labour pains until now' (Romans 8.22). The physical, the material, the created world is acutely aware of both its beauty and its brokenness, and longs for its redemption. Where, today, might our prayers and actions join in that chorus of longing?

Lord of the hosts of heaven,
our salvation and our strength,
without you we are lost:
guard us from all that harms or hurts
and raise us when we fall;
through Jesus Christ our Lord.

COLLECT

Wednesday 12 February

Joel 2.1-17

'... return to me with all your heart' (v.12)

Again we are in 'Ash Wednesday territory', with large parts of today's reading familiar from that great penitential liturgy in which many of us will engage in only a few short weeks. Striking, however, and not normally read on Ash Wednesday, is the description of the Lord's army. We hear a description of a well-trained and well-rehearsed attack, with disciplined and motivated soldiers charging, scaling the walls, each following their own oft-practised lines of attack, and swarming into windows of houses before them. This is uncomfortable language when used of God whom we love and turn to for forgiveness.

How important, therefore, to keep reading beyond verse 11 today. If our God is one of justice, our God is one of mercy also. God calls, 'return to me with all your heart'. Does our heart turn towards God? Are there parts of it that we defend and keep locked down? When God arrives, will there be doors standing open or a drawbridge firmly raised? As many of our forebears in the faith have taught, we need to heed the reminder in John's first letter (1 John 4.16) that God is love, and love only, and that we get into a pickle when we disorder our own love. That's where we begin to close doors and windows that ought to be open to God.

COLLECT

O God,
you know us to be set
in the midst of so many and great dangers,
that by reason of the frailty of our nature
we cannot always stand upright:
grant to us such strength and protection
as may support us in all dangers
and carry us through all temptations;
through Jesus Christ our Lord.

| *Reflection by* **Tom Clammer**

Psalm **37***
Joel 2.18-27
John 16.1-15

Thursday 13 February

Joel 2.18-27

'... the pastures of the wilderness are green' (v.22)

As we move through chapter two, the great theme of deliverance emerges. The language continues to be a mixture of the military and the agricultural, and the message is one both of salvation from attack, and of abundant harvest. Detailed biblical and historical analysis of this passage will reveal the circumstances in which these verses were first written, where rescue from real armies, and deliverance from famine, were matters prayed for daily.

As we read this passage today, in the context of what came yesterday and what may come tomorrow, what we receive is the absolute promise of God that no matter what besets us, no matter what the circumstances of this day, it is goodness, fruitfulness and salvation that God would gift to us. Reading this in a world still full of armies and hunger is a challenge. These promises, these prophecies, are at once wonderful and unsettling. We are invited into a vision of the kingdom of God, and to believe that vision even while we move through a world that sometimes tells a very different story. This is the challenge and the adventure of prophecy. How might we hold on to this vision, and how might it shape our prayers today?

Lord of the hosts of heaven,
our salvation and our strength,
without you we are lost:
guard us from all that harms or hurts
and raise us when we fall;
through Jesus Christ our Lord.

COLLECT

Friday 14 February

Joel 2.28-end

'I will pour out my spirit' (v.29)

Once again, we are on familiar ground with the opening words of today's passage. Now we are in 'Holy Spirit territory', and that liturgical connection might be helpful for us as we ponder the more difficult lines of this prophecy. What happens between Ash Wednesday and the feast of Pentecost is, of course, the Passion, death and resurrection of Jesus. When we read of 'portents in the heavens and on the earth', when we think about darkness and blood, we are not only sitting firmly in the tradition of the Old Testament prophets; we are also in the story of Good Friday.

There is a cost to love. There is a cost to our salvation. And the price, for Christ, is darkness and blood. That action, that utterly self-emptying offering, is indeed amazing grace, and the gift to us is the closeness and intimacy of the Holy Spirit. Faced with that extraordinary act of love, do we dare to see visions? Do we dare to dream dreams? When was the last time we prayed that prayer? Maybe that's a task for today: to pray once again for the Holy Spirit of God to make us receptive to the dreams and visions that might inspire us for the living of our Christian faith today.

COLLECT

O God,
you know us to be set
in the midst of so many and great dangers,
that by reason of the frailty of our nature
we cannot always stand upright:
grant to us such strength and protection
as may support us in all dangers
and carry us through all temptations;
through Jesus Christ our Lord.

| *Reflection by* **Tom Clammer**

Psalms 41, **42**, 43
Joel 3.1-3, 9-end
John 16.23-end

Saturday 15 February

Joel 3.1-3, 9-end

'... all the stream beds of Judah shall flow with water' (v.18)

Among the most striking words in today's reading have to be in verse 10, where the prophet exhorts people to 'beat your ploughshares into swords and your pruning hooks into spears'. We are so used to the text from Isaiah 2 (and its parallel in Micah 4), where the prophet speaks of entirely the opposite: a time when, 'they shall beat their swords into ploughshares', and a vision of peace is held before our eyes. Joel seems to be describing something rather different here in the closing verses of his prophecy, and it feels rather uncomfortable. The five verses that are omitted from today's reading are verses describing the revenge that God will take upon Tyre, Sidon and Philistia, and reading them is very unsettling.

Perhaps the key message to take from this short and strange book of the Bible is summed up in verse 18, where the agricultural imagery returns and we hear that 'all the stream beds of Judah shall flow with water'. Drill down through the military and agricultural metaphors and we find the repeated promise that God is faithful to us, and that life and vitality will return. Any sense of abandonment and isolation, or a drying up of our faith, is set within the utterly unbreakable fidelity of God.

Lord of the hosts of heaven,
our salvation and our strength,
without you we are lost:
guard us from all that harms or hurts
and raise us when we fall;
through Jesus Christ our Lord.

COLLECT

Monday 17 February

Psalm **44**
Ecclesiastes 1
John 17.1-5

Ecclesiastes 1

'Vanity of vanities! All is vanity' (v.2)

Over the next two weeks we will journey with the Teacher through an exploration of what surely everyone must ask at some time in their lives: What is it all about? What is the meaning of life? How do we make sense of what at times can feel like a futile existence, as we stand on a tiny rock hurtling at 67,000 miles per hour around a ball of fire, in a seemingly infinite universe, with the only fact about which we can be sure being that we will die.

Who is our companion in this journey? Is it the wisest of Old Testament Kings, the mighty Solomon? The jury is out, but does it matter? The Teacher is one who has pondered the meaning of life and tried to make sense of it but who has concluded that it is meaningless, futile, deceptive, unreliable, brief – vanity. So far, so depressing. Or is it?

As we continue to recover from the 'the Covid years', the anecdotal evidence seems to be that people are reassessing their lives. Faced with a world that feels increasingly unstable, and where once trusted institutions that used to win our respect prove themselves to be untrustworthy, the question 'What is it all about?' is not far from people's lips. As Christians we have an answer. Can the musings of the Teacher help us better to engage with those who are seeking?

COLLECT

Almighty God,
who alone can bring order
to the unruly wills and passions of sinful humanity:
give your people grace
so to love what you command
and to desire what you promise,
that, among the many changes of this world,
our hearts may surely there be fixed
where true joys are to be found;
through Jesus Christ our Lord.

| *Reflection by* **Jan McFarlane**

Psalms **48**, 52
Ecclesiastes 2
John 17.6-19

Tuesday 18 February

Ecclesiastes 2

'... for all is vanity and a chasing after wind' (v.17)

We don't have to look far to see where we're encouraged to search for a meaningful or successful existence. Advertising often leads the way. Popular television follows. In this regard not much has changed over the thousands of years since the Teacher sought to make sense of life. The acquisition of wealth, possessions, property and a luxurious lifestyle; the 'delights of the flesh' in the form of casual or exploitative sex, or even the so-called 'higher pursuits' of acquiring knowledge, academic prowess, or promotion to the 'top job' – the Teacher has tried them all. But he is quite clear, 'All of it is meaningless, a chasing after the wind.'

The Church is often preoccupied, obsessed even, with trying to attract young people. 'Growing younger' features in many a mission statement and strategy. And, of course, it is vitally important that children and young people grow up knowing something of our Christian faith. But it's no surprise to me that in our congregations the majority are often those of riper years. They have spread their wings, sought meaning in their careers or in the pursuit of wealth or possessions, and as retirement beckons, and the lure of 'gilded things' diminishes, and the end of life is contemplated, the Church is the place where those big questions about the meaning of life can be explored. Just as long as we're not too busy chasing after the young, who are themselves often busy chasing after the wind.

Eternal God,
whose Son went among the crowds
and brought healing with his touch:
help us to show his love,
in your church as we gather together,
and by our lives as they are transformed
into the image of Christ our Lord.

COLLECT

Wednesday 19 February

Psalm **119.57-80**
Ecclesiastes 3.1-15
John 17.20-end

Ecclesiastes 3.1-15

'... it is God's gift that all should eat and drink and take pleasure in all their toil' (v.13)

The poem that makes up the first eight verses of today's passage has captured the imagination of those who might not realize that they are, after all, familiar with the Bible, thanks to the song version by American rock band The Byrds. The fourteen couplets covering the whole range of life experiences, from birth to death, resonate with that part of us that longs for there to be some sort of order and purpose to our existence.

But the Teacher reflects on how little we can influence our lives; how all our toil is futile because our times are in God's hands. Made as we are in God's image, we have a sense of time and of eternity, and yet seemingly can do little about it. Is this a prison? Or is it freedom?

The conclusion reached is that we should stop striving, receive our food and drink and our work as gifts from God, and cease fretting about things we cannot change. Perhaps we can hear echoes of Jesus' teaching in the sixth chapter of Matthew's Gospel, that we should consider the lilies of the field and the birds of the air who are provided for by God, and not worry about tomorrow, instead seeking first the kingdom of God and his righteousness and trusting that 'all these things will be given to you as well'.

COLLECT

Almighty God,
who alone can bring order
to the unruly wills and passions of sinful humanity:
give your people grace
so to love what you command
and to desire what you promise,
that, among the many changes of this world,
our hearts may surely there be fixed
where true joys are to be found;
through Jesus Christ our Lord.

| *Reflection by* **Jan McFarlane**

Psalms 56, **57** (63*)
Ecclesiastes 3.16 – end of 4
John 18.1-11

Thursday 20 February

Ecclesiastes 3.16 – end of 4

'A threefold cord is not quickly broken' (4.12)

Perhaps of all the challenges that cause people to question the meaning of life and the existence of God, there is none more powerful than injustice. Those of us who talk often with those searching for faith frequently encounter the age-old conundrum, 'Why do bad things happen to good people?' and the sense of injustice that accompanies that question. The Teacher is not immune and examines the elements of human existence that cause him to wonder what life is all about. Why do the powerful oppress the powerless? Why do we see still, centuries on from when the Teacher wrote, economic exploitation of the poor, jealousy, competitiveness and greed, with the odds usually favouring the oppressor rather than the oppressed?

Sometimes the writings of the Teacher seem to ramble a little, and we shouldn't be too worried if we can't keep up. But he seems to conclude that it's in community where God's love and justice are to be found. Not one person going all out to be top dog, but each of us helping and supporting the other, lifting each other up when we fall, and forming bonds that cannot easily be broken. At the cathedral where I serve, we often refer to our congregation, including the housebound who worship with us online, as our church 'family'. If loneliness is the 'new epidemic' as it has sometimes been described, doesn't the Church have something very precious to offer?

Eternal God,
whose Son went among the crowds
and brought healing with his touch:
help us to show his love,
in your church as we gather together,
and by our lives as they are transformed
into the image of Christ our Lord.

COLLECT

Reflection by **Jan McFarlane** | 79

Friday 21 February

Psalms **51**, 54
Ecclesiastes 5
John 18.12-27

Ecclesiastes 5

'The lover of money will not be satisfied with money' (v.10)

If asked what would make them happiest in life, I suspect many people would touch on the subject of wealth, often a close second – but only just – to health. The idea that riches will guarantee happiness cause those with little spare cash to buy lottery tickets or to risk 'a flutter on the horses'. And yet, as the Teacher reflects, those who have great riches often don't rest content but keep striving for more, or spend time and energy worrying what will happen if their wealth is suddenly taken from them. There is no doubt that struggling to buy food or to pay energy bills is a huge source of anxiety for many, and in that sense money matters very much. The problem comes when we assume that the more we have, the happier we will be, and the more meaning our lives will have.

Not so, says the Teacher. We come into this world naked and we will leave this world naked. There are no pockets in a shroud. While everyone needs enough to live, acquiring great riches is not the answer to the deepest questions of life. Centuries later Jesus picks up this theme when he teaches us not to store up riches where rust and moths can attack, or where thieves can steal, but to find true riches in our relationship with God – something that is truly priceless.

COLLECT

Almighty God,
who alone can bring order
to the unruly wills and passions of sinful humanity:
give your people grace
so to love what you command
and to desire what you promise,
that, among the many changes of this world,
our hearts may surely there be fixed
where true joys are to be found;
through Jesus Christ our Lord.

| *Reflection by* **Jan McFarlane**

Saturday 22 February

Ecclesiastes 6

'All human toil is for the mouth, yet the appetite is not satisfied'
(v. 7)

The Teacher concludes that no matter how long we live, it is never long enough, as there is never time to sit back from the acquisition of wealth and possessions in order to enjoy them, and so we die, leaving someone else to benefit from all our work. This, he concludes, is futile. It is all vanity. Children and long life – understood by Israel to be the signs of God's blessing – are not worth much if there isn't time to benefit from them. If that's all there is to life, then surely it would be better not to be born.

'All human toil is for the mouth,' the Teacher declares. We toil to satisfy our physical need and desires, and yet are never satisfied. In the same way that a sugary treat is enjoyed but soon leaves us hungry again as our blood sugar levels rise and then plummet, so nothing we earn ultimately scratches where we are itching. We are always searching for more.

As Christians we know that we can direct those who are seeking to the one who is the bread of life, who satisfies all our hungers. We know we can go to the water of life so that we shall never thirst again. The fourth-century theologian Augustine of Hippo's famous saying is an apt conclusion: 'You have made us for yourself, O Lord, and our hearts are restless until they find their rest in you.'

Eternal God,
whose Son went among the crowds
and brought healing with his touch:
help us to show his love,
in your church as we gather together,
and by our lives as they are transformed
into the image of Christ our Lord.

COLLECT

Monday 24 February

Ecclesiastes 7.1-14

'... and the day of death, [better] than the day of birth' (v.1)

In the first six chapters of Ecclesiastes, the Teacher has been at pains to present to his audience proof that life without a personal relationship with God is meaningless. It is all vanity. And so how are we to make the most of a futile existence? The Teacher doesn't take the path trodden by the authors of other ancient wisdom literature and suggest we end our own lives because life is pointless. Instead he encourages us to examine our lives and choose the lesser of two evils.

The day of our death, the Teacher suggests, is better than the day of our birth. Birth leads to a finite life, but death is infinite. And as death is forever, then we would be better to spend our time preparing for it, rather than wasting our time in the 'house of mirth'. We probably don't feel inclined to take the Teacher's words too literally, and to spend the rest of our days without laughter, but the idea that we should consider our death is surely wise.

Perhaps as those who believe in resurrection, and who understand that death is nothing to be feared if we believe in Jesus Christ, we might begin to help others understand that death is part of life, and to remove some of its fear by refusing to shy away from using the word itself (sensitively of course), rather than opting for the gentler, but perhaps avoidant, 'passed away'.

COLLECT

Almighty God,
you have created the heavens and the earth
and made us in your own image:
teach us to discern your hand in all your works
and your likeness in all your children;
through Jesus Christ your Son our Lord,
who with you and the Holy Spirit reigns supreme over all things,
now and for ever.

Reflection by **Jan McFarlane**

Psalm **73**
Ecclesiastes 7.15-end
John 19.17-30

Tuesday 25 February

Ecclesiastes 7.15-end

'... there are righteous people who perish in their righteousness'
(v.15)

Besides the conundrum of why bad things happen to good people, perhaps the most searching questions we are asked is why those we might consider evil often seem to thrive. If anything makes us question the meaning of life, surely it is this. Why do 'righteous people perish in their righteousness' and 'wicked people prolong their life in their evildoing'. If God is a God of justice, then how is this just?

As I write, I am spending much time with a couple whose teenage daughter was killed in a collision with a car. She was simply in the wrong place at the wrong time, and neither she nor the driver was at fault. It was simply an accident. All I can do is sit with her parents, listen to them and support them, and not avoid them for fear of not knowing what to say. The temptation in such circumstances is to resort to platitudes, but that will not do. We simply don't know why this happened. It makes no sense. It is deeply unfair.

It's my hope and prayer that those parents may one day learn to live with the questions. It is my even more fervent prayer that one day they will come to know the one who walks with us 'through the valley of the shadow of death' so that we may 'fear no evil' and ultimately find comfort and hope (Psalm 23).

Almighty God,
give us reverence for all creation
and respect for every person,
that we may mirror your likeness
in Jesus Christ our Lord.

COLLECT

Reflection by **Jan McFarlane** | 83

Wednesday 26 February

Ecclesiastes 8

'Wisdom makes one's face shine' (v.1)

Sometimes reading Ecclesiastes can make our heads hurt. We might almost have reached the stage of dreading picking up our Bibles knowing that we're in for another passage about life being nothing but vanity. And then, a crumb of hope. Wisdom makes our faces shine.

The hardness of countenance the Teacher refers to can be seen all around us. We live in a world that appears largely to have turned its back on God. The human race is self-reliant, we trust in our own strength. When things don't turn out as we think they should, we're confused. We question. And eventually we conclude that 'all is vanity'. There is little meaning. There isn't much justice. It simply isn't true that if you work hard and live a decent life, you will be rich and happy. No wonder then that stress and anxiety levels are at an all-time high. Perhaps we simply need to work harder? Try harder? Our brows are furrowed.

As Christians we have something very precious to offer to those who are trying to find meaning through sheer hard work and the acquisition of material goods. We believe in the One who creates, redeems, sustains us. Life does have a meaning if we believe in a beginning and an end and then a new beginning: resurrection hope. Why are our churches then so slow to share such good news with those around us? – with faces that shine!

COLLECT

Almighty God,
you have created the heavens and the earth
and made us in your own image:
teach us to discern your hand in all your works
and your likeness in all your children;
through Jesus Christ your Son our Lord,
who with you and the Holy Spirit reigns supreme over all things,
now and for ever.

| *Reflection by* **Jan McFarlane**

Psalm **78.1-39***
Ecclesiastes 9
John 20.1-10

Thursday 27 February

Ecclesiastes 9

'... their deeds are in the hand of God' (v.1)

As the Teacher begins to move towards some sort of conclusion, God enters, stage left. The Teacher has tried in vain to make sense of a life without God. He has examined the evidence before him and has found it wanting. Life makes no sense: all is vanity, as he has kept saying. There is neither logic nor meaning to our existence. There are no laws that mean if we do 'this', then 'that' will automatically follow. Life is random. So we're back in the company of the Greek philosopher Epicurus who advises to 'eat, drink and be merry, for tomorrow we die'.

The Teacher is left to conclude that as life makes no earthly sense, it must make heavenly sense. We can conclude only that our lives are in God's hands. We are left dependent on the mysteries of divine providence.

Being a Christian does not mean that nothing bad will ever happen to us. When I was diagnosed with cancer ten years ago, there were those who questioned how God could let such a thing happen to one of his priests. I never once asked 'why me?' Why shouldn't it have been me? Bad things happen to those who try to do their best in life, like everyone else. But we do have the assurance that we are in God's hands. Not in the way the Teacher meant, but in the sense that God holds us in the palm of his hands, and never, ever lets us go.

Almighty God,
give us reverence for all creation
and respect for every person,
that we may mirror your likeness
in Jesus Christ our Lord.

COLLECT

Friday 28 February

Psalm **55**
Ecclesiastes 11.1-8
John 20.11-18

Ecclesiastes 11.1-8

'... at evening do not let your hands be idle' (v.6)

The Teacher is at pains to point out that despite concluding that our times are in God's hands and human life apart from God makes no earthly sense, we shouldn't be tempted just to sit back and do nothing. We shouldn't conclude that because we can't control our destinies, we can be idle and simply let life happen to us. There is still the need to seize the day, to make the most of our lives, to do what we can with what we've been given, and to prepare for our futures as carefully as possible.

We are to be diligent simply because so much of life is a mystery. We understand a little of how cells divide in the womb and new life is created, but we don't know where the resulting child's spirit or character comes from. It's like the wind that blows where it wishes, as Jesus will later teach Nicodemus (John 3.8).

Ultimately, the Teacher concludes, we are to let God take care of the mysteries of this world – mysteries we will never understand this side of heaven – while we get on with the day-to-day tasks of everyday life. Mystery is often seen in opposition to scientific fact. But even the greatest minds understand that the more we think we know, the more we realize we don't know. Mystery is all we are left with. Best then to embrace it willingly.

COLLECT

Almighty God,
you have created the heavens and the earth
and made us in your own image:
teach us to discern your hand in all your works
and your likeness in all your children;
through Jesus Christ your Son our Lord,
who with you and the Holy Spirit reigns supreme over all things,
now and for ever.

| *Reflection by* **Jan McFarlane**

Saturday 1 March

Ecclesiastes 11.9 – end of 12

'The end of the matter: all has been heard' (12.13)

The Teacher reaches his conclusion. He has reviewed 'all the toil under the sun'. He has contemplated the brevity of life and the infinite death that comes to us all. He has urged us not to be passive passengers in life, but to make the most of all that has been given to us, working hard and enjoying our food and drink, while knowing that our times are not in our hands and that life is often neither fair nor just. He has concluded that left to our own devices, humans can find little that makes sense of life, for the things that in our youth we believe will bring fulfilment and joy, ultimately bring neither, at least not in any lasting and meaningful sense.

At the last, the Teacher concludes, life is a mystery and we are in God's hands. We are then to fear God and keep his commandments – 'for that is the whole duty of everyone'. The seventeenth-century Westminster Catechism teaches (before the advent of inclusive language):

'What is the chief end of man?
Man's chief end is to glorify God, and to enjoy him forever.'

We are to let go of striving to make sense of our lives and instead turn our attention to God. And then to learn what sense God wants to make of our lives. And to discover that, with God, our lives have purpose and meaning. And they are far from vanity.

Almighty God,
give us reverence for all creation
and respect for every person,
that we may mirror your likeness
in Jesus Christ our Lord.

COLLECT

Monday 3 March

John 3.1-21

'How can these things be?' (v.9)

Jesus does not answer Nicodemus but throws a question back: 'Are you a teacher of Israel, and yet you do not understand these things?' The conversation is profoundly ironic, and it invites the reader to participate in developing a multilayered meaning.

Nicodemus tries to test how his understanding of God fits with what Jesus does. He operates with his received categories of how God relates to humanity, but Jesus offers something new. His long-held religious understanding does not help him comprehend the two levels of meaning in 'born again' or 'born from above'. We need to be willing to challenge our own presuppositions and embrace new ways of understanding to see how God acts in Jesus.

Nicodemus does not get the point that physical birth into his faith community is not enough. Nor does he understand that he needs to be part of a new community. In verse 11, the conversation moves on from a personal to a communal level, as Jesus uses 'we' and 'you' (plural). They become representatives of two communities. The second birth that Jesus talks about makes one born into the new community of Jesus. Nicodemus hopes to continue as a secret admirer, visiting Jesus under cover of darkness. But the gospel challenge is to walk in the light and make a commitment to an alternative community. But for many, like Nicodemus, such a change in social location is as impossible as re-entering their mother's womb.

COLLECT

Almighty Father,
whose Son was revealed in majesty
before he suffered death upon the cross:
give us grace to perceive his glory,
that we may be strengthened to suffer with him
and be changed into his likeness, from glory to glory;
who is alive and reigns with you,
in the unity of the Holy Spirit,
one God, now and for ever.

Reflection by **John Perumbalath**

Psalms 87, **89.1-18**
Jeremiah 2.1-13
John 3.22-end

Tuesday 4 March

John 3.22-end

'He must increase, but I must decrease' (v.30)

The complaint from John's disciples about the success of Jesus' ministry is an indication of the rivalry between the followers of two men, which may have continued into the time that the Gospel of John was being written towards the end of the first century (see Acts 19.1-7). John tries to shift his disciples' perspective by speaking about 'receiving' from heaven in verse 27. The issue is not about receiving more members to one's group but about receiving God, which can only happen if given by heaven.

John's joy at Jesus' success reminds us that what takes precedence over the acclamation of one's own work or ministry is the success of the gospel. John knows his ministry is already successful as it had prepared the ground for and revealed the Messiah to Israel (John 1.31). There would not be any place for competitions or turf battles among the people of God if we understood our particular and limited roles in God's story.

John finds his joy in his subordination to Jesus. Once Jesus' ministry began, John had no function. John models the role of disciples in all ages and their willingness to play second fiddle. John's attitude rebukes every movement or church that points to itself as the way to God. It enables us not to let our self-importance be wounded by the success of other disciples. It helps us recognize our own role positively but gladly embrace the potentially greater roles of our fellow servants.

Holy God,
you know the disorder of our sinful lives:
set straight our crooked hearts,
and bend our wills to love your goodness
and your glory
in Jesus Christ our Lord.

COLLECT

Wednesday 5 March
Ash Wednesday

Psalm **38**
Daniel 9.3-6, 17-19
1 Timothy 6.6-19

1 Timothy 6.6-19

'… there is great gain in godliness with contentment' (v.6)

Keeping a holy Lent involves paying attention to how we live. How we regard and use money are among the most important ways in which Christian understanding challenges and transforms sinful cultural norms. These attitudes and practices are part of making a 'good confession', which is a commandment for believers, not an optional extra in Christian life.

If we are to have a proper Christian attitude, it is necessary to understand 'gain' and 'profit' beyond material terms. The author writes of death in verse 7. The dead have no use for money, but their godliness and personal integrity (the word translated as contentment could mean integrity too) are spoken of as 'great gain' beyond the grave.

The instruction of what to avoid and what to pursue comes from the ethical discourses of antiquity: it portrays what kind of character is expected of the people of God. We cannot simply flee away from the love of money, or from the vices referred to in verse 4, without consciously embracing a spiritual disposition and moral character. This is expanded in terms of six virtues – righteousness, godliness, faith, love, endurance and gentleness.

Formation of this spiritual and moral character is traditionally a focus of Lent. This will lead us to do good, to be generous and rich in good works. This passage offers us so much material for reflection on the usual Lenten themes of piety, detachment and giving.

COLLECT

Almighty and everlasting God,
you hate nothing that you have made
and forgive the sins of all those who are penitent:
create and make in us new and contrite hearts
that we, worthily lamenting our sins
and acknowledging our wretchedness,
may receive from you, the God of all mercy,
perfect remission and forgiveness;
through Jesus Christ our Lord.

| *Reflection by* **John Perumbalath**

Thursday 6 March

John 4.1-26

'Jesus said to her, "Give me a drink".' (v.7)

Jesus' action here is in serious violation of the prevailing cultural code. It transcended all the barriers of gender, race and religion that existed at that time. There were clear boundaries between 'chosen people' and 'rejected people', and between male and female. Also, that this woman came to fetch water at noon rather than joining the social occasion in the morning or evening suggests that she was already an outsider in her own community.

Jesus disregards the woman's protest of the impropriety of the situation and brings up her past and the present not to shame her, but to take away their power in showing how little they affect how God accepts her. What Jesus offers her is a role reversal: instead of her being the one who gives water, she could become the one who receives. And Jesus names obvious and hidden thirsts to deepen the woman's awareness of both.

By tendering direct questions and diverting her distracting responses by more intimate questions, both gain a deeper knowledge of the other and realize that water in the well is not the endpoint of this conversation, but just its beginning. Bodily needs for basic sustenance and a spiritual tapestry of relationship are woven into this encounter that leads to further questioning, the healthy airing of confusion, impassioned testimony, defensive disbelief, and confession of faith. The story shows us how effective faith conversations might take place and how God meets us where we are and receives us.

Holy God,
our lives are laid open before you:
rescue us from the chaos of sin
and through the death of your Son
bring us healing and make us whole
in Jesus Christ our Lord.

COLLECT

Reflection by **John Perumbalath** | 91

Friday 7 March

John 4.27-42

'He cannot be the Messiah, can he?' (v.29)

The woman has now moved from protest and doubt to confession and witness. The content of her witness seems tentative, in the form of a question rather than a convincing statement, but it's enough to lead her villagers to Jesus. Bearing compelling witness does not depend on our absolute certainty in everything we say but on our honest willingness to share what we have experienced with an invitation to 'come and see'.

Jesus' disciples do not seem to be in a different place than that of the Samaritan woman when they come back with food. The misunderstanding, wordplay, and double meaning that we found in the previous conversations are here too in the conversation between Jesus and his disciples about food and harvest. Despite being close followers of Jesus, they still lacked understanding.

Jesus speaks with the disciples about his vocation and the vocation of all his witnesses, setting out some general principles. They are to feed on a different food: the food of doing the will of God. They do not need to wait for a future harvest: the fields are always ripe for God's witnesses. And, finally, they are not to do all the work. We build on the labour of others and leave space for others to continue after us.

COLLECT

Almighty and everlasting God,
you hate nothing that you have made
and forgive the sins of all those who are penitent:
create and make in us new and contrite hearts
that we, worthily lamenting our sins
and acknowledging our wretchedness,
may receive from you, the God of all mercy,
perfect remission and forgiveness;
through Jesus Christ our Lord.

Reflection by **John Perumbalath**

Psalm **71** *or.* 96, **97**, 100
Jeremiah 4.1-18
John 4.43-end

Saturday 8 March

John 4.43-end

'Go; your son will live' (v.50)

The first sign in Cana of water changed into wine had revealed Jesus' glory. Here, in the second, he is revealed as life-giver. The royal official moves from a request for help, through astonished realization of Jesus' power, to a firm commitment to Jesus. He approached Jesus for healing of his son, but he also receives the gift of faith. Jesus now draws to himself a family identified with royal court, in addition to the Jewish disciples and Samaritans he has already gathered, building his diverse beloved community.

Faith based on a sign is not enough, but it can be a stage on the way to a relationship with the one to which the sign points. It is the presence of God that transforms Jesus' acts from miracles to signs. Signs hold together the spiritual and physical in the same way as they are held together in the life of Jesus, the Word incarnate. It is not the miracle itself, but the presence of God at work within the miracle that leads to faith.

Yet here it is physical healing that provides a glimpse of God's character in Jesus. God knows that we human beings experience the spiritual only through our physicality, and we need to remember this as we witness to Christ today. It was both physical and material realities that would become 'signs' of God's presence and glory.

Holy God,
our lives are laid open before you:
rescue us from the chaos of sin
and through the death of your Son
bring us healing and make us whole
in Jesus Christ our Lord.

COLLECT

Monday 10 March

John 5.1-18

'Stand up, take your mat and walk' (v.8)

The sick man here represents those who have given up on healing, fallen into apathy and in their hopelessness, tend to rely on pity. Jesus refuses to play the self-pity game, ignores the question of who is to blame, and tells the man to get up and walk. He rises and steps out in faith. Faith brings healing of a limitation, restoration of purpose and hope, and the prospects of a fruitful life. And the healing is more than physical: the restoration that Jesus offers is holistic: 'Do not sin anymore, so that nothing worse happens to you.'

Jesus' compassion takes the paralytic seriously. 'Do you want to be made well?' is a question that respects the dignity and freedom of the sick person. Encouraging a desire to be made well is a compassionate act towards someone who has, to all intents and purposes, given up hope.

The episode also speaks about the cost of ministry and the price we might have to pay in the ministry of liberation. We do not know whether the healed man was collaborating with Jesus' enemies, or it was simply a case of innocent answers to their probing questions. In any case, the healing provokes a negative reaction among them. For his enemies, Jesus was breaking the Sabbath rules, but Jesus affirmed that God worked on the Sabbath. We cannot restrain God's work through the regulations and traditions we establish for ourselves.

COLLECT

Almighty God,
whose Son Jesus Christ fasted forty days in the wilderness,
and was tempted as we are, yet without sin:
give us grace to discipline ourselves in obedience to your Spirit;
and, as you know our weakness,
so may we know your power to save;
through Jesus Christ our Lord.

| *Reflection by* **John Perumbalath**

Psalm **44** *or* **106*** (*or* 103)
Jeremiah 5.1-19
John 5.19-29

John 5.19-29

'... those who hear will live' (v.25)

Having identified himself with the Father in the previous episode, Jesus goes on to talk in depth about the dynamic divine unity in today's reading. He makes a distinction between himself and God but without any functional difference: 'whatever the Father does, the Son does likewise.' The relationship between the Father and the Son cannot be reduced to a rational formula; rather it points to the mystery of God's nature.

Some scholars simplify the fourth evangelist's teaching about the future as realized: John teaches that God's future is already come in Jesus Christ. Verses 26-27 are clear in speaking about the here and now. But John's theology is not devoid of future hope. Verses 27-29 presuppose a future resurrection and judgement. Like John, we need to hold this tension between present and future: the Christ has come but the Christ is still to come.

The discourse also lays out the expected outcome of God's work through his Son. People need to 'hear'. Hearing is not only listening to the words but also receiving and accepting the message. This enables them to 'live' or have eternal life, a life that begins with God now. And those who have this life from Christ will be doers of good. Accepting God, enjoying eternal life and doing good are essential ingredients of the life expected of us.

Heavenly Father,
your Son battled with the powers of darkness,
and grew closer to you in the desert:
help us to use these days to grow in wisdom and prayer
that we may witness to your saving love
in Jesus Christ our Lord.

COLLECT

Reflection by **John Perumbalath**   95

Wednesday 12 March

John 5.30-end

'There is another who testifies on my behalf ... ' (v.32)

Jesus affirms that God alone is an adequate witness: that the Father who sent him has testified on his behalf. God does not witness directly but through a variety of mediators. Jesus lists some of these, helping us to know where we can find God's witness. Jewish law required two or three witnesses in serious allegations (e.g. Deuteronomy 17.6; Numbers 35.30) and in his ongoing debate with the Jews, Jesus here summons witnesses to support his case.

God uses human agency. The first witness Jesus calls for is John the Baptist, the one who came to prepare his way. The Evangelist has already established the Baptist's testimony earlier in the Gospel. Jesus then speaks about a testimony greater than John's – the works of God that Jesus does. Jesus' enemies often had a problem with Jesus' works. They sometimes found it difficult to reject his works as being from the devil because of the popularity he was gaining. Equally, they could not reject these works in God's name because they would then be seen as having rejected God.

Finally, Jesus moves on to the witness that his critics cannot avoid – the scriptures. His critics claimed their beliefs and practices were rooted in scripture: they often weaponized scripture to discredit him. They uphold scripture religiously and often literally, but they fail to read it with an openness to hear what God might be saying through it.

COLLECT

Almighty God,
whose Son Jesus Christ fasted forty days in the wilderness,
and was tempted as we are, yet without sin:
give us grace to discipline ourselves in obedience to your Spirit;
and, as you know our weakness,
so may we know your power to save;
through Jesus Christ our Lord.

| *Reflection by* **John Perumbalath**

Thursday 13 March

John 6.1-15

'But what are they among so many people?' (v.9)

The feeding of the five thousand is the only miracle story we find in all four Gospels. John uses it in a specific way that prepares us for Jesus' discourse on the bread of life. Jesus' action in taking, giving thanks and distributing the loaves will trigger thoughts of the eucharist for many readers. Jesus, meeting his hearers where they are, uses everyday substance from their daily lives and leads them to a life-changing choice.

But the occasion here where Jesus' glory is revealed is one of normal human need: hunger. There is no jumping straight into the spiritual need without dealing first with the immediate physical need. The miracle shows Jesus' concern for both This is a story that reveals God's compassionate love, and with the overtones of the Eucharist, it resonates strongly with Jesus' sacrificial self-giving in response to the human condition.

We need also to pay attention to the other characters in the story. Philip's answer expresses his despair at Jesus' question and reflects our general helplessness in the face of challenging situations of human need. Andrew jumps in with helpful information about the boy's lunch pack although he thought it inadequate. The boy, though, is willing to offer what he had, although very simple (barley was inferior to wheat). As Desmond Tutu said, 'The divine miracle requires the thoroughly inadequate human contribution.' God creates abundance from the very little that we can offer.

Heavenly Father,
your Son battled with the powers of darkness,
and grew closer to you in the desert:
help us to use these days to grow in wisdom and prayer
that we may witness to your saving love
in Jesus Christ our Lord.

COLLECT

Reflection by **John Perumbalath** | 97

Friday 14 March

John 6.16-27

'It is I; do not be afraid' (v.20)

Today's reading describes the most dramatic self-revelation of Jesus to this point in John's Gospel. Jesus' demonstration of power over the sea followed by an 'I am' saying presents a claim to speak both for and as God. There is no confession of faith from the disciples as in Matthew's account of this story (14.33) nor confusion among them as in Mark's (6.51-52). This is more about what Jesus does, and less about the impact of his revelation.

Jesus walks across the sea and brings his disciples safely to their destination. This is so unlike what the crowd had expected when they sought to make him king. He is not presented here as a candidate for public position and power but rather as God's own presence coming to his disciples. Jesus moves away from the crowd that wants him to be king and instead reveals himself in the midst of the disciple's fears.

The crowd reappears (v.22) and, in response to or in search of Jesus' signs, goes to the other side of the lake to meet him. The crowd represents the struggle of those who are open to believing, but neither the scriptures nor the signs lead them to a deeper commitment. The evangelist is building his invitation to all his readers to move from simple openness to faith in the presence of a sign to a mature faith that will no longer depend on signs.

COLLECT

Almighty God,
whose Son Jesus Christ fasted forty days in the wilderness,
and was tempted as we are, yet without sin:
give us grace to discipline ourselves in obedience to your Spirit;
and, as you know our weakness,
so may we know your power to save;
through Jesus Christ our Lord.

Reflection by **John Perumbalath**

Saturday 15 March

John 6.27-40

'Sir, give us this bread always' (v.34)

The question 'What must we do to perform the works of God?' suggests that the crowd is beginning to accept Jesus' challenge to think beyond physical food and to consider the things of God. When they go looking for a sign again, Jesus brings them back to the concerns beyond material food by speaking about the bread from heaven.

The crowd seems to be suggesting that, despite their hunger, they don't really know what they want. Jesus then focuses the conversation, speaking not about 'works' – the good deeds that make up life – but about a single 'work': to believe in the one who has been sent. But this requirement of faith has challenging implications for discipleship: believing is not for self-satisfaction or gain.

We might read 'all that he has given me' as implying that there are others who are not given to him. But John's emphasis on 'believing' necessitates that we hold human and divine responsibility in tension. Both God and humans play a role in having faith. God gives us the bread from heaven, but we must seek and receive it, acknowledging our hunger and thirst that bread and water alone cannot fulfil (v.35). This bread is given by God in the person of Christ and we receive him in the 'work' of faith.

Heavenly Father,
your Son battled with the powers of darkness,
and grew closer to you in the desert:
help us to use these days to grow in wisdom and prayer
that we may witness to your saving love
in Jesus Christ our Lord.

COLLECT

Reflection by **John Perumbalath** | 99

Monday 17 March

John 6.41-51

'I am the living bread' (v.51)

It is still the case that whatever question you ask children in church or school worship someone is likely to give the answer 'Jesus'. After all, it has a fair chance of being right and may well satisfy the vicar at least in the short term. The crowd Jesus addresses also prefers to stick to the expected answers about where Jesus comes from: his parentage rather than his claim that he is the bread of life come down from heaven. Like their ancestors in the wilderness, who were content once they knew they could collect manna every day, they are looking for bread to satisfy them now rather than the bread of eternal life.

In this season of Lent, we recall Jesus' words in the wilderness, that human beings 'cannot live by bread alone'. We pray for God to give us 'our daily bread' in the Lord's Prayer and in doing so are grateful for both physical and spiritual sustenance, for manna for the day and the bread of life for eternity.

Then, as now, there are those who because of the loud voices of many religious people claiming that they are in the right cannot hear the life-giving words of Jesus. Today might we listen more deeply into situations and be open to answers beyond our expectations that only Jesus can bring?

COLLECT

Almighty God,
you show to those who are in error the light of your truth,
that they may return to the way of righteousness:
grant to all those who are admitted
    into the fellowship of Christ's religion,
that they may reject those things
    that are contrary to their profession,
and follow all such things as are agreeable to the same;
through our Lord Jesus Christ.

| *Reflection by* **Justine Allain Chapman**

Psalm **50** *or* **132**, 133
Jeremiah 8.1-15
John 6.52-59

John 6.52-59

'... whoever eats me will live because of me' (v.57)

Several members of my family are coeliac. If they eat anything made with wheat or containing gluten they become ill. So now we look for bread made with some other kind of flour, and that goes for communion wafers too. Having to make changes to the basics of what we ate was irritating, disappointing and expensive, but change was necessary for us to eat together and provide healthy and nourishing meals.

Far beyond God providing manna or a household sharing food, Jesus describes himself as the bread of life; believers eating his human flesh and swilling it down with his human blood. It was a shocking and distasteful image then, and even though as Christians we can quickly shift from thoughts of cannibalism to the Eucharist, it is still vivid and uncomfortable.

Real participation in Christ and Christ's body goes beyond intellectual assent or good table manners. Communion with Christ is a sharing and abiding in the divine life force that transforms us. We participate in this communion individually and as one body, seeking a holiness and wholeness that attends not only to our minds and bodies, but also to our social and political relating. Our 'amen' when we receive the Sacrament at Holy Communion is our acceptance that we are ever becoming the body of Christ, together.

If you eat bread today, might you acknowledge Christ as the bread of life and pause to abide in him?

Almighty God,
by the prayer and discipline of Lent
may we enter into the mystery of Christ's sufferings,
and by following in his Way
come to share in his glory;
through Jesus Christ our Lord.

COLLECT

Reflection by **Justine Allain Chapman**

Wednesday 19 March

Joseph of Nazareth

Psalms 25, 147.1-12
Isaiah 11.1-10
Matthew 13.54-end

Matthew 13.54-end

'Is not this the carpenter's son?' (v.55)

'Tall poppy syndrome' is a term from Australia and New Zealand and it occurs when peers think you are getting above your station, too successful or boastful, and cut you down to size by criticism and exclusion. In Nazareth the people were astounded by Jesus' teaching, but bewildered and resentful that one of their own should have gained such wisdom and attention. Jesus identified this as what happens to prophets – they are without honour in the place where they come from. So, because of their unbelief, Jesus did not do many deeds of power.

Today we honour Joseph of Nazareth who was no tall poppy. His calling was hidden and humble as he protected both the reputation and life of the family given to him – he was a righteous man, unwilling to expose Mary to public disgrace (Matthew 1.19). If the people's unbelief prevented Jesus working deeds of power, Joseph's belief and care for his family enabled God's works of power to be revealed, for Jesus was shaped by the compassion, faith and practical wisdom he saw in Joseph. It was Joseph's belief in God's guidance through dreams and angels, putting his trust in God's working within Mary and giving Jesus his protection and an occupation, that gave shape to the divine life on earth.

Might we, as we remember Joseph, rather than cut someone down, show that we believe in them, knowing that such belief opens human life to the power of God?

COLLECT

God our Father,
who from the family of your servant David
raised up Joseph the carpenter
to be the guardian of your incarnate Son
and husband of the Blessed Virgin Mary:
give us grace to follow him
in faithful obedience to your commands;
through Jesus Christ our Lord.

| *Reflection by* **Justine Allain Chapman**

Thursday 20 March

John 7.1-13

'... show yourself to the world' (v.4)

It was hard every Sunday night to find something for our primary-school-aged children to 'Show and Tell' in school the next morning. We would affectionately call it 'Bring and Brag', not realizing then that later those same children would, along with us adults too, experience the pressures of social media requiring us to show something of our lives by a post and picture.

Jesus' brothers wanted to send him to Jerusalem to the festival so he and his works would be widely known, they said, but also so that they too could see how credible he was.

Sukkot, or the festivals of Booths, or Tabernacles, remembers the time of journeying through the wilderness. Households now as then make a temporary shelter, a *sukkah*, thankful for a more secure life as they celebrate God's protection and provision at that exposed and uncertain time where there was little to boast about.

In the forty days in the wilderness Jesus resisted the temptation to show off just as he did at this festival: conscious that his time is not yet at hand, he holds back.

In our culture of superficial news and constant scrutiny we, like Jesus, can be pushed to brag or to take up rather than give space. Today might we join Jesus in pondering that even when there are only temporary and insubstantial shelters to protect us, it is God in whom we find security?

Almighty God,
you show to those who are in error the light of your truth,
that they may return to the way of righteousness:
grant to all those who are admitted
into the fellowship of Christ's religion,
that they may reject those things
that are contrary to their profession,
and follow all such things as are agreeable to the same;
through our Lord Jesus Christ.

COLLECT

Reflection by **Justine Allain Chapman** | 103

Friday 21 March

Psalms 40, 41 *or* 142, 144
Jeremiah 10.1-16
John 7.14-24

John 7.14-24

'Do not judge by appearances' (v.24)

As I gained experience as a school teacher, I shifted from teaching a subject, focusing on the content, to teaching the students. I became aware of how I could enable a year group, class or individual genuinely to learn, be inspired and make connections with other subjects and with their lives.

Jesus inspired astonishment in his hearers as he taught. Much of this was to do with the way in which his words rang true – how he met people's yearnings with life-giving words. His words, he says, are not his own nor for his glory, but will resonate deeply and be accepted as God's by anyone who seeks to do the will of God.

Jesus' hearers, proud of being law-abiding, circumcized on the sabbath, but condemned him for healing on the sabbath. Their judgement of him did not come from a place of openness to learning, change or growth.

Honing our judgements so that we look beyond appearances is what Jesus asks of his hearers. Rather than seeking to be persuaded of an opinion or being on the right side of an argument, might we cultivate openness to judging another's words by the good they bring about? Pray today that those decisions we have been a part of bear fruit, with the humility to change our mind if they do not.

COLLECT

Almighty God,
you show to those who are in error the light of your truth,
that they may return to the way of righteousness:
grant to all those who are admitted
    into the fellowship of Christ's religion,
that they may reject those things
    that are contrary to their profession,
and follow all such things as are agreeable to the same;
through our Lord Jesus Christ.

Reflection by **Justine Allain Chapman**

Psalms 3, **25** *or* **147**
Jeremiah 10.17-24
John 7.25-36

Saturday 22 March

John 7.25-36

'... his hour had not yet come' (v.30)

In the popular science fiction television series *Doctor Who*, the Doctor is a Time Lord, one of an ancient race from the planet Gallifrey. Taking various human forms over time, the Doctor saves worlds from catastrophes by preventing the timeline from being subverted, because in the Tardis, they can travel through time. The Doctor does not always arrive with much time to spare, but being present to intervene at a key moment is the nature of the mission.

Jesus, present from the beginning of time (John 1.1), avoids being arrested several times because his 'hour has not yet come'. His movements are hard to track. He speaks of staying a little longer but then going where no one else can go. Living within time, Jesus is conscious of events gaining pace and coming together, of disciples he must prepare, of teaching he wants to convey, and the anticipation of suffering and death.

Approaching the third Sunday of Lent we see time marching on. Greek has two words for time: *chronos* is time that can be measured; *kairos* moments are those that change the nature of things, such as a pregnant woman knowing that it is time for her baby to come. These different experiences of time are always present in our lives. I am increasingly aware of the subtleties and mystery of the way God works in the world, how openness to God through prayer enables encounters in time to shimmer with grace from above. Be open to notice this action of God today.

Almighty God,
by the prayer and discipline of Lent
may we enter into the mystery of Christ's sufferings,
and by following in his Way
come to share in his glory;
through Jesus Christ our Lord.

COLLECT

Monday 24 March

John 7.37-52

'Out of a believer's heart shall flow' (v.38)

In positive psychology the concept of flow describes the experience of being fully immersed in a feeling of energized focus. It is not overwhelming or understimulating but a joyful melting of action and consciousness. We might describe the things that absorb us, such as climbing or painting, where we experience 'being in the zone' or the flow state.

At the festival of Sukkot, the crowd sees the golden pitcher of water brought from the Pool of Siloam to the Temple and hears Jesus using the image of water to call the thirsty to him. He promises that believers who drink of him will experience his life flowing through them, as a river, steady and continuous, bringing life to all that surrounds it. It is such a contrast to the conflictual discussions among the crowd, the Temple police and the religious leaders – none of whom can decide whether Jesus' words are astounding or deceptive, his origins of God or of Galilee.

Nicodemus tried to stem the antagonism to Jesus by suggesting he is given a fair hearing. He already knew that Jesus requires something more than mental assent, that we must be born from above (John 3.3). Then, as now, Jesus calls us to change from within. As you pray, invite Jesus to transform you from within, sweeping away whatever may stem the flow of his life within your heart.

COLLECT

Almighty God,
whose most dear Son went not up to joy
but first he suffered pain,
and entered not into glory before he was crucified:
mercifully grant that we, walking in the way of the cross,
may find it none other than the way of life and peace;
through Jesus Christ our Lord.

| *Reflection by* **Justine Allain Chapman**

Psalms 111, 113
1 Samuel 2.1-10
Romans 5.12-end

Tuesday 25 March
Annunciation of Our Lord
to the Blessed Virgin Mary

Romans 5.12-end

'... the free gift is not like the trespass' (v.15)

Paul's discussion of trespass and law could be symbolized by a quill made of a single feather. He dips the tip into ink again and again to make sense of the dynamics of salvation, of the work God brought about through Christ. He contrasts Adam and Christ, sin and grace, obedience and disobedience and, implicitly, Eve and Mary.

On this day when we celebrate the angel Gabriel announcing to Mary that she will bear Jesus, it is a symbol of the angel's wings, swift and vast, feathers soft and strong, which reveals the contrast between sin and grace – that the free gift is not like the trespass. Only the unmerited gift of grace can undo the dominance of death and bring about the promise of life, eternal in its scope.

Mary's welcome of the angel's words that she was the 'favoured one' (Luke 1.28) begins the most profound upward spiral of grace in the life of humanity. Whereas sin separates us from God, the angel's words lead Mary to bear God's Son living a life of grace where God is at work. The method is not transactional but relational, and by the incarnation the opposites of human and divine, heaven and earth, come together as one. Dualism gives way to all things being held together in Christ (Colossians 1.17).

Today, might you notice where a vicious cycle could, by the flutter of an angel's wing, become a spiral of grace?

We beseech you, O Lord,
pour your grace into our hearts,
that as we have known the incarnation of your Son Jesus Christ
by the message of an angel,
so by his cross and passion
we may be brought to the glory of his resurrection;
through Jesus Christ our Lord.

COLLECT

Wednesday 26 March

John 8.12-30

'Whoever follows ... will have the light of life' (v.12)

The origin of the word 'Lent' comes from 'lengthening' because the days, in the northern hemisphere, are getting longer with less darkness and more light. Light and darkness are themes that run through John's Gospel with their double meanings of natural sight, daylight and insight or enlightenment.

As Lent progresses, although there are more hours of daylight, the darkness of human minds, proud and afraid, closes in around Jesus and threatens his life. Jesus declares himself to the 'light of the world' and that his followers need never walk in darkness because they have the light of life.

The experience of suffering, our own or another's, can feel like the descent of darkness immobilizing us. As with a beam of light from a torch showing us the next step, but little more, what really matters often becomes clear; we are able to walk forward because we experience love and fellowship, compassion and care. It is afterwards, when we look back on those times, that we might gain insight.

In the darkness of our world today in what form do we see the light that is Christ? If there seems to be more darkness than light, perhaps pray in these words written by a Jewish prisoner on the wall of the Nazi concentration camp: 'I believe in the sun, even when it is not shining. I believe in love, even when there's no one there. I believe in God, even when he is silent.'

COLLECT

Almighty God,
whose most dear Son went not up to joy
    but first he suffered pain,
and entered not into glory before he was crucified:
mercifully grant that we, walking in the way of the cross,
may find it none other than the way of life and peace;
through Jesus Christ our Lord.

| *Reflection by* **Justine Allain Chapman**

Psalms **56**, 57 *or* 14, **15**, 16
Jeremiah 14
John 8.31-47

John 8.31-47

'… you choose to do your father's desires' (v.44)

Many people who have obtained their DNA profile have perhaps done so in order to deepen their sense of identity, or to gain some understanding of the strengths and vulnerabilities of their character. It's not for the fainthearted because you don't know what will be revealed. It can be deeply unsettling to discover a propensity for a life-limiting illness, or to learn that you are not actually biologically related to your grandfather. Our DNA profiles can tell us something about the way in which we have been shaped, but not who we are or how to respond to new knowledge about ourselves.

Jesus challenged the sense of entitlement his Jewish hearers felt in being descended from Abraham. He declared that for his disciples the truth about who he was and what they could become would set them free. But his proud hearers could not accept that they were not free. Seemingly having forgotten about being slaves in Egypt and seeking to kill Jesus they were, he said, the children of the devil who is the father of lies and a murderer. True descendants of Abraham would show his example of faith and character.

In Christ we have an identity where we are born anew and given power to become children of God (John 1.13). The legacy of the truth about anything in our past or background can be redeemed in Christ. Is there anyone that God calls you today to set free?

Eternal God,
give us insight
to discern your will for us,
to give up what harms us,
and to seek the perfection we are promised
in Jesus Christ our Lord.

COLLECT

Reflection by **Justine Allain Chapman**

Friday 28 March

John 8.48-end

'... whoever keeps my word will never see death' (v.51)

Earlier in chapter 8 we read of Jesus' response to the scribes and Pharisees, and to the woman brought by them accused of adultery (8.1-11). She might well have been stoned, had Jesus not held up a mirror reflecting her persecutors' sin back to them.

The crowd in the Temple were by now unreceptive to Jesus and especially to the notion that they were not children of Abraham. Jesus experiences the violence of a crowd ready again with their stones, but this time they are for him. The woman was silenced by her experience. We know that Jesus will remain silent in the face of the final accusations against him, but before then, the crowd's insults and tone are menacing and the capacity to hear him further diminished.

By his dealings with people and by his teaching, Jesus tried to enable his hearers experience life with God as eternal and present in the here and now. Their argumentative response is a long way from such a spiritual path.

We should not be surprised that there are times when our Christian understanding of what it is to be human compels us to think and act differently from others around us. Nor that there are times when we cannot speak but must remain silent, withdrawing to reflect and pray. What will be the tone of our engagement with others today?

COLLECT

Almighty God,
whose most dear Son went not up to joy
   but first he suffered pain,
and entered not into glory before he was crucified:
mercifully grant that we, walking in the way of the cross,
may find it none other than the way of life and peace;
through Jesus Christ our Lord.

Reflection by **Justine Allain Chapman**

Psalm **31** *or* 20, 21, **23**
Jeremiah 16.10 – 17.4
John 9.1-17

Saturday 29 March

John 9.1-17

'… who sinned, this man or his parents?' (v.2)

It is natural for human beings to look for reasons for and causes of the way things are. It expands our knowledge, but it doesn't necessarily lead to any real insight or transformation. Bessel van der Kolk in the bestseller *The Body Keeps the Score: Mind, brain and body in the transformation of trauma*, identified the devastating effects of psychological trauma on the mind and body's development. Rather than focus on the causes, he movingly describes innovative treatments that can reactivate the brain's natural neuroplasticity and the tremendous power of our relationships to heal our minds and our bodies, opening the way to a new life post-trauma.

In a culture of blame, Jesus' disciples ask about causes – whether it was the parents' sin or the sin of the blind man himself that caused the blindness. Later, the crowd and the Pharisees want to know the reasons for the blind man's recovery of sight. Jesus is judged as a sinner, not one who has healing power from God, because he has healed on the sabbath. In both cases, the question about who should be judged a sinner motivates the questions about causes.

Judgementalism does not lead to healing and transformation. Today, notice the tendencies of your natural curiosity and pray that God may direct them towards insight and healing.

Eternal God,
give us insight
to discern your will for us,
to give up what harms us,
and to seek the perfection we are promised
in Jesus Christ our Lord.

COLLECT

Reflection by **Justine Allain Chapman**   111

Monday 31 March

Psalms 70, **77** *or* 27, **30**
Jeremiah 17.5-18
John 9.18-end

John 9.18-end

'Surely we are not blind, are we?' (v.40)

Today's passage concludes the meditation on blindness and sight that began in chapter 8. It opens with a classic example of how people with disabilities are patronized by those who assume they can't speak for themselves, epitomized in the phrase 'Does he take sugar?' The religious authorities question the man's parents, assuming they will somehow know more than he does! His parents quite rightly reply, 'Ask him...he will speak for himself.'

And he certainly does. He dismantles the arguments of the 'authorities', and ends up wryly asking them if they too want to be Jesus' disciples, and they, like so many entitled people when they lose an argument, just revert to insult and exclusion: 'They drove him out.'

And then comes the real encounter with Jesus, and it's noteworthy that Jesus sought the man out, not the other way round. In the conversation that ensues Christ opens the man's eyes a second time, but this time he is granted spiritual sight and insight, and he recognizes Christ as Messiah, and worships him. And at precisely this moment of insight Jesus speaks his judgement against those who make themselves wilfully blind. Of course, we'd like to identify with the man born blind, transformed by Jesus, surely *we* are not blind, are we? But this story won't let us go so easily. We lift our eyes from the page wondering what our own wilful blindness might be concealing from us.

COLLECT

Merciful Lord,
absolve your people from their offences,
that through your bountiful goodness
we may all be delivered from the chains of those sins
which by our frailty we have committed;
grant this, heavenly Father,
for Jesus Christ's sake, our blessed Lord and Saviour.

| *Reflection by* **Malcolm Guite**

Psalms 54, **79** *or* 32, **36**
Jeremiah 18.1-12
John 10.1-10

John 10.1-10
'I am the gate' (vv.7, 9)

We begin a chapter exploring what it means to call Jesus the Good Shepherd, a chapter that draws deeply on the daily experience of a pastoral people and also on the rich vein of pastoral imagery and metaphor in the Old Testament. But before we come to him as shepherd, Jesus offers an image of himself as a gate or door, in one of the seven key I AM sayings of this gospel: 'I AM the gate of the sheep.'

There is a local context for this saying: the sheep folds in the hill country were circular stone wall enclosures, with no door or roof, but a gap through which the sheep could pass into the safety of the enclosure and across which the shepherd would lie, making himself the door so that all who came or went must step across him. So, Jesus invites us to come in and go out through him. That phrase may itself be an echo of the promised blessing of Psalm 121.8, now fulfilled in Christ: 'The Lord will keep your going out and your coming in from this time on and for evermore.'

But there is something about Christ himself as a door that goes beyond this pastoral context. We come in prayer through Christ to the Father. In John 1.51 Christ becomes Jacob's ladder, becomes 'the very gate of heaven' or, in the words of John the Divine, 'a door open in heaven' (Revelation 4.1).

COLLECT

Merciful Lord,
you know our struggle to serve you:
when sin spoils our lives
and overshadows our hearts,
come to our aid
and turn us back to you again;
through Jesus Christ our Lord.

Wednesday 2 April

Psalms 63, **90** *or* **34**
Jeremiah 18.13-end
John 10.11-21

John 10.11-21
'I am the Good Shepherd' (v.11)

Now we come to the central I AM saying of this chapter: 'I AM the Good Shepherd.' The saying is so often given sentimental illustration that we miss the shock and scandal of it. By saying I AM (*ego eimi* in Greek) Jesus is identifying himself with Yahweh, the great I AM, and by saying that he is *the* Good Shepherd, he is claiming to be the same Lord and Shepherd who is proclaimed mysteriously in Psalm 23. I say mysteriously, because in verse 4 the psalmist claims that this Shepherd-Lord will lead us even through death itself: 'Even though I walk through the valley of the shadow of death... you are with me.'

The first hearers of this psalm must have been mystified. They knew that shepherds *lead* their sheep, pioneer the path for them, and that the sheep follow because they know the shepherd and trust that he has found a way through. How could Yawheh lead us through the gate of death? For he is immortal and cannot die! And then comes Jesus and says, 'I am He. I lay down my life for the sheep', and we note, with a sharp, tender shock, that the promise of Psalm 23 is preceded by the agony of Psalm 22, the crucifixion psalm. It is the agony of the one that makes the blessing of the other possible.

COLLECT

Merciful Lord,
absolve your people from their offences,
that through your bountiful goodness
we may all be delivered from the chains of those sins
which by our frailty we have committed;
grant this, heavenly Father,
for Jesus Christ's sake, our blessed Lord and Saviour.

| *Reflection by* **Malcolm Guite**

Psalms 53, **86** *or* **37***
Jeremiah 19.1-13
John 10.22-end

Thursday 3 April

John 10.22-end

'The Father and I are one' (v.30)

John carefully locates this moment of revelation in time and place. It's set at the festival of the rededication of the Temple – Hannukah, the festival of lights – and is set in the Temple, specifically Solomon's Porch, which ran along one side of the court of the Gentiles. The one who said 'I am the Light of the world' now deepens his claim on a day that recalls the lights rekindled in the newly cleansed Temple when every other light had gone out.

The Temple was the meeting place of God and humanity, and now Jesus reveals that the true Temple, the true meeting place of God and humanity, comes to them as a person. The Temple has come to life and is now more than a mere meeting place, it is a place of union: 'the Father and I are One'. And this declaration does not take place, as one might have expected, in the sanctuary – the holy centre – but on the edge, the court of the Gentiles, the edge that is precisely the meeting place of Jew and Gentile. It is here that Jesus reveals, not only for one race or religion, but for all, that he and the Father are one.

'They tried to arrest him, but he escaped from their hands.' He escapes also from ours. We cannot confine the God-Human, the Human-God, to our categories, he breaks them all and walks free, beckoning us instead into his mystery.

Merciful Lord,
you know our struggle to serve you:
when sin spoils our lives
and overshadows our hearts,
come to our aid
and turn us back to you again;
through Jesus Christ our Lord.

COLLECT

Reflection by **Malcolm Guite** | 115

Friday 4 April

Psalm **102** *or* **31**
Jeremiah 19.14 – 20.6
John 11.1-16

John 11.1-16

'Let us also go, that we may die with him' (v.16)

Thomas is a distinctive and attractive character among the twelve, and no more so than at this moment. He is often given to doubts, difficulties and gloomy prognostications – a natural pessimist. But at the same time he is strong-willed, intensely loyal and ready to do the right thing whatever the cost, which paradoxically makes the company's pet pessimist an encouraging person to be with! Others, swayed by naive optimism, begin an enterprise, and then when difficulties arise, give up. Thomas, by contrast, assumes that they are facing defeat but chooses to be with Jesus anyway and urges the others to do the same. One is reminded of Gimli's great one-liner in the film of the Lord of the Rings: 'Certainty of death. Small chance of success. What are we waiting for?' Or the words of the Earl when the English are losing the Battle of Maldon:

'Will shall be the sterner, heart the bolder,
spirit the greater as our strength lessens.' (Tolkien's translation)

C.S. Lewis, too, created a character in his Narnia novels whose role is very like that of 'doubting Thomas': Puddleglum, the perpetually pessimistic Marsh Wiggle, who for all his gloomy prognostications, doubts and difficulties, is the one who hangs on to the quest and even says, 'I'm going to live like a Narnian even if there is no Narnia.'

Happily most churches have someone like this, someone who sees all the difficulties, but also stays to see them through.

COLLECT

Merciful Lord,
absolve your people from their offences,
that through your bountiful goodness
we may all be delivered from the chains of those sins
which by our frailty we have committed;
grant this, heavenly Father,
for Jesus Christ's sake, our blessed Lord and Saviour.

Reflection by **Malcolm Guite**

Psalms **32** *or* 41, **42**, 43
Jeremiah 20.7-end
John 11.17-27

Saturday 5 April

John 11.17-27

'If you had been here ...' (v.21)

John takes us from the most mind-expanding cosmic theology to the most intimate human experience, in almost the same breath, and no wonder, for John's contention is that because the Word was made flesh, great theology happens precisely in and through human intimacy, not least the intimacy of death and mourning.

Here Martha confronts Jesus with one of those agonizing 'if onlys' that haunt and torment the bereaved: 'If only I'd known..., if only he hadn't taken that route..., if only I could have been there...' And now the sharpest of these that almost blames the very person who has come to share your grief: 'If you had been here, my brother would not have died.' Jesus will soon be pierced by nails and a spear, but this too is heart-piercing, and he will hear it a second time from Martha's sister, Mary. He takes it, he absorbs it, but he is not thwarted by its implicit anger and accusation; he still has words of hope and comfort to bring.

If you visit the bereaved on behalf of the Church, you stand where Jesus stands here, amid the anger and the accusation, so often directed, as it must be, at God: 'If only he had intervened as surely he could – but no – he let us all down.' The only way to hear these things is to hear them in and with Jesus, and to meet them with his compassionate love.

Merciful Lord,
you know our struggle to serve you:
when sin spoils our lives
and overshadows our hearts,
come to our aid
and turn us back to you again;
through Jesus Christ our Lord.

COLLECT

Reflection by **Malcolm Guite** | 117

Monday 7 April

Psalms **73**, 121 *or* **44**
Jeremiah 21.1-10
John 11.28-44

John 11.28-44

'… he cried with a loud voice' (v.43)

'He speaks – and listening to his voice
New life the dead receive.'

In these lines from his famous hymn 'And can it be', Charles Wesley
was alluding obliquely to the raising of Lazarus. The prologue to
John's Gospel is in one sense the prologue and underpinning of every
single episode in the whole book. John wants us to know that the
one who 'cried out with a loud voice' is the Word himself, the one
who spoke the cosmos into being. He is the Lord whose voice is
celebrated in Psalm 29: 'The voice of the Lord is over the waters…The
voice of the Lord is powerful; the voice of the Lord is full of majesty.'
And now this primal creative voice speaks from within its own
creation and raises the dead. And yet in this very passage, only a few
verses earlier, this same all-powerful voice is weeping, sharing our
tears, experiencing with us our misery and grief.

This gets to the heart of the matter. The Word really was made flesh.
He is fully human and feels from within all the pain and devastation
of our griefs, the 'thousand natural shocks that flesh is heir to'
(*Hamlet*, Act 3, Scene 1). And that is why, even in this life, he can
raise us too from the dead. He has been in the places where we are
dead or dying: the heartbreak, the fear, the failure. Even as he weeps
with us, his creating voice raises and releases us.

COLLECT

Most merciful God,
who by the death and resurrection of your Son Jesus Christ
delivered and saved the world:
grant that by faith in him who suffered on the cross
we may triumph in the power of his victory;
through Jesus Christ our Lord.

| *Reflection by* **Malcolm Guite**

Tuesday 8 April

John 11.45-end

'... better for ... one man to die' (v.50)

It is remarkable that whatever is said of Jesus in the Gospel, even misunderstandings or downright attacks, he takes and transforms into blessings, not on himself, but on us. They call him 'the friend of sinners' to denigrate him, and he is forever, and to our immense blessing, the friend of sinners, for he came to befriend us. Mary Magdalene 'mistook' him for a gardener, but he was in truth The Gardener, who had planted the garden of the world, who had turned the garden of mourning into the garden of resurrection, and he is a gardener to Mary's heart, wintry with grief, for, as Lancelot Andrewes said, 'with one word he makes all green again'.

So here Caiaphas, thinking that he speaks of nothing more than political expediency, suggests that Jesus should be sacrificed to save the nation, a sordid attempt to make the end justify the means, but Jesus fulfils his words in a far better way and far beyond his imaginings, for he dies to save not just one nation but the whole world, indeed the cosmos (*ton kosmon* is how John puts 'world' in 3.16).

From here on Jesus is a wanted man, in many senses. Those who gather for the Passover are looking for him with hope as a Messiah, those who want to preserve the status quo are looking for him to destroy him. The great question is 'Will he come?'

COLLECT

Gracious Father,
you gave up your Son
out of love for the world:
lead us to ponder the mysteries of his passion,
that we may know eternal peace
through the shedding of our Saviour's blood,
Jesus Christ our Lord.

Reflection by **Malcolm Guite**

Wednesday 9 April

Psalms **55**, 124 *or* **119.57-80**
Jeremiah 22.20 – 23.8
John 12.1-11

John 12.1-11

'The house was filled with the fragrance' (v.3)

After so much public drama and political tension, and before the violent climax of his story, John gives us by contrast this poignant, intimate interlude: the anointing at Bethany. As so often in the gospels, the behaviour of the men contrasts unfavourably with that of the women. Many commentators rightly contrast Judas and Mary. Judas sees only the price of the perfume, whereas Mary, with her extravagant gesture, recognizes the infinite value of her saviour's love. Here Judas illustrates perfectly Oscar Wilde's quip that a cynic is one 'who knows the price of everything and the value of nothing'. The real poetry of this moment, though, is the way Mary's love anticipates Christ's death yet somehow gestures beyond it, something I tried to intimate in a poem of my own:

> Come close with Mary, Martha, Lazarus,
> So close the candles flare with their soft breath,
> And kindle heart and soul to flame within us
> Lit by these mysteries of life and death.
> For beauty now begins the final movement,
> In quietness and intimate encounter,
> The alabaster jar of precious ointment
> Is broken open for the world's true lover.
> The whole room richly fills to feast the senses
> With all the yearning such a fragrance brings,
> The heart is mourning but the spirit dances,
> Here at the very centre of all things,
> Here at the meeting place of love and loss
> We all foresee and see beyond the cross.

(From *Sounding the Seasons*)

COLLECT

Most merciful God,
who by the death and resurrection of your Son Jesus Christ
delivered and saved the world:
grant that by faith in him who suffered on the cross
we may triumph in the power of his victory;
through Jesus Christ our Lord.

Reflection by **Malcolm Guite**

Psalms **40**, 125 *or* 56, **57** (63*)
Jeremiah 23.9-32
John 12.12-19

Thursday 10 April

John 12.12-19

'... the world has gone after him' (v.19)

Once again something is said of Jesus that is far truer than those who utter it could have imagined. The crowds that surged towards Jesus on Palm Sunday were devout Jews, there in Jerusalem for the Passover, the very ceremony that distinguished Jews from the rest of the world and defined them as a nation: a chosen and exceptional people.

The psalm they quoted in their Hosannas, Psalm 118, was a distinctly messianic and royal psalm. The prophecy they saw fulfilled in Jesus' riding on a donkey was a distinctive prophecy to them alone. Both those who welcome Jesus and those who oppose him at this moment are Jewish people, taking a position about whether or not he is the longed-for Messiah. Perhaps the Pharisees only meant 'the whole world' as an exaggerated synonym for 'this big Passover crowd – our fellow Jews', but the word they use for 'the whole world' at this point is the very word Jesus uses earlier in John 3.16 for his universal mission 'God so loved the world ('*ho kosmos*') that he sent his only Son.'

This deeper, more inclusive meaning of the word, this evocation of a mission of love to the Gentiles, is about to have its beginning in the very next verse of this Gospel when 'some Greeks' ask to see Jesus.

Gracious Father,
you gave up your Son
out of love for the world:
lead us to ponder the mysteries of his passion,
that we may know eternal peace
through the shedding of our Saviour's blood,
Jesus Christ our Lord.

COLLECT

Reflection by **Malcolm Guite** | 121

Friday 11 April

Psalms **22**, 126 *or* **51**, 54
Jeremiah 24
John 12.20-36*a*

John 12.20-36*a*

'The hour has come ...' (v.23)

Back in chapter 2 of his Gospel, John set up a kind of tension and suspense in his narrative when Jesus says to his mother at the wedding at Cana, 'My hour has not yet come.' Thereafter we are always asking ourselves, 'When will it come? When is the moment we are waiting for?' Not just a sign, like the miracle at Cana, but the full revelation of who Jesus is.

Now, ten chapters later, that tension is released, that promise is fulfilled, and he announces at last, 'The hour has come!' And the fulfilment is initiated, not by some grand miracle or fulfilment of ancient prophecy, but with the arrival of 'some Greeks', a group of complete strangers who, according to the Jewish view, are not even supposed to be part of this story. This is so shocking and unexpected that Philip, whom the Greeks probably approached because he had a Greek name, goes off to consult Andrew, and then the two of them, stymied by this development, go to see Jesus, which is what Philip should have done in the first place.

It wouldn't be the only time that the question of 'who belongs?', 'who can come to Jesus?' was met by the Church with embarrassment and prevarication; we are in the middle of such a moment now with issues of sexuality and gender identity, but there is no doubt of Jesus' response: 'Welcome them, my death and my resurrection are for the whole world.'

COLLECT

Most merciful God,
who by the death and resurrection of your Son Jesus Christ
delivered and saved the world:
grant that by faith in him who suffered on the cross
we may triumph in the power of his victory;
through Jesus Christ our Lord.

| *Reflection by* **Malcolm Guite**

Saturday 12 April

John 12.36*b*-end

'I have come as light into the world' (v.46)

Once more we hear that glorious, all-inclusive little phrase 'the world' – *ton kosmon* – ringing out from Jesus' lips, as John deftly returns us to the great theme of light shining in darkness, a theme he had announced in his prologue and developed so powerfully in chapters 8 and 9. We are not merely to long for light, or to 'believe in the light', or even to 'have the light'; we are, in a breathtaking command and promise, to 'become children of light'! For that is our truest life.

Did we not hear in the prologue, 'In him was life and the life was the light of all people' (John 1.4)? And now, in the presence of the Gentiles, and, with them, the whole world for which he dies, Jesus explicitly proclaims: 'I have come as the light of the world.' This is a light that does more than simply illuminate, it calls us into personal communion, something I tried to express in my sonnet on Christ as light:

[Light] shimmers through translucent leaves in summer,
Or spills from silver veins in leaden skies,
It gathers in the candles at our vespers
It concentrates in tiny drops of dew,
At times it sings for joy, at times it whispers,
But all the time it calls me back to you.
I follow you upstream through this dark night
My saviour, source, and spring, my life and light.

(from *Parable and Paradox*)

Reflection by **Malcolm Guite**

Monday 14 April
Monday of Holy Week

Psalm 41
Lamentations 1.1-12*a*
Luke 22.1-23

Lamentations 1.1-12*a*

'... all her friends have dealt treacherously with her' (v.2)

Lamentations graphically describes the devastation of Jerusalem and the appalling suffering of her people: brutal slaughter, people enslaved or turned into refugees, children starving, women raped, the destruction not only of homes and public and religious buildings but also of a culture, a political community, and a whole way of life, and betrayal by 'all her friends'. In the face of all this, the overwhelming response is lament. This is as relevant to our world as it was then. If our prayer does not include lament, we are not seeing the world as it is – or the Church as it is, or ourselves as we are. It is right to lament, grieve, cry out, weep, mourn, be in anguish.

Holy Week is a time for lament, for realistically facing up to what and who have gone terribly wrong. This is a way of realizing the scale of our salvation, and what it was that faced Jesus, 'the Lamb of God who takes away the sin of the world' (John 1.29). This unique person, who is utterly at one with God and with us, engages with the depths of suffering, sin and death. A key element in this is that one of his close friends, Judas, betrayed him.

Why is breaking trust so fundamental? I think it is because what Jesus most desires is mutual love – between himself and us, and among ourselves. But without mutual trust that is impossible.

COLLECT

Almighty and everlasting God,
who in your tender love towards the human race
    sent your Son our Saviour Jesus Christ
to take upon him our flesh
and to suffer death upon the cross:
grant that we may follow the example of his patience and humility,
and also be made partakers of his resurrection;
through Jesus Christ our Lord.

| *Reflection by* **David Ford**

Psalm 27
Lamentations 3.1-18
Luke 22. [24-38] 39-53

Tuesday 15 April
Tuesday of Holy Week

Luke 22. [24-38] 39-53

'Father, … not my will but yours be done' (v.42)

The Greek word *thelēma* means 'desire' as well as 'will', as here and in the Lord's Prayer. In Israel's scriptures, and in the teaching of Jesus, at the heart of God's will and desire for us is that we find our fulfilment in loving God with all our heart, mind and strength, and loving our neighbours as ourselves.

Jesus embodies such love, and twice in the Gospel of Luke we are given an insight into how he resists temptations to let other desires have priority. At the beginning of his ministry the temptations involve his desires for food, for worldly power and glory, and for doing spectacular, impressive signs (Luke 4.1-13). Here, at the climax of his life, the temptation is to turn away from the depths of suffering, sin and death in his crucifixion. His ultimate test is to be willing to go that way of love 'to the end' (John 13.1), in loving solidarity with all who suffer, sin and die, and to lay down his life in order to open up to others his own deep relationship of love with his Father and with all who trust him.

We live in cultures saturated with stimuli to desires of many sorts. To receive and trust Jesus is to begin to have our desires continually inspired and transformed by him. In this, the prayer of Jesus himself is crucial – and still continues (Hebrews 7.25).

COLLECT

True and humble king,
hailed by the crowd as Messiah:
grant us the faith to know you and love you,
that we may be found beside you
on the way of the cross,
which is the path of glory.

Reflection by **David Ford**

Wednesday 16 April

Wednesday of Holy Week

Psalm 102 [*or* 102.1-18]
Wisdom 1.16 – 2.1; 2.12-22
or Jeremiah 11.18-20
Luke 22.54-end

Luke 22.54-end

'I am not!' (v.58)

What relationships are at the heart of our identity? With whom do we really belong?

As Jesus is put on trial, someone says to Peter, 'You also are one of them.' Peter's 'I am not!' is not only a lie, it denies his core identity, who he has become through Jesus calling him, giving him a new name and community. In the trial, Jesus' identity is central: Messiah (Christ)? Son of Man? Son of God? King of the Jews? In stark contrast to Peter, Jesus refuses to deny such dangerous religious and political identities and is condemned to be crucified.

Holy Week is a time to consider and renew our core identity. In many Christian communities today, as in the early Church, Easter is a time for baptisms and renewal of the promises made in baptism. Baptism is about our fundamental identity, centred on being baptized into the death and resurrection of Jesus, and belonging utterly to God and to each other 'in Christ'.

Other forms of belonging (family, gender, race, class, nation, job, politics, culture, friendships, networks, online groups, etc.) may harmonize with this or be in tension with it. In our situation of identities in conflict, we need continual wise discernment, and freedom from fear, in order to decide, given the utter primacy of our baptism, on the extent and quality of our commitment to other identities and relationships.

COLLECT

Almighty and everlasting God,
who in your tender love towards the human race
   sent your Son our Saviour Jesus Christ
to take upon him our flesh
and to suffer death upon the cross:
grant that we may follow the example of his patience and humility,
and also be made partakers of his resurrection;
through Jesus Christ our Lord.

| *Reflection by* **David Ford**

Psalms 42, 43
Leviticus 16.2-24
Luke 23.1-25

Thursday 17 April
Maundy Thursday

Luke 23.1-25

'Pilate asked him, "Are you the king of the Jews?"' (v.3)

In Luke's account, the accusations against Jesus when he is brought before the Roman governor are angled towards Pilate's interests in public order, taxes for the Emperor and claims to be a king. In the Roman Empire the only people who could be kings were those appointed by the Emperor, and any others were treated as rebels.

The reply of Jesus to Pilate's question is, 'You say so.' We can understand why this is not a 'yes' or 'no' response.

From the beginning of Luke's Gospel, Jesus is associated with 'the throne of his ancestor David ... and of his kingdom there will be no end' (1.32-33). But, as the Gospel unfolds, there are many surprises about the sort of king he is. He resists the tempting offer of power over all the kingdoms of the world. He inaugurates the 'kingdom of God' with healings, exorcisms, forgiveness, good news for the poor, uncomfortable news for the rich and teaching about the shockingly generous love of God for us, and about our love for our neighbours. Little children and daring friendships with prostitutes and hated tax collectors are central to this kingdom.

But, above all, this kingdom is inseparable from who Jesus is and what happens to him. Maundy Thursday reveals his upside-down power of loving, humble service: 'I am among you as one who serves.' How could Pilate have begun to understand this sort of king? How can we?

True and humble king,
hailed by the crowd as Messiah:
grant us the faith to know you and love you,
that we may be found beside you
on the way of the cross,
which is the path of glory.

COLLECT

Friday 18 April
Good Friday

Genesis 22.1-18
'Here I am!' (vv.1, 7, 11)

'Here I am!' Abraham says this three times – to God, who calls him by name, 'Abraham!'; to his only, beloved son, Isaac, calling him, 'Father!'; and to 'the angel of the Lord' calling him, 'Abraham! Abraham!' In this test, who Abraham is in his deepest relationships, his 'I am', is at stake. Is utter trust in God at the heart of his identity? Is God utterly trustworthy? Can God be trusted with our most precious and intimate relationships? Is breaking trust with God something worse even than the death of those we love – who are ultimately all in God's hands?

'Here I am!' On Good Friday, Jesus, the beloved Son of God, who has said to his Father, 'See, I have come to do your will' or 'your desire', gives himself utterly in love for his Father and for us. It is the deepest mystery, this 'once for all' event. It is central to the 'I am' of Jesus, to the 'I am' of God, and to the love in which we are invited to trust, as Abraham trusted.

'Here I am!' As we stand at the foot of the cross, how do we receive the One who calls each of us by name, and gives himself for us and to us?

COLLECT

Almighty Father,
look with mercy on this your family
for which our Lord Jesus Christ was content to be betrayed
    and given up into the hands of sinners
    and to suffer death upon the cross;
who is alive and glorified with you and the Holy Spirit,
one God, now and for ever.

| *Reflection by* **David Ford**

Psalm 142
Hosea 6.1-6
John 2.18-22

Saturday 19 April
Easter Eve

John 2.18-22

'What sign can you show us ... ?' (v.18)

Jesus identifies the Temple, which he has earlier called 'my Father's house' (his family home), with his body, which will be destroyed, and then 'in three days I will raise it up'. This is the greatest of all the signs in John's Gospel, the death and resurrection of Jesus, which creates the new family home. This home is nothing less than himself and his love: 'Abide in me as I abide in you ... As the Father has loved me, so I have loved you: abide in my love' (John 15.4, 9). Approaching death he prays, 'As you, Father, are in me and I am in you, may they also be in us, so that the world may believe that you have sent me ...' (John 17.21). What a home!

But good homes can cost a lot. Today, on Holy Saturday, we sit with the dark mystery of death itself. What was happening when Jesus was dead? Death had happened to him, along with suffering, sin and evil. *But he had also happened to death, suffering, sin and evil*. This unique person – utterly human and mortal, yet also utterly divine – dies and also transforms death itself, along with suffering, sin and evil. 'In three days I will raise it up.' The ultimate sign that death, and the darkness of suffering, sin and evil, do not in reality have the last word, is that Good Friday and Holy Saturday lead into Easter Day.

COLLECT

Grant, Lord,
that we who are baptized into the death
of your Son our Saviour Jesus Christ
may continually put to death our evil desires
and be buried with him;
and that through the grave and gate of death
we may pass to our joyful resurrection;
through his merits,
who died and was buried and rose again for us,
your Son Jesus Christ our Lord.

Reflection by **David Ford** | 129

Monday 21 April

Monday of Easter Week

Psalms **111**, 117, 146
Song of Solomon 1.9-27
Mark 16.1-8

Mark 16.1-8

'He has been raised' (v.6)

The resurrection of Jesus is a God-sized event. This key text is what scholars call a 'divine passive': 'He has been raised – by God.' God is free to do something unique, surprising, utterly good and without parallel. The nearest parallel to the resurrection is creation itself. Resurrection from death echoes creation from nothing. Both can be understood as free acts of God's wisdom, delight and love.

All through this week, readings from the Gospels are accompanied by readings from the Song of Solomon, which ecstatically celebrates creation and love together, evoking Adam and Eve in the Garden of Eden:

'Ah, you are beautiful, my beloved, truly lovely,
our couch is green ...
Awake, O north wind,
and come, O south wind!
Blow upon my garden,
that its fragrance may be wafted abroad ... '
(Song of Solomon 1.16, 4.16)

Such poetry of love, joy and adoration has helped to inspire century after century of creative responses to the risen Jesus, and this continues around the world.

Mark's testimony to the resurrection of Jesus is clear and brief (most scholars agree that the original text of this Gospel ended at 16.8). But he gives us the essential: Jesus 'who was crucified ... has been raised'.

COLLECT

Lord of all life and power,
who through the mighty resurrection of your Son
overcame the old order of sin and death
to make all things new in him:
grant that we, being dead to sin
and alive to you in Jesus Christ,
may reign with him in glory;
to whom with you and the Holy Spirit
be praise and honour, glory and might,
now and in all eternity.

130 | *Reflection by* **David Ford**

Psalms 112, 147.1-12
Song of Solomon 2.8-end
Luke 24.1-12

Tuesday 22 April
Tuesday of Easter Week

Luke 24.1-12

'... he went home, amazed at what had happened' (v.12)

This is the beginning of amazement without end. It is amazement at something that is good beyond imagining. It is the ultimate sign of death overcome, of evil and sin defeated, of deep, superabundant life, joy, love, and glory without end. It is the ultimate good news. Above all, it is amazement at *someone* who is good beyond imagining, embodying the love, wisdom, mercy, joy, life and very being of God. To trust this news fully and wholeheartedly is to enter into the amazement of a love supreme, a love that is utterly mutual, and whose height, depth, length and breadth are immeasurable, and continually enriching.

The Song of Solomon knows a mutual love like this:

'The voice of my beloved! ...
Arise, my love, my fair one ...
for your voice is sweet,
and your face is lovely ... '

Peter's first amazement (John 21.15-19) led into a life of mutual love ('Do you love me?'... 'Yes, Lord ... ') and loving service ('Feed my lambs ... '). And that first amazement continued: 'By his great mercy he has given us a new birth into a living hope through the resurrection of Jesus Christ ... Although you have not seen him, you love him, and ... you believe in him and rejoice with an indescribable and glorious joy' (1 Peter 1.3, 8).

Let us receive this news with amazement, trust and joy, and be born anew into a community of celebration, living hope and loving service.

God of glory,
by the raising of your Son
you have broken the chains of death and hell:
fill your Church with faith and hope;
for a new day has dawned
and the way to life stands open
in our Saviour Jesus Christ.

COLLECT

Reflection by **David Ford** | 131

Wednesday 23 April

Wednesday of Easter Week

Psalms 113, 147.13-end
Song of Solomon 3
Matthew 28.16-end

Matthew 28.16-end

'I am with you always' (v.20)

Wherever we are right now, and whatever the time of day, the most important truth about our place and time is this – 'I am with you.' It follows that the most important question for anyone who thinks of becoming, or has become, a disciple (which simply means 'learner') is one that risks beginning to trust this unseen presence of the crucified and resurrected Jesus, and asks him, 'Who are you?'

If you're prepared to take this risk, then be prepared for surprises. You are beginning an ongoing, daily journey of learning and loving. More fundamentally, it is a journey of 'being with' someone who is present with you, and whose greatest desire is to be trusted to teach and love us. This happens through prayer and worship, through reading and rereading the Bible, through daring friendships and loving service, through being part of a community that is both local and has 'disciples (or learners) of all nations' (it's currently estimated that there are over two billion Christians worldwide), and through the ordinary and extraordinary events and relationships of life.

There will be doubts and downs as well as ups – '... they worshipped him, but some doubted'. But be confident that perseverance in desiring and seeking will be rewarded: 'I sought him whom my soul loves ... but found him not ... but he gave no answer ... I found him whom my soul loves ... and would not let him go' (Song of Solomon 3.1, 4).

Why be confident? Because it really is true – 'I am with you always.'

COLLECT

Lord of all life and power,
who through the mighty resurrection of your Son
overcame the old order of sin and death
to make all things new in him:
grant that we, being dead to sin
and alive to you in Jesus Christ,
may reign with him in glory;
to whom with you and the Holy Spirit
be praise and honour, glory and might,
now and in all eternity.

| *Reflection by* **David Ford**

Psalms 114, 148
Song of Solomon 5.2 – 6.3
Luke 7.11-17

Thursday 24 April
Thursday of Easter Week

Song of Solomon 5.2 – 6.3
'I am my beloved's and my beloved is mine' (6.3)

This is fully mutual love. In the San people, or Bushmen, of the Kalahari Desert, a husband and a wife call each other 'utterly my man', 'utterly my woman'. The Song, too, has an intensity of mutual belonging, rooted in passionate desire, '... my inmost being yearned for him'.

This utter mutuality is also set within a community: 'the flock of your companions ... the mighty men of Israel ... O Daughters of Jerusalem ...'. And the community is set within a glorious, vibrant world of nature, bursting with plant and animal life. This is both imaginative ('I am a rose of Sharon, a lily of the valley ... My beloved is like a gazelle ... Your eyes are pools in Heshbon') and literal – vineyards, orchards, pastures, figs, apples, spring flowers, cliffs, wilderness, goats, foxes, lions, leopards and, above all, gardens, all evoke Eden. But there is also the realism of urban life and violence: 'they beat me, they wounded me'.

The resurrection of the crucified Jesus resonates with the violence and the wounds, with the abundant life of a new creation and a new community, and with the mutuality of lovers. In a garden, Mary Magdalene meets the risen Jesus, 'supposing him to be the gardener'. Then, in what is perhaps the most moving moment of mutuality in the New Testament, 'Jesus said to her, "Mary!" She turned and said to him in Hebrew, "Rabbouni!" (which means Teacher)' (John 20.16).

We, too, are called by name by the risen Jesus.

God of glory,
by the raising of your Son
you have broken the chains of death and hell:
fill your Church with faith and hope;
for a new day has dawned
and the way to life stands open
in our Saviour Jesus Christ.

COLLECT

Friday 25 April

Friday of Easter Week

Psalms 115, 149
Song of Solomon 7.10 – 8.4
Luke 8.41-end

Luke 8.41-end

'Do not fear. Only believe, and she will be saved' (v.50)

'Your faith has made you well.'
'Only believe.'

The Greek for 'faith' is *pistis*, for 'believe' it is *pisteuson*. Once, over lunch with a leading New Testament scholar, she said, 'I tell my students: in our culture, these words are best translated in the first instance as 'trust'.' Both the woman healed of haemorrhages and Jairus, whose daughter is brought back to life, trust Jesus.

The response of Jesus to the needs of each is not simply clinical cure, but a fully personal, tender relationship. To the woman he says: 'Daughter, your trust has made you well: go in peace'; to Jairus' daughter, 'Child, get up!' Then he directs those in the room to give her something to eat.

'I am my beloved's, and his desire is for me.'

The deepest desire of Jesus is to love and to be loved, for which it is vital that we trust him. Can our desire for him grow to match his for us? When, in his prayer in John 17.20-26, he faces death and looks beyond it to us – his future disciples 'who will trust in me' – his ultimate desire is for us to be united in trust and love with himself and his Father, and with each other, for the sake of the world to which he has been sent in love.

'Do not fear.'

What fears stop us trusting Jesus wholeheartedly, and being sent together into the world in love, as he was sent?

COLLECT

Lord of all life and power,
who through the mighty resurrection of your Son
overcame the old order of sin and death
to make all things new in him:
grant that we, being dead to sin
and alive to you in Jesus Christ,
may reign with him in glory;
to whom with you and the Holy Spirit
be praise and honour, glory and might,
now and in all eternity.

| *Reflection by* **David Ford**

Psalms 116, 150
Song of Solomon 8.5-7
John 11.17-44

Saturday 26 April

Saturday of Easter Week

John 11.17-44

'I am the resurrection and the life' (v.25)

The raising of Lazarus is the culminating 'sign' in Jesus' public ministry. Its purpose, he says in prayer to his Father, is that people 'may believe/trust/have faith that you sent me', and this leads into the climactic moment of the drama: Jesus 'cried with a loud voice, "Lazarus, come out!". The dead man came out ...'.

'I am the resurrection and the life' opens up the depth of this sign, and is the high moment of its meaning. This sign points to who Jesus is. It is the culmination of many earlier moments that give further content to the Prologue's headline, 'in him was life' (1.4 – read, for example, 4.14, 6.35, 8.12). And it anticipates what is to come: 'I am the way, and the truth, and the life' (14.6). Jesus is the 'I am' – a name unique to God, and is also fully human, weeping for his dead friend, 'greatly disturbed in spirit and deeply moved'.

Above all, this sign points to the ultimate mystery, in which both death and resurrection happen to Jesus. The result is the best imaginable news for all of us: the crucified and resurrected Jesus is the 'I am' of God who is present with us and for us on both sides of death. In life, in death, he is utterly trustworthy. And, as with his friend Lazarus, he calls each by name into life with him in ongoing love.

God of glory,
by the raising of your Son
you have broken the chains of death and hell:
fill your Church with faith and hope;
for a new day has dawned
and the way to life stands open
in our Saviour Jesus Christ.

COLLECT

Reflection by **David Ford** | 135

Monday 28 April

George, martyr,
patron of England

Psalms 5, 146
Joshua 1.1-9
Ephesians 6.10-20

Joshua 1.1-9

'... the Lord your God is with you wherever you go' (v.9)

Our scripture reading is going to feel a bit lumpy this week. We would usually be reading John 20–21 straight through but, because of the date of Easter, two feast days get transferred into this week, joining the feast of Philip and James, which we keep on Thursday, and enriching our worship in quite interesting ways. Today we keep the Feast of St George. This comes with some attendant militaristic images, and quite a lot of talk of possession of territory, both of which feel a bit uncomfortable, particularly in association with the Holy Land.

A useful antidote to some of the more martial language used in some celebrations of St George is God's clear direction to Joshua that vital to his ministry is going to be keeping 'the book of the law' at the very heart of all that he does. Attending to God's voice, in prayer and engagement with scripture, is not an add-on or an option: it is the key to a successful journey. In this season of Easter we might take the opportunity to review how we listen to, and for, the voice of God. How do you listen to that promise that 'the Lord ... will be with you wherever you go'?

COLLECT

God of hosts,
who so kindled the flame of love
in the heart of your servant George
that he bore witness to the risen Lord
by his life and by his death:
give us the same faith and power of love
that we who rejoice in his triumphs
may come to share with him the fullness of the resurrection;
through Jesus Christ our Lord.

Psalms 37.23-end, 148
Isaiah 62.6-10
or Ecclesiasticus 51.13-end
Acts 12.25 – 13.13

Tuesday 29 April

Mark the Evangelist

Isaiah 62.6-10

'... build up, build up the highway' (v.10)

Today's reading from Isaiah is full of fascinating job descriptions! There are sentinels, builders of highways, clearers of stones, flag raisers (which is what 'lifting up an ensign' means), and perhaps most strikingly, *reminders* of the Lord. What does it mean to be 'you who *remind* the Lord'? It seems here to refer to prayer, to a constant holding before God of the people and their situations. As such it is a reassurance that our daily intercessions are important, legitimate and part of our relationship with the divine.

Today is the feast of Mark the Evangelist, author of the earliest of the four canonical Gospels. There is an urgency about his Gospel. Most commentators note how many times the word 'immediately' occurs within the 16 chapters of Mark. This fits in well with these verses from Isaiah, with their air of excitement, watchfulness and preparation. We can almost imagine people scurrying about clearing the road, raising flags, looking out from the walls eagerly, looking for the Lord. Is this us? Are we ready? Are we eager? Words like 'steadfast' and 'enduring' are often used to describe the sort of faith we ought to have, and those are good words, but how often do we consider how 'eager', how full of expectation our faith is? Are we daily raising the flag in anticipation of God's arrival? Food for thought on this great feast day.

Almighty God,
who enlightened your holy Church
through the inspired witness of your evangelist Saint Mark:
grant that we, being firmly grounded
in the truth of the gospel,
may be faithful to its teaching both in word and deed;
through Jesus Christ our Lord.

COLLECT

Wednesday 30 April

Psalms 16, **30** *or* 119.1-32
Deuteronomy 3.18-end
John 20.19-end

John 20.19-end

'Thomas ... was not with them when Jesus came' (v.24)

Scripture is completely silent on the question of where Thomas was when the other disciples had their first encounter with the risen Christ. Might he have been delayed on the way? Could he not face gathering with his friends, overwhelmed with grief and despair over the death of his mentor and master Jesus? Might the answer be far more prosaic, and perhaps he was out shopping, preferring to lose himself in mundane activity after all the drama of recent days? We simply do not know.

What we do know is that Thomas' encounter, a week later than his friends, gives both reassurance and hope to all of us who pursue our Christian journey with a mixture of faith and doubt, hope and despair, optimism and pessimism. We want to believe but some days, some weeks, it seems very hard indeed. How wonderful to have a figure like Thomas to look to; someone who knows what it is to doubt profoundly, to want proof, but who is also so receptive to Jesus that actually when the moment comes, he doesn't need to touch Christ's hands or side after all. We all have ups and downs in our journey of faith, and Thomas reminds us that we are in good company.

COLLECT

Almighty Father,
you have given your only Son to die for our sins
and to rise again for our justification:
grant us so to put away the leaven of malice and wickedness
that we may always serve you
in pureness of living and truth;
through the merits of your Son Jesus Christ our Lord.

Psalms 139, 146
Proverbs 4.10-18
James 1.1-12

Thursday I May
Philip and James, Apostles

Proverbs 4.10-18

'Keep hold of instruction; do not let go' (v.13)

There is some pleasing symmetry in the fact that today we keep the feast of Philip and James, sandwiched in between readings from the closing chapters of the Gospel according to John. It is in the very first chapter of John's Gospel that we learn much about Philip. Philip is the third disciple to be called by Jesus (John 1.43), and he is the second person to go and bring a friend to meet this mysterious Galilean preacher who has so captivated him (John 1.45). Philip brings Nathanael to meet Jesus, and the two of them become numbered among the twelve apostles, and we still look to them today for inspiration in the way of discipleship.

Today's words from the Proverbs are advice from a parent to a child, words from long before the time of Philip, James and Jesus, and they present a pattern of life to be followed. Wisdom is to be cherished and desired. Instruction, in other words being willing to learn and be formed, should be guarded because it is the way to life. In Jesus, Philip, James and countless others through the years found that wisdom and instruction have a name and a face. Christ is God incarnate: in Christ, all God's promises come to meet us.

Almighty Father,
whom truly to know is eternal life:
teach us to know your Son Jesus Christ
as the way, the truth, and the life;
that we may follow the steps
of your holy apostles Philip and James,
and walk steadfastly in the way that leads to your glory;
through Jesus Christ our Lord.

COLLECT

Friday 2 May

Psalms 57, **61** *or* 17, **19**
Deuteronomy 4.15-31
John 21.15-19

John 21.15-19

'... do you love me?' (vv. 15, 16, 17)

The final chapter of St John's Gospel is quite wonderful, with the whole chapter set on the seashore at breakfast time. We missed the first fourteen verses yesterday as we were paying attention to Saints Philip and James, so do go back and read those because they set the scene for our readings today and tomorrow. This interaction between Peter and Jesus has so many layers and associations. Our Roman Catholic brothers and sisters see in the conversation part of the establishing of the papacy, and leadership ministry in the Church more generally: 'Feed my sheep, tend my lambs.' Biblical scholars point out that several different words for 'love' are used in this exchange. The first word, *'agape'*, which Jesus uses the first two times he asked Peter the question, refers to a deep, sacrificial, godly love. Peter, when he responds, uses the word *'phileo'* instead, which refers much more to brotherly, familial love. What is interesting is that the third time Jesus asks the question, he, too, uses the word *'phileo'*. Perhaps an example of Jesus meeting Peter where he is, with typical compassion and care?

Above all, what we see here is an individual talking to his Saviour about how much he loves him. This is something that we all struggle with because words run out and we are weak, but we still want to try. And we learn that truly loving God is not without risk: to love is to follow, and following might lead us to risky places. Follow we must, however, and Eastertide is a good time to recommit to follow the God who knows everything about us, and who knows that we love him.

COLLECT

Almighty Father,
you have given your only Son to die for our sins
and to rise again for our justification:
grant us so to put away the leaven of malice and wickedness
that we may always serve you
in pureness of living and truth;
through the merits of your Son Jesus Christ our Lord.

Reflection by **Tom Clammer**

Psalms 63, **84** *or* 20, 21, **23**
Deuteronomy 4.32-40
John 21.20-end

Saturday 3 May

John 21.20-end

*'I suppose that the world itself could not contain the books
that would be written' (v.25)*

The Gospel according to St John has two endings. We read the first
one on Wednesday, when we heard that 'Jesus did many other signs
in the presence of the disciples' (20.30), and that the author's
purpose in writing down some of them in the Gospel is to encourage
faith in the reader. Here again, in what seems like a restressing of
how important this message is, we have a similar but even more
beautifully phrased verse, which evokes in the mind a never-ending
library crammed with books telling the wondrous story of works and
deeds of Jesus Christ, the Son of God.

There's a temptation to read the final verse of St John's Gospel as
somewhat rhetorical, if very beautiful, but of course as Christians we
believe that Jesus Christ continues to work through his body here on
earth. If that is true, and the Jesus of two thousand or so years ago
who breakfasted on the lakeside is also working where we live,
where we work, where we breakfast, then actually those books are
still filling up with the stories of what Christ is doing. There are also
many other things that Jesus did and some of them he is doing right
now, in and through us.

Risen Christ,
for whom no door is locked, no entrance barred:
open the doors of our hearts,
that we may seek the good of others
and walk the joyful road of sacrifice and peace,
to the praise of God the Father.

COLLECT

Reflection by **Tom Clammer** | 141

Monday 5 May

Ephesians 1.1-14

'Blessed be the God and Father of our Lord Jesus Christ' (v.3)

The opening of Ephesians feels like being hit by water from a theological fire hose. Word after word, phrase after phrase, idea after idea tumble over each other as Paul praises God for all he has done in Christ, for the world and, particularly, for those in Christ. If it feels a lot in English, it's even more in Greek! Verses 3-14 are a single sentence joined together by lots of clauses. The translators have been kind to us, dividing Paul's prose into sentences to give us a better chance of keeping up with him.

These verses underpin the whole of the rest of the epistle. They describe who Paul* thinks God to be, who Christ is, and what difference this makes to the Ephesians. As a result, Paul has clear ideas about how the Ephesians should relate to one another and how they should act, which he unpacks throughout the rest of the letter.

Few of us would write something quite so theologically articulate or dense as we find in these verses but, if you were challenged to write down what you believed about God, what difference this makes to you and how you live your life, I wonder what you might say?

*Some scholars question whether or not Paul wrote Ephesians. For the sake of ease, and as there is no room for a long discussion of the options, I am assuming that the author of this epistle is Paul.

T	Almighty Father,
C	who in your great mercy gladdened the disciples
E	with the sight of the risen Lord:
L	give us such knowledge of his presence with us,
L	that we may be strengthened and sustained by his risen life
O	and serve you continually in righteousness and truth;
C	through Jesus Christ our Lord.

| *Reflection by* **Paula Gooder**

Psalms **98**, 99, 100 *or* 32, **36**
Deuteronomy 5.22-end
Ephesians 1.15-end

Ephesians 1.15-end

'I have heard of your faith' (v.15)

Being on social media can be a depressing experience. Although some platforms are better than others, the overwhelming function of social media seems to be the telling and retelling of bad news about both people and institutions. While it would be lovely to think that Christian social media is different, sadly it isn't.

It's striking, therefore, to note Paul's warm opening to the Ephesians in which he talks about what he has heard about them – their faith in the Lord Jesus and their love towards all the saints. The social media of Paul's day (i.e. letters and messengers) had delivered such good news about the Ephesians that he never ceased to give thanks for them as he remembered them in his prayers. This is not to imply that the Ephesians were perfect: as the letter unfolds, it is clear that they were not. Even in this opening section, Paul has cause to pray that God will give the Ephesians a spirit of wisdom and revelation.

Nevertheless, this opening chapter focuses on the good news that Paul has heard of the Ephesians' faith and action. I often wonder how different our churches would be if we focused on similarly inspirational stories about our fellow Christians – stories of their faith and love. What would happen if we talked about that all the time instead of the bad news that crowds in on us so often?

Risen Christ,
you filled your disciples with boldness and fresh hope:
strengthen us to proclaim your risen life
and fill us with your peace,
to the glory of God the Father.

COLLECT

Wednesday 7 May

Psalm **105** *or* **34**
Deuteronomy 6
Ephesians 2.1-10

Ephesians 2.1-10

'God ... made us alive together in Christ' (v.5)

When was the last time you felt fully and truly alive?

One of Paul's most significant images is that of death and life. Although he only used it three times, each one is important. He described dying and rising with Christ in baptism (Romans 6.1-14). He referred to it in 2 Corinthians 5.14-21 to talk about Christ dying and rising on our behalf and he uses it here and in Colossians 2.8-15 to talk about being dead through sin and raised to life with Christ.

The implication of Paul's language is that those who are in Christ should experience 'life in all its fullness', to borrow a phrase from one translation of John 10.10. But what does this mean? Anyone who imagines that it indicates that Christians will be full of endless vitality is sure to be disillusioned quite quickly.

The hint to what 'life' means can be found in today's opening verse, through reference to its opposite. The Ephesians were 'dead through the trespasses and sins in which you once lived'. Sin by its nature cuts us off from God and from each other. Conversely, being 'in Christ' establishes a deep and lasting connection with God and with each other. Being alive, in Paul's mind, then, is an experience of being fully and truly connected, both to God and to one another.

As is clear throughout Ephesians, our calling is to live this out in everything that we say and do.

COLLECT

Almighty Father,
who in your great mercy gladdened the disciples
    with the sight of the risen Lord:
give us such knowledge of his presence with us,
that we may be strengthened and sustained by his risen life
and serve you continually in righteousness and truth;
through Jesus Christ our Lord.

| *Reflection by* **Paula Gooder**

Psalm **136** *or* **37***
Deuteronomy 7.1-11
Ephesians 2.11-end

Thursday 8 May

Ephesians 2.11-end

'... you are citizens ... and members of the household of God' (v.19)

The words we use to describe 'belonging' are significant. They tell us a lot about how we think we will behave towards those to whom we belong. For example, if we talk of brothers and sisters, we invoke families and the notion of life-long relationships; whereas if we talk of colleagues or associates, we more readily imagine a relationship that exists in a work environment.

Throughout his writings, Paul used a range of different images of belonging from brothers and sisters to saints; from ecclesia (or Church) to the 'body of Christ'. They all provide different shades of understanding of what belonging to each other in Christ means. The images in this passage – 'citizens with the saints and members of the household of God' – are particularly important, especially when we contrast them with what the Ephesians are not – 'strangers and aliens' – in other words people who by right do not belong and have no rights.

The linking together of citizens with household members is especially noteworthy. The phrase stresses, more strongly than almost anything else could have done, that those who are in Christ are beloved and welcome, they have rights of dignity and inheritance. In short, they truly belong.

Paul's challenge to the Ephesians is to behave to each other as though they believe this to be true. It is a challenge that remains as relevant today as it did when Ephesians was written.

Risen Christ,
you filled your disciples with boldness and fresh hope:
strengthen us to proclaim your risen life
and fill us with your peace,
to the glory of God the Father.

COLLECT

Reflection by **Paula Gooder** | 145

Friday 9 May

Psalm **107** or **31**
Deuteronomy 7.12-end
Ephesians 3.1-13

Ephesians 3.1-13

'This is the reason that I … am a prisoner' (v.1)

In my Christian life I am often reminded of the Laurel and Hardy quip: 'Well, here's another fine mess you've gotten me into.' It makes me wonder whether we would still say 'yes' to God's call on our lives if we knew where it would lead us.

In a similar vein, I wonder whether Paul would have said 'yes' in his encounter with the risen Christ on the road to Damascus if he had known it would land him in prison. In this passage, he certainly draws a direct line from the mystery made known to him by revelation to becoming a servant of the gospel and hence the reason he is in prison.

We can never know whether Paul would have said the same 'yes' to God if he had known what the consequences would be. No more than we can know if any one of us would have said 'yes' if we'd known that it would sometimes take us to difficult places. What we can know is that Paul shows no hint of regret in this passage, quite the opposite, in fact. He talks of the grace and of the boundless riches of Christ given to him.

In other words, no matter what the consequences, the glorious gift of God in Christ Jesus makes our 'yes' to God unfailingly the best decision we could ever take.

COLLECT

Almighty Father,
who in your great mercy gladdened the disciples
   with the sight of the risen Lord:
give us such knowledge of his presence with us,
that we may be strengthened and sustained by his risen life
and serve you continually in righteousness and truth;
through Jesus Christ our Lord.

Reflection by **Paula Gooder**

Ephesians 3.14-end

'... rooted and grounded in love' (v.17)

Just when we have recovered from Paul's first rich theological opening statement (1.3-14), we encounter another passage that is an equally dense, single sentence. Verses 14-19 are, again, in Greek, a single sentence in which Paul lays out what he prays for the Ephesians. The prayer reaches its climax at the end of verse 19, where Paul prays that the Ephesians might be 'filled with all the fullness of God'.

Powerful as this prayer is, it is not the most famous phrase in this passage. Much more well known is something that Paul prays almost in passing: 'as you are being rooted and grounded in love'. It is a beautiful image, even if it contains one of Paul's favoured mixed metaphors. The first word refers to roots, as in a plant, and the second to foundations, as in a building. In other words, the love of Christ nourishes us and causes us to grow, while at the same time establishing firm foundations on which we can stand and which give us long-term stability.

We miss the point of what Paul is talking about, though, if we pull that one phrase out on its own. The reason why we are rooted and grounded in love is not for its own sake but, ultimately, so that we can be strengthened to experience the full indwelling of God. What this means is something that can be comprehended only in prayer.

Risen Christ,
you filled your disciples with boldness and fresh hope:
strengthen us to proclaim your risen life
and fill us with your peace,
to the glory of God the Father.

COLLECT

Reflection by **Paula Gooder**

Monday 12 May

Psalms **103** *or* **44**
Deuteronomy 9.1-21
Ephesians 4.1-16

Ephesians 4.1-16

'... lead a life worthy of the calling to which you have been called'
(v.1)

Often, when speaking about the fruit of the Spirit (listed in the famous passage found in Galatians 5.22-23), people slip and talk about 'fruits of the Spirit'. This may seem small and incidental but is quite important. The fruit of the Spirit is all the characteristics Paul describes in those verses, so calling them the fruits of the Spirit could imply that you can pick and choose – joy but not patience; peace but not love.

Something similar is going on in this passage. Paul talks about characteristics of a life 'worthy of the calling to which you have been called' marked by humility, gentleness, patience, bearing with one another in love and maintaining the unity of the Spirit. These are all non-negotiable. You can't pick one and neglect the others. In contrast, later in the passage Paul talks of the different gifts Christ has given: that some would be apostles, prophets, etc. From this list, we can expect to receive one gift, but not all.

The reason why this is so important is that the characteristics of a Christian life – all of them – should be lived out in each of the callings. In other words, you can't say that because I'm a prophet I don't need to be gentle or patient. We spend a lot of time talking about 'gifts' but I wonder what would happen if we spent as long discussing exactly what it looks like to inhabit the characteristics of a Christian calling?

COLLECT

Almighty God,
whose Son Jesus Christ is the resurrection and the life:
raise us, who trust in him,
from the death of sin to the life of righteousness,
that we may seek those things which are above,
where he reigns with you
in the unity of the Holy Spirit,
one God, now and for ever.

Reflection by **Paula Gooder**

Tuesday 13 May

Ephesians 4.17-end

'Let no evil talk come out of your mouths' (v.29)

Live as though you believe all this to be true.

One of the striking features of the end of nearly all Paul's epistles is that he moves into what you might call the 'so what?' questions. In other words, having laid out profound and eloquent theology, he moves on to the question of the difference it all makes to the way in which we live our lives. Ephesians is no exception.

Halfway through chapter 4, Paul turns his attention to how we should live, and his views are characteristically uncompromising, though vary in the extent of their challenge. His strictures against lying and stealing are only what we might expect. But how many of us can honestly say that we have never stayed angry overnight? Or allowed words to come out of our mouths that did not build up those around us? Or been bitter or contentious?

Just when we might be wondering how exactly we are meant to achieve and maintain this kind of model behaviour, the chapter ends with positive advice: be kind, compassionate and forgiving. As so often in his letters, Paul balances what we should not do with what we should. A life lived in kindness, compassion and forgiveness will leave little room for those bad habits that he condemns and, in any case, is a very good place to begin.

COLLECT

Risen Christ,
faithful shepherd of your Father's sheep:
teach us to hear your voice
and to follow your command,
that all your people may be gathered into one flock,
to the glory of God the Father.

Reflection by **Paula Gooder** |149

Wednesday 14 May

Matthias the Apostle

Psalms 16, 147.1-12
1 Samuel 2.27-35
Acts 2.37-end

Acts 2.37-end

'... with glad and generous hearts' (v.46)

It is tempting to look at the past with the nostalgia of rose-tinted spectacles. Whether that past consists of what used to happen ten or twenty years ago, or when we were young, or, as here, what happened at the start of it all.

People often look at Acts 2 as the ultimate nostalgic account of what Christianity was like at the very start. With hindsight, it looks idyllic: the earliest Christians spent time together in the Temple, presumably devoting themselves to the apostles' teaching; they broke bread and ate together; they praised God, were thought well of and grew numerically every day.

It is probably worth reminding ourselves at this point that this idyll did not last. Only four chapters later (6.1-7) we read of the first grand falling out between Greek speakers and Hebrew speakers because they didn't think they were being treated equally.

So, does the harsh light of reality spoil the earlier idyll? I would argue not. The reality of Christian existence – just as with all human existence – is that arguments will break out and unity will crumble, but even though this is the case, we shouldn't give up on the vision. One phrase stands out as key here: 'with glad and generous hearts'. Whatever happens in our lives together as Christians, having 'glad and generous hearts' will contribute enormously to our longed-for unity.

COLLECT

Almighty God,
who in the place of the traitor Judas
chose your faithful servant Matthias
to be of the number of the Twelve:
preserve your Church from false apostles
and, by the ministry of faithful pastors and teachers,
keep us steadfast in your truth;
through Jesus Christ our Lord.

| *Reflection by* **Paula Gooder**

Thursday 15 May

Ephesians 5.15-end

'... live, not as unwise people, but as wise' (v.15)

It is hard to resist the sinking feeling that comes when you know that this passage, and others like it, are approaching in the lectionary readings. So much has been written about them over the years that it is hard to read them with anything like clear sight.

Beginning to read this passage about how husbands and wives relate to one another in verse 15, though, does give an interesting lens through which to regard what Paul is saying. The key, he says, is to live 'wisely'. The word 'wise' is important because it doesn't just mean 'clever' but also implies 'skilled,' 'smart in practical matters', 'savvy' as we might say today. In other words Paul is advising skill and practical nous for negotiating our most important relationships and goes on to talk about giving thanks to God at all times as the foundation of how we live.

Wisdom and thanksgiving then form the bedrock of relationships that are expressed in mutual respect for each other. Although much has been made of the husband being head of his wife, the majority of the passage is about how a husband should love his wife and treat her with the utmost respect.

This passage is never going to be an easy one to read in our society, which is so different from the one Paul is addressing here, but the principles of mutual love and respect shine through it all.

COLLECT

Almighty God,
whose Son Jesus Christ is the resurrection and the life:
raise us, who trust in him,
from the death of sin to the life of righteousness,
that we may seek those things which are above,
where he reigns with you
in the unity of the Holy Spirit,
one God, now and for ever.

Reflection by **Paula Gooder** | 151

Friday 16 May

Ephesians 6.1-9

'... doing the will of God from the heart' (v.6)

If the end of Ephesians 5 is hard to read, the beginning of chapter 6 is no easier. Here Paul turns his attention to children's relationships with their parents and slaves to their masters. Particularly in the case of slaves and masters, there is so much that we might wish Paul had said that he did not.

What is interesting, though, is that the main focus in these passages is on how to live as a Christian in a situation you do not have the ability to change. In this case, slaves could not change their masters' rights over them but they could choose how to live as slaves and this is what Paul addresses here.

Paul's advice feels a little similar to the parable of the sheep and the goats in Matthew 25.31-46. There, Jesus lauds those who fed the hungry or clothed the naked because they did it as if for him. Here, slaves are encouraged to act as though they are slaves of Christ, doing God's will from the heart and serving with enthusiasm 'as to the Lord'.

This does not make Paul's silence on the subject of slavery any easier to accept but it does provide food for thought. In situations where we have no power or any ability to change anything, we can change ourselves, living wholeheartedly and with enthusiasm as though for God.

COLLECT

Almighty God,
whose Son Jesus Christ is the resurrection and the life:
raise us, who trust in him,
from the death of sin to the life of righteousness,
that we may seek those things which are above,
where he reigns with you
in the unity of the Holy Spirit,
one God, now and for ever.

| *Reflection by* **Paula Gooder**

Psalm **34** *or* **68**
Deuteronomy 15.1-18
Ephesians 6.10-end

Saturday 17 May

Ephesians 6.10-end

'... the whole armour of God' (v.11)

One of Paul's most evocative images is that of the putting on the whole armour of God.

In two different verses in this letter Paul mentions being in prison (3.1, 4.1) and in this passage he talks of being 'an ambassador in chains'. In prison, Paul would have been very familiar with the armour of a Roman soldier. It is possible, indeed, that his reflections about the armour of God in 6.10-17 were inspired by watching the soldiers who guarded him donning their armour each day.

The majority of items in a soldier's armour are protective: the belt, the breastplate, the shield and the helmet all protect the soldier from harm. Even the shoes, mentioned in verse 15, exist to protect the feet. Only the sword existed both to protect and to attack. This provides an insight into what Paul had in mind here. Christians would face an onslaught from rulers, authorities, cosmic powers and spiritual forces of evil. Just as the lives of the Roman soldiers who guarded him depended on the quality of their armour for survival, so Christians would rely in the same way on truth, righteousness, the proclamation of peace, faith and salvation.

Today, warfare is conducted completely differently. This raises the question of what everyday images we might draw on today – medical? constructional? technological? – to achieve a similarly vibrant image of the characteristics we need to survive as Christians.

Risen Christ,
faithful shepherd of your Father's sheep:
teach us to hear your voice
and to follow your command,
that all your people may be gathered into one flock,
to the glory of God the Father.

COLLECT

Reflection by **Paula Gooder**

153

Monday 19 May

Psalm **145** *or* **71**
Deuteronomy 16.1-20
1 Peter 1.1-12

1 Peter 1.1-12

'... chosen to be sprinkled by his blood' (v.2)

Having the right understanding of sacrifice is crucial for a healthy spiritual life. We tend to think of sacrifices as something that we offer to God and that please him because they are costly. This might be true of pagan sacrifices but not of the sacrificial spirituality of the Old Testament and of its metaphorical application to the death of Christ and the lives of Christians.

Whenever we hear this word we should remind ourselves of its etymology, *sacrum facere*, to 'make something sacred or holy', that is pleasing to God. Also, we should remember that this is impossible for us. In the Old Testament the ritual use of blood was based on the belief that it does not belong to us but to God because it is the symbol of the life only God can give: 'The life of the flesh is in the blood; and I have given it to you for making atonement for your lives on the altar; for, as life, it is the blood that makes atonement' (Leviticus 17.11).

In the New Testament we are taught that blood is synonymous not only with life but with love – because love alone can unite us to God and to each other. It is by *his* (Christ's) *blood that we are sprinkled*, says Peter. It is by Christ's love that whatever we do and are becomes sacrifice, is made holy, makes the impossible possible: give joy to God.

COLLECT

Almighty God,
who through your only-begotten Son Jesus Christ
have overcome death and opened to us the gate of everlasting life:
grant that, as by your grace going before us
    you put into our minds good desires,
so by your continual help
we may bring them to good effect;
through Jesus Christ our risen Lord.

| *Reflection by* **Luigi Gioia**

Tuesday 20 May

1 Peter 1.13-end

'... you were ransomed ... with the precious blood of Christ'
(v.18-19)

The idea that Christ saved us by paying a 'ransom' has long misled the theological imagination of Christians. Slaves could indeed be freed by paying a ransom to their masters. When this image is applied to the sacrifice of Christ, though, the emphasis is not on the payment – unless we want to go down the rabbit hole of conjecturing a transaction between God and the devil. The emphasis is on the deliverance.

Blood means love. Whenever blood is mentioned in reference to Christ it means the love that led him to give his life freely for us. We killed him, but he forgave us and broke the bondage of 'an eye for an eye' once and for all. The way he died obtained for us the freedom to achieve the impossible: to turn the other cheek. Non-violence and forgiveness are no longer the expression of resignation, powerlessness and weakness. They have become the highest possible expression of love.

This is the deliverance Christ won for us by his sacrifice: his love can now make our lives, our desires, our motives a sacrifice too. No physical blood-offering could ever achieve this feat: unite us to God and to each other (which is the literal meaning of 'atonement'), and deliver us from the slavery of hatred, violence and retaliation.

Risen Christ,
your wounds declare your love for the world
and the wonder of your risen life:
give us compassion and courage
to risk ourselves for those we serve,
to the glory of God the Father.

COLLECT

Reflection by **Luigi Gioia**   155

Wednesday 21 May

Psalms **30**, 147.13-end *or* **77**
Deuteronomy 18.9-end
1 Peter 2.1-10

1 Peter 2.1-10

'... let yourselves be built into a spiritual house, to be a holy priesthood' (v.5)

'This is the sacrifice of Christians,' says Augustine, 'that we who are many become one body in Christ' (*City of God* 10.6). Forgiving others, loving them as Christ has loved us, can be costly. It is not the cost, though, that makes forgiveness and love 'sacrifices'. Rather, forgiveness and love make us 'holy' (*sacrum facere*) in that they 'atone': they join us to God and to one another, and, as Peter says, they build us into a spiritual house.

God had already made this clear in the Old Testament: he does not want the blood of animals but mercy and justice. Or, rather, he asked his people to perform ritual sacrifices as a sign of their commitment to worship God by loving him with all their heart and by caring for the poor and the stranger. Once we were not a people because greed, jealousy and suspicion ruled our hearts, divided us from others and emptied our religious practices of their meaning. There is no point in bringing an offering to the altar if I harbour resentment against someone in my heart.

Perfect love remains beyond our reach in this life but we can still become one body with Christ and with one another if we never become resigned to our divisions and patiently, daily, obstinately renew our commitment to forgiving and caring.

COLLECT

Almighty God,
who through your only-begotten Son Jesus Christ
have overcome death and opened to us the gate of everlasting life:
grant that, as by your grace going before us
    you put into our minds good desires,
so by your continual help
we may bring them to good effect;
through Jesus Christ our risen Lord.

Psalms **57**, 148 *or* **78.1-39***
Deuteronomy 19
1 Peter 2.11-end

Thursday 22 May

1 Peter 2.11-end

'Christ ... suffered for you, leaving you an example' (v.21)

When we hear that Christ died for our sins we might be tempted to depart from history and to imagine a timeless tribunal where an angry God exacts the punishment we deserve on someone willing to take our place. History tells us that Jesus was murdered not by God but by Roman soldiers following a political and religious conspiracy sanctioned by a mob. He was betrayed not by God but by his disciples and friends. Ultimately it was our idolatry that caused his death.

Our desire is for a domesticated God whom we can contain in our temples and propitiate with our well-choreographed offerings – a God who does not upset our established order nor the pursuit of our wellbeing by making us accountable for those in need. Killing Jesus was a desperate attempt to silence his intolerable call to replace greed with care, indifference with love. But we had underestimated the power of his determination to love us to the end. Forgiveness was the last gasp of the crucified and the first breath of the risen body. Just as divine breath made us alive at the beginning so Christ's Spirit now makes our lives holy: sacrifices that can truly please our God.

Risen Christ,
your wounds declare your love for the world
and the wonder of your risen life:
give us compassion and courage
to risk ourselves for those we serve,
to the glory of God the Father.

COLLECT

Reflection by **Luigi Gioia** | 157

Friday 23 May

Psalms **138**, 149 *or* **55**
Deuteronomy 21.22 – 22.8
1 Peter 3.1-12

1 Peter 3.1-12

'... repay with a blessing' (v.9)

Sacrifices in scripture are a form of blessing. The relationship between the two shines out of the book of Psalms. Blood sacrifices were performed to seal the covenant with God, renew it and purify the people whenever they forfeited it. They were not mere rituals. The blood of animals belonged to God, and when both the people and the altar representing God were sprinkled with it, this signified their communion, their atonement (coming into one).

God, though, wanted not just a ceremonial commitment but the heart of his people. He wanted to help them to recognize that their freedom, their land, the produce of the earth and their own lives are a divine gift. This is why blessing and giving thanks for every aspect of life came to be seen as a sacrifice in itself, even without the symbolic role played by blood: 'Those who bring thanksgiving as their sacrifice honour me' (Psalm 50.23).

Blessing other people, even those who hurt us, is the sacrifice that truly pleases our God: it attunes our minds and hearts with the Father who never ceases to send his blessing on all of us and makes 'his sun rise on the evil and on the good, and sends rain on the righteous and on the unrighteous' (Matthew 5.45).

COLLECT

Almighty God,
who through your only-begotten Son Jesus Christ
have overcome death and opened to us the gate of everlasting life:
grant that, as by your grace going before us
   you put into our minds good desires,
so by your continual help
we may bring them to good effect;
through Jesus Christ our risen Lord.

| *Reflection by* **Luigi Gioia**

Psalms **146**, 150 *or* **76**, 79
Deuteronomy 24.5-end
1 Peter 3.13-end

1 Peter 3.13-end

'For it is better to suffer for doing good, if suffering should be God's will' (v.17)

Does God will us to suffer? The answer is an emphatic no. Peter's sentence is a shortcut. It is not God but the way things are that, sadly, makes suffering inevitable in life. Scripture is clear: God did not desire death, illness, the pain of work and childbirth, and especially not the suffering we inflict on each other on a daily basis because of our instinct to thrive or survive at the expense of others. Suffering has the potential to warp our souls, to deprive us of our dignity and to harden our hearts.

The way Jesus embraced suffering imbued it with new meaning. The suffering that others inflict on us has no more to be simply endured but can now be embraced in order to break the circle of retaliation: violence will stop with me, it will not reverberate from me onto others. Then the suffering we endure because the way things are (especially illness and death) becomes the place where the Crucified abides with us. The hope of the resurrection deprives it of its damaging potential. The love, faith and hope we can now infuse in suffering make it a sacrifice, something that atones, that unites us to God and to others.

Risen Christ,
your wounds declare your love for the world
and the wonder of your risen life:
give us compassion and courage
to risk ourselves for those we serve,
to the glory of God the Father.

COLLECT

Reflection by **Luigi Gioia** | 159

Monday 26 May

1 Peter 4.1-11

'... love covers a multitude of sins' (v.8)

The spilling of blood in the ritual sacrifices of the Old Testament expressed God's determination to help us overcome our unfaithfulness to his covenant. Of course, symbolic blood was not enough to atone, not enough to make us one with him and others. What we needed was a transformation of our hearts of stone into hearts of flesh (Ezekiel 36.26). His law had to be inscribed not merely on tablets of stone, but in our hearts.

In other words, God had to awaken in us a love for him and for one another that matched his love for us. Jesus came, and apparently little changed – neither then, nor now. Christians are just as unfaithful as the people who agreed to love God with their whole hearts at the foot of Mount Sinai but pined after the gods of Egypt the moment they were in need again. We are still mired in a multitude of sins, but a new invincible love is now at work in history. Nothing can stop its course. We might delay it but we can never outmatch its power. Now is the time of patience and forgiveness, both God's and ours. Not only with others but first of all with ourselves.

COLLECT

God our redeemer,
you have delivered us from the power of darkness
and brought us into the kingdom of your Son:
grant, that as by his death he has recalled us to life,
so by his continual presence in us he may raise us
    to eternal joy;
through Jesus Christ our Lord.

Reflection by **Luigi Gioia**

Psalms 124, 125, **126**, 127 *or* 87, **89.1-18**
Deuteronomy 28.1-14
1 Peter 4.12-end

1 Peter 4.12-end

'... rejoice in so far as you are sharing Christ's sufferings' (v.13)

How do we share in Christ's sufferings? Imagine that someone has hurt you unjustly or maliciously ruined your reputation. Being unfairly wronged does not make you like Christ and the suffering remains yours. You need to want to forgive this person because you believe that this is how the power of the resurrection changes human history; this is how it transforms your own heart and possibly even the heart of the perpetrator.

A Christian is called to believe that Christ has inaugurated a new creation, a new order of things. It is as if gravitational power had been inverted: we are no more pulled downwards but towards the new focal point of God's love – and the more we allow ourselves to be attracted by this love, the closer we get to one another. We are given eyes to see this new reality and a yearning to consent to its appeal.

Our instinct of self-preservation, our emotions and the prevailing mentality of the world might still make this hard. It might cost us. It will take time – because forgiveness is a process. But Christ opened the way, and much more than *we* sharing *his* suffering, it is *he* who shares *ours*. What makes the whole difference is that we suffer as those who are no longer alone, and as those who have hope. We suffer as Christians.

Risen Christ,
by the lakeside you renewed your call to your disciples:
help your Church to obey your command
and draw the nations to the fire of your love,
to the glory of God the Father.

COLLECT

Reflection by **Luigi Gioia**   161

Wednesday 28 May

1 Peter 5

'Cast all your anxiety on him' (v.7)

The struggles of life, the prospect of suffering, our wavering motivation, our hesitant faith, our unresolved inner insecurity: many are the triggers of the pangs of anxiety that wake us up in the middle of the night when darkness is all that we can see, literally and figuratively. How are we supposed to cast this anxiety on the Lord? Peter echoes Jesus' sermon on the mountain by reminding us that God cares for us.

There is something to be cherished in anxiety: it reminds us that we are not in control of our life. Even were we to expand our capabilities, the span of all that worries us is too wide for us to manage. All we can cope with is the burden of this particular day. And, as it happens, only this present moment is real, on it alone we can act. The people of Israel was ordered to collect manna only for one day – everything that exceeded their daily consumption went off. The Lord's Prayer teaches us to ask for bread not for the week or the year, but for the day.

The remedy for anxiety is humility: stay close to the humus – the ground – and stick to the only reality that matters, this present moment. The greatest certainty of our faith is that God is faithful and will never leave our side. There is true empowerment – and freedom – in trust and acceptance.

COLLECT

God our redeemer,
you have delivered us from the power of darkness
and brought us into the kingdom of your Son:
grant, that as by his death he has recalled us to life,
so by his continual presence in us he may raise us
    to eternal joy;
through Jesus Christ our Lord.

Reflection by **Luigi Gioia**

Psalm 110
Isaiah 52.7-end
Hebrews 7. [11-25] 26-end

Thursday 29 May
Ascension Day

Hebrews 7. [11-25] 26-end

'… this he did once for all when he offered himself' (v.27)

Our wrongdoings alienate us from others or result from our indifference to others. Others might still be physically close but disappear from our radar. The prodigal son goes to a distant country because he perceives his father's love as an intolerable restriction to his freedom. Sin is not an offence in need of reparation, but the opening of a gulf between ourselves and God, or between ourselves and others, which in time widens to the point of becoming unbridgeable. Hence the powerlessness of our sacrifices: they cannot atone any more, they cannot make us 'at one' with others and with God. Only the cross bridges this gulf: its horizontal beam embraces the whole of humanity and its vertical beam reunites us with God. Only the span of Christ's love is large and high enough. Only his risen body can be present to all people and to all times, remain on earth with us and be seated at the right hand of the Father.

At his Ascension Christ disappears visibly from one place to become invisibly present and active everywhere and forever: 'I am with you, until the end of times' are Jesus' last reported words in Matthew's gospel (28.20). Now his offer of himself can reach us wherever we are. Thanks to this offer we are truly atoned: we are made one, once and for all.

COLLECT

Grant, we pray, almighty God,
that as we believe your only-begotten Son
our Lord Jesus Christ
to have ascended into the heavens,
so we in heart and mind may also ascend
and with him continually dwell;
who is alive and reigns with you,
in the unity of the Holy Spirit,
one God, now and for ever.

Reflection by **Luigi Gioia** | 163

Friday 30 May

Galatians 5.13-end

'… you were called to freedom' (v.13)

We tend to oppose freedom and accountability. Having to take God or others into account means consenting to an endless cycle of obligations: giving up my time, energies and money, putting other people's needs above mine. We are willing to do this for the people we love, but extending such generosity to the stranger or to those who cannot give us anything in return would stretch us too thin, would threaten our inner resources and be unrealistic. Indeed, the freedom to love as selflessly as Jesus or the saints did is the work of a lifetime.

We underestimate how far benevolence can go and how much it replenishes while it gives; far from depleting us, it can unlock inner resources we were not aware of. Paul assures us that these resources are provided for. Patience, kindness, generosity and all the other inner dispositions he lists are not resolutions we should muster out of nowhere, but gifts at our disposal – if only we are willing to make use of them. They are like the bread Jesus multiplied for the five thousand: they flow all the more plentifully in order that we freely give. They are the bread we can ask only for this day and we are assured that, today, we will not be lacking. More patience, kindness and generosity might be needed another day but obtaining them will be the task of the prayer of that day.

COLLECT

Grant, we pray, almighty God,
that as we believe your only-begotten Son
   our Lord Jesus Christ
to have ascended into the heavens,
so we in heart and mind may also ascend
and with him continually dwell;
who is alive and reigns with you,
in the unity of the Holy Spirit,
one God, now and for ever.

| *Reflection by* **Luigi Gioia**

Psalms 85, 150
I Samuel 2.1-10
Mark 3.31-end

Saturday 31 May
Visit of the Blessed Virgin
Mary to Elizabeth

Mark 3.31-end

'... standing outside, they sent to him and called him' (v.31)

Obsessive concern about who has the right to be inside and who should be kept outside is one of the most unfailing signs that a Christian Church, denomination, community or congregation has become deeply dysfunctional. That this issue should arise from time to time is part of what life in common inevitably entails. That such debates should tear a community apart signals that something crucial about Jesus' message has been forgotten.

Jesus came for outsiders. He keeps looking for us to the extent that we acknowledge how much we remain outside too, despite our best efforts. Surrounding ourselves with walls leaves outside not only the people we deem undesirable, but the God whose overriding concern is for the lost sheep.

Jesus' own mother did not escape this temptation. She and the rest of Jesus' family thought they could own him, claim him for themselves. They thought themselves as the only insiders. Their entitlement excluded them from the circle of those who remain close to Jesus not because they think they have a right to him but because they have understood how much they keep needing his mercy and his care.

COLLECT

Mighty God,
by whose grace Elizabeth rejoiced with Mary
and greeted her as the mother of the Lord:
look with favour on your lowly servants
that, with Mary, we may magnify your holy name
and rejoice to acclaim her Son our Saviour,
who is alive and reigns with you,
in the unity of the Holy Spirit,
one God, now and for ever.

Reflection by **Luigi Gioia** | 165

Monday 2 June

Psalms **93**, 96, 97 *or* **98**, 99, 101
Numbers 27.15-end
1 Corinthians 3

1 Corinthians 3

'You are God's temple ... God's spirit dwells in you' (v.16)

How did you come to faith? Were you born into a Christian family and immersed daily in faith as you grew? Perhaps an event in your life led to a spiritual experience with the living God. Did a particular person lead you to Christ, intentionally or by accident? Maybe your faith, planted early through infant baptism, began to blossom as the Spirit grew within you. Perhaps you are still waiting for that moment.

For several years, the major focus of ministry was for me in vocational discernment, during which I encountered hundreds of people's faith stories. Some conversions were very ordinary, some extraordinary and a few miraculous. But every story was authentic, unique and beautiful. God has a remarkable ability to draw people into the body of Christ and fill them with the Holy Spirit. God longs to take up residence in us. We are God's temple where God's Spirit dwells. This is equally true for us as individuals and as the Christian community.

The young Corinthian Church struggled with divisions and factions. Paul tells them that it doesn't matter who was instrumental in bringing them to faith. Jesus Christ as the foundation of faith is what really matters. Faith built on that foundation will determine the robustness of the structure, its longevity and witness. Lives lived with Jesus as the foundation, and the Spirit dwelling within, will become recognizable as God's beautiful, spacious, inclusive and holy temple.

COLLECT

O God the King of glory,
you have exalted your only Son Jesus Christ
with great triumph to your kingdom in heaven:
we beseech you, leave us not comfortless,
but send your Holy Spirit to strengthen us
and exalt us to the place where our Saviour Christ is gone before,
who is alive and reigns with you,
in the unity of the Holy Spirit,
one God, now and for ever.

| *Reflection by* **Catherine Williams**

Psalms 98, **99**, 100 or **106*** (*or* 103)
I Samuel 10.1-10
I Corinthians 12.1-13

Tuesday 3 June

1 Corinthians 12.1-13

'Jesus is Lord' (v.3)

Competition is awakened in us from an early age and promoted as a positive thing. Our society celebrates and rewards winners, the best and the greatest. Honours, prizes, medals and trophies abound in many of our endeavours. It starts at school and continues throughout our lives. It's so hard-wired into us that we barely notice. I had an extraordinary experience several years ago while on placement in the Church of South India. I attended an end-of-term celebration at a local Christian college, whose remit was to take failing young people and give them a second chance by building confidence and unlocking their gifts. During the ceremony, each student took the microphone and with appropriate pride told everyone all they had achieved during the year including any qualifications they had gained. After each contribution everyone in the hall stood up, cheered, clapped and shouted, joining in the joy of success. Everyone was the best. Everyone was celebrated equally. The memory is etched on my heart.

Whoever we are, if we can say that 'Jesus is Lord' then we have the Spirit dwelling within us, and we are blessed with gifts to enable the body of Christ to flourish. The Christian community is a living, breathing force for transformation, made in God's image, incorporated into Christ and animated by the Holy Spirit. Each of us has something special to bring and each contribution is to be equally honoured, celebrated and developed to bless and transform the world.

> Risen, ascended Lord,
> as we rejoice at your triumph,
> fill your Church on earth with power and compassion,
> that all who are estranged by sin
> may find forgiveness and know your peace,
> to the glory of God the Father.

COLLECT

Reflection by **Catherine Williams** | 167

Wednesday 4 June

Psalms 2, **29** or 110, **111**, 112
1 Kings 19.1-18
Matthew 3.13-end

Matthew 3.13-end

'... he came up from the water' (v.16)

Our word 'baptism' comes from the Greek term meaning to immerse or submerge, to be overwhelmed or waterlogged. Traditionally, converts to Judaism underwent baptism in special ceremonial baths. John breaks with convention by baptizing his fellow Jews in the flowing waters of the Jordan. Flocking to John, they express an overwhelming need to repent and receive forgiveness. Jesus comes too. John in turn is overwhelmed by the humility of Jesus, asking for baptism. Why does the sinless Lamb of God need to repent? Jesus is showing solidarity with his people, preparing himself for ministry, opening himself to the overwhelming love of his Father, and receiving the Spirit's equipping for all that lies ahead as he steps into the identity of Israel's suffering servant.

The river's flowing water echoes Ezekiel's vision (47.1-12) in which he sees the water of life spreading from the Temple sanctuary out into the world. The water flows into the Arabah region bringing new life and fruitfulness to the lowest place on earth, the Dead Sea, where nothing can survive. Ezekiel paddling in the waters is quickly drenched and overwhelmed. Jesus, surfacing from his overwhelming baptismal waters, hears his Father's affirmation and receives the Spirit. His place within the Godhead is revealed.

What new life and fruitfulness has come with your baptism? How is it to be God's beloved child, overwhelmed by divine love and affirmation? How does it feel to be waterlogged with Jesus?

COLLECT

O God the King of glory,
you have exalted your only Son Jesus Christ
with great triumph to your kingdom in heaven:
we beseech you, leave us not comfortless,
but send your Holy Spirit to strengthen us
and exalt us to the place where our Saviour Christ is gone before,
who is alive and reigns with you,
in the unity of the Holy Spirit,
one God, now and for ever.

| *Reflection by* **Catherine Williams**

Psalms **24**, 72 *or* 113, **115**   **Thursday 5 June**
Ezekiel 11.14-20
Matthew 9.35 – 10.20

Matthew 9.35 – 10.20

'… no bag for your journey' (10.10)

If you've flown on a budget airline recently, you'll know that the 'free' baggage allowance has significantly shrunk. It takes considerable skill to fit a week's holiday packing into a small holdall that fits under your seat. We are left pondering what to leave behind, and what we can buy, borrow or go without when we get to our destination.

For the twelve, commissioned by Jesus, the baggage allowance is non-existent. They are to go with just the clothes on their backs and to trust that everything they need will be provided in response to the good news of the kingdom they bear. This news and the authority to heal, cleanse, exorcize and offer peace are weighty enough – no need for the extra burden of bags, money or a change of clothes. Where God's message is received, they will be welcomed and shown hospitality. Where it is not, they should move on swiftly and not look back.

How lean and keen is the Church to enter the areas where people are hungry to hear that God loves them beyond measure? The Good News of the Kingdom is sufficient for life in all its fullness. Why then are we clinging on to so much that holds us back and why do we constantly bemoan the lack of resources? Jesus warns that the task of bringing in the Kingdom may be demanding but with the Spirit on board we have all we require.

Risen, ascended Lord,
as we rejoice at your triumph,
fill your Church on earth with power and compassion,
that all who are estranged by sin
may find forgiveness and know your peace,
to the glory of God the Father.

COLLECT

Reflection by **Catherine Williams**

Friday 6 June

Psalms **28**, 30 *or* **139**
Ezekiel 36.22-28
Matthew 12.22-32

Matthew 12.22-32

'... the kingdom of God has come to you' (v.28)

Once, I almost saw a tiger in the depths of the jungle, only I was looking in the wrong direction. Those facing forward in the jeep caught the striped flash of the tiger in the undergrowth. I turned my head, but she was gone. So annoyed and disappointed were those of us who missed the sighting, some began to question whether it had happened. They suggested that the tiger sighting was a made-up story to goad us. How easily we hit out at others when we feel left out or things don't go the way we want.

The Pharisees see Jesus heal a disabled man but are wrong-footed by the miracle. Jesus has power where they have none. Perhaps they don't want to believe that God is working through Jesus, the itinerant preacher, rather than through them and so they denounce the healing as a work of the deceiver: Satan. Rather than celebrating the extraordinary way that the kingdom of God is among them, the religious authorities take steps to discredit the goodness they see. Jesus cleverly wraps them up in their own arguments but warns them not to misinterpret or dismiss God's creative and ground-breaking Spirit. It's unforgivable to deny or condemn the Spirit's work, suggests Jesus.

This passage makes us uncomfortable and with good reason. How often do we ignore or discredit God's Spirit working among us, because her presence doesn't fit neatly with our limited perceptions of God?

COLLECT

O God the King of glory,
you have exalted your only Son Jesus Christ
with great triumph to your kingdom in heaven:
we beseech you, leave us not comfortless,
but send your Holy Spirit to strengthen us
and exalt us to the place where our Saviour Christ is gone before,
who is alive and reigns with you,
in the unity of the Holy Spirit,
one God, now and for ever.

| *Reflection by* **Catherine Williams**

Psalms 42, **43** *or* 120, **121**, 122
Micah 3.1-8
Ephesians 6.10-20

Ephesians 6.10-20

'... and having done everything ... stand firm' (v.13)

I've recently moved from a small town to a rural estate setting. Unexpectedly, the move has necessitated a change of wardrobe. I now require warm hard-wearing clothing for outdoor countryside events together with very smart outfits for social occasions with the local landowner. My younger self would have baulked at such conventions. My wiser and more mature self has learned the importance of respecting local culture and customs when offering ministry in traditional settings. Wearing appropriate clothing helps enormously!

Paul, under house arrest, writes to the persecuted Ephesian Christians encouraging them to take hold of God's strength in their endeavours. Baptized into Christ they have put on Jesus like a new set of clothes. Paul describes this clothing as a battle kit, which protects them from the enemy. We may have a variety of reactions to this imagery of the whole armour of God. However, as members of Christ's body, it's good to be reminded of the Christian virtues with which we were clothed at our baptism. They come from within and, unlike a christening gown, are permanent. Truth holds us together. Righteousness covers our heart. We walk with peace. Our mind knows we are saved. We carry our faith before us and our words inspired by the Spirit cut through to where they are most needed. All of this comes from the living God whose strength empowers us to stand firm, pray constantly and be attentive to all around.

Risen, ascended Lord,
as we rejoice at your triumph,
fill your Church on earth with power and compassion,
that all who are estranged by sin
may find forgiveness and know your peace,
to the glory of God the Father.

COLLECT

Monday 9 June

Psalms 123, 124, 125, **126**
Job 1
Romans 1.1-17

Job 1

'... blessed be the name of the Lord' (v.21)

Set in Uz, beyond Israel, and involving no characters identifiable as Israelite, the Book of Job has a universal and timeless quality. It explores the theme of human response to suffering in the presence of God and resonates with people of any background.

This opening feels like a folk tale, describing a man of extraordinary goodness, living in extraordinary prosperity, upon whom calamities of extraordinary intensity suddenly fall. Many of us will have experienced sudden and traumatic loss or will know people who have. Job's story seizes our attention, evokes our sympathy and perhaps triggers our deepest fears.

The breathless, repetitive way in which disasters are announced, one upon another, has an unreal, even comic, character to it. We can visualize the storyteller holding his captive audience in half incredulous suspense. With Job's response at the end of the chapter, though, the tone changes dramatically. We hear one simple, solemn note as Job turns in humility to the Lord. This sets the tone of the whole book: for better or worse, in wisdom or confusion, Job's focus will always be on God.

Telling the story of his own Christian faith, St John Henry Newman began with his mind resting on 'the thought of two and two only absolute and luminously self-evident beings – myself and my Creator'. We could say the same of Job, as through his book we learn of our own, never-ending relationship with the God who made us.

COLLECT

O Lord, from whom all good things come:
grant to us your humble servants,
that by your holy inspiration
we may think those things that are good,
and by your merciful guiding may perform the same;
through our Lord Jesus Christ.

| *Reflection by* **Michael Ipgrave**

Tuesday 10 June

Job 2

'All that people have they will give to save their lives' (v.4)

Questions of motivation are important in the book of Job. Job questions God's motivations throughout, but rabbinic readers also highlighted the question of Job's motivation. Why does he live a life of such righteousness? 'Does Job fear God for nothing?' asks Satan (1.9). Now Satan pushes home the point as he receives permission to afflict Job in his very being, saving only his life.

Does Job live a good and pious life out of love for God or fear? Born of his observations of human nature, Satan predicts that the basis for Job's uprightness will be revealed as self-preserving fear rather than other-serving love.

As to whether Job passes or fails this test, the rabbinic readers were divided. He was compared to Abraham, the supreme exemplar of service of God springing from love rather than fear. For many, the comparison was to Abraham's advantage, with at best grudging acknowledgment that Job's motivations were not entirely selfish.

In any time of great testing, questions of motivation can suddenly become evident in a painful experience of self-revelation. Whatever the verdict on ourselves, as Christians we look to one who was the perfect man, in whom perfect love cast out fear.

O Lord, from whom all good things come:
grant to us your humble servants,
that by your holy inspiration
we may think those things that are good,
and by your merciful guiding may perform the same;
through our Lord Jesus Christ.

COLLECT

Reflection by **Michael Ipgrave** | 173

Wednesday 11 June

Barnabas the Apostle

Psalms 100, 101, 117
Jeremiah 9.23-24
Acts 4.32-end

Jeremiah 9.23-24

'... let those who boast boast in this' (v.24)

Nicknames sometimes succinctly express who somebody is. That is true of Barnabas, 'son of encouragement' – one of the most attractive personalities in the New Testament. In Acts, he is often associated with Paul, but there is also mention of a serious disagreement that caused them to part ways. We do not know the details, but Paul probably was not the easiest work colleague or travelling companion. Unlike Paul, who seemed to be unable not to talk about himself, there is no record of Barnabas boasting.

Such reticence or modesty is not because Barnabas lacked admirable qualities. The three categories of wisdom, strength and wealth, which Jeremiah mentions as grounds for self-promotion, were all present in Barnabas. He must have been wise to be trusted by the apostles as emissary to the first Christians in Antioch. He was physically imposing: at Lystra, where he and Paul were taken for the gods in human form, it was Barnabas who was likened to the mighty figure of Zeus. And he was wealthy: he freely gave a field to lay at the apostles' feet for the good of the early community. But wherever we read of Barnabas, we read of one whose only source of pride was in his service of the Lord.

I can call to mind several Barnabas figures I have known – people who have enriched the lives of others with their generosity, their kindness, their wisdom, the sheer attractiveness of their personality. I thank God for each of them, as I know what an encouragement they are to us all.

COLLECT

Bountiful God, giver of all gifts,
who poured your Spirit upon your servant Barnabas
and gave him grace to encourage others:
help us, by his example,
to be generous in our judgements
and unselfish in our service;
through Jesus Christ our Lord.

| *Reflection by* **Michael Ipgrave**

Psalms **143**, 146
Job 4
Romans 2.17-end

Job 4

'... now it has come to you' (v.5)

This speech of Eliphaz is unlikely to help Job. When we encounter enormous personal grief or loss, it is often our experience that the words of others are of little help, and may in some cases renew the pain we feel. This is true of Eliphaz's presentation, which largely reiterates conventional wisdom about the security of the innocent under God's protection – a wisdom that Job knows to be disproved by his own experience. There is a particular brutality (whether intentional or not) in the reference to evil doers perishing 'by the breath of God', given that all Job's own children have been killed by a great wind (the words 'breath' and 'wind' are the same in Hebrew).

Despite the insensitivity of his language, Eliphaz is astute in pointing out to Job that it is easy to give counsel to others in their sufferings, and hard to experience the like sufferings oneself: 'Now it has come to you!' For those in caring professions, personal loss and pain can hit particularly hard for just this reason.

Eliphaz's good intentions, though, should not be discounted. Before he says anything, he and his companions have already sat on the ground with Job for seven days, during which 'no one spoke a word for they saw that his suffering was very great'. That silent presence alongside the suffering was Eliphaz's most helpful contribution; the same is usually true for us too.

COLLECT

O Lord, from whom all good things come:
grant to us your humble servants,
that by your holy inspiration
we may think those things that are good,
and by your merciful guiding may perform the same;
through our Lord Jesus Christ.

Reflection by **Michael Ipgrave**

Friday 13 June

Psalms 142, **144**
Job 5
Romans 3.1-20

Job 5

'To which of the holy ones will you turn?' (v.1)

In his dire situation of loss and grief, Job must feel that the very fabric of the cosmos is turned against him. It's natural, then, that he should look for support from supernatural sources; it is presumably to these that the phrase 'the holy ones' refers. Jewish commentators interpret these as the angels or 'sons of God' gathered before the Lord at the outset of Job's story, and explain that Eliphaz is emphasizing to Job the pointlessness of enlisting their aid, since it was in their presence that God commissioned Satan to inflict his sufferings.

Rather than turn to any intermediary, Eliphaz counsels Job to bring his case directly to God. He follows this with a psalm-like hymn to the divine power over both the natural world and human affairs. In Job's circumstances, Eliphaz's pious words might have felt rather unconvincing, his assurances of divine protection belied by the raw facts of Job's suffering.

Nevertheless, Job would indeed take his cry direct to God. In so doing, he will be brought to a vision of God's reality far more expansive, strange and terrifying, yet ultimately far more redemptive than the formulae Eliphaz has on offer. When we experience anguish for ourselves, we too may find that our vision of God's reality is broken and remade. When we are alongside those going through such a process of breaking and remaking, we must humbly recognize that we are on holy ground.

COLLECT

O Lord, from whom all good things come:
grant to us your humble servants,
that by your holy inspiration
we may think those things that are good,
and by your merciful guiding may perform the same;
through our Lord Jesus Christ.

| *Reflection by* **Michael Ipgrave**

Psalm **147**
Job 6
Romans 3.21-end

Saturday 14 June

Job 6

'... my words have been rash' (v.3)

When he engages in dialogues with his interlocutors, Job acknowledges that he has spoken 'rashly' – the same word used by Obadiah to describe the slurred and reckless speech of a drunkard. This obstreperous Job is in sharp contrast to the self-contained figure of the first two chapters, who receives news of successive calamities in dignified silence. It is as the former – an exemplar of patient trust – that Job is remembered in the New Testament (James 5).

Job was generally criticized by Jewish commentators for his rash speech; the rabbis historically sided with his companions' positions in the dialogues that form the heart of this book. Today, though, our sympathies are mostly with Job. We can not only excuse, but may positively approve, his at times savage outspokenness in tackling head on the pious conventionalities of his 'comforters'.

For those experiencing intense loss and pain, an expectation that they should speak with propriety and restraint can feel burdensome; part of Job's contemporary appeal lies in his frankness, honesty and unbounded self-expression. But we must also remember that no set of calamitous experiences has a single victim, but affects several people. Job's wife suffered as much as he did, and she surely would have been further hurt by some of the things Job said and the way he said them. There is a solidarity in suffering, but it requires gentle consideration and care for one another among those sharing in adversity.

O Lord, from whom all good things come:
grant to us your humble servants,
that by your holy inspiration
we may think those things that are good,
and by your merciful guiding may perform the same;
through our Lord Jesus Christ.

COLLECT

Reflection by **Michael Ipgrave** | 177

Monday 16 June

Psalms 1, 2, 3
Job 7
Romans 4.1-12

Job 7

'... you watcher of humanity' (v.20)

'What are humans?', Job asks. His language echoes Psalm 8, but it becomes clear that Job sees God very differently from the Psalmist. For the latter, God's constant 'mindfulness' of humans is a sign of the honour in which he holds them: 'a little lower than the angels'. In a bitter parody of this vision, Job, himself the plaything of one of God's angels, experiences divine surveillance as oppressive, wearing, nightmarish.

The theme of God's observation of humans appears elsewhere in the Hebrew Scripture, most famously Psalm 139, where the writer confesses that there is nowhere he can escape God's presence. There, though, God's all-knowing oversight is experienced as a beneficent and healing acceptance. Job, in the desolation of his spirit, is in a different place: God is for him at best an exacting tyrant, at worst a malevolent foe.

This attitude demonstrates the extreme pressure that Job is feeling. We cannot blame him for that; we may well feel similarly at times of crisis and loss. What is remarkable and admirable about Job is that, in all this, he holds on to God as the primary reality of his life. Even though he cannot trust him, he does not doubt that his life is fundamentally oriented towards God.

Jesus will also speak of the constant oversight of God for all, reaching even to the smallest sparrow, and will assure his people that the divine gaze is always for their good and their protection.

COLLECT

Almighty and everlasting God,
you have given us your servants grace,
by the confession of a true faith,
to acknowledge the glory of the eternal Trinity
and in the power of the divine majesty to worship the Unity:
keep us steadfast in this faith,
that we may evermore be defended from all adversities;
through Jesus Christ our Lord.

| *Reflection by* **Michael Ipgrave**

Tuesday 17 June

Job 8

'... he delivered them into the power of their transgression' (v.4)

More than his companions, Bildad the Shuhite relies on *a priori* reasoning in his arguments. Beginning from the principle that God could not subvert the general laws of retributive justice, he concludes that Job's experience must be the result of some act of lawbreaking. He does not directly accuse Job of sin, but makes an even more offensive claim: that the destruction of Job's children must be the consequence of their evil deeds.

This is both unwarranted and unkind. There is no evidence of wrongdoing on the part of Job's offspring; to the contrary, Job 1 assigns their death to an unpredictable cause: a great wind from the desert. In his zeal to defend God from any suggestion of injustice, Bildad goes far beyond the evidence.

He also, perhaps unintentionally, displays callous and brutal cruelty in his words to Job. There are few more painful experiences than to lose a child – unless it be to lose ten, as Job did. Job's tender remembrance of his lost children would be lacerated by Bildad's casual remark that their fate was of their own deserving. Bildad has crossed the line at which intended comfort becomes experienced cruelty, and religious zeal turns into censorious torment.

It's easy for us to discern this catastrophic misstep as we read the text. But there is a bit of a Shuhite in each of us. Whenever we seek to defend God's cause in a suffering world, sometimes we need the painful witness of Job to hold back our zealous assurance.

Holy God,
faithful and unchanging:
enlarge our minds with the knowledge of your truth,
and draw us more deeply into the mystery of your love,
that we may truly worship you,
Father, Son and Holy Spirit,
one God, now and for ever.

COLLECT

Wednesday 18 June

Psalm 119.1-32
Job 9
Romans 5.1-11

Job 9

'... he passes me by' (v.11)

In this response to Bildad the Shuhite, Job spends little time addressing him. Rather, he speaks of God. On one hand, he imagines putting his case before him. On the other, he knows God would spare no time for him to do this.

So he says, forlornly: 'He passes me by and I do not see him.' The Lord 'passing by' is the experience of Abraham in covenant-making as a flaming torch passes through the sacrificial birds, Moses on Sinai, granted a vision of the Lord's 'back', and Elijah hearing the still small voice on Horeb. In all these encounters, the same verb is used as here in Job 9. But unlike Abraham, Moses or Elijah, Job is granted no sign of divine communication, let alone favour.

Although a man of piety, Job is not one of God's people; maybe it is not surprising he receives no such affirmation. But, precisely because he is not one of the chosen, his longing for a direct encounter with God, which is not granted, can speak powerfully to us, especially when we experience both intense longing for God and utter brokenness by God. For Christians, this foreshadows the agony in Gethsemane. Our faith is that in the face of the crucified and risen Christ we will see and will be seen by a merciful God.

COLLECT

Almighty and everlasting God,
you have given us your servants grace,
by the confession of a true faith,
to acknowledge the glory of the eternal Trinity
and in the power of the divine majesty to worship the Unity:
keep us steadfast in this faith,
that we may evermore be defended from all adversities;
through Jesus Christ our Lord.

| *Reflection by* **Michael Ipgrave**

Psalm 147
Deuteronomy 8.2-16
1 Corinthians 10.1-17

Thursday 19 June

Day of Thanksgiving for the
Institution of Holy Communion
(Corpus Christi)

Deuteronomy 8.2-16

'[He] fed you with manna in the wilderness' (v.16)

One rule of human nature is that we often don't value anything deeply until it has been removed from us. Another, related, rule is that becoming accustomed to something of value gradually makes us take it for granted and fail to appreciate its worth. Both phenomena lie behind this passage. The text depicts Moses encouraging the people to look forward to their settled abundant life in the promised land, and from there to remember the wilderness years, and God's provision of the life-giving manna from heaven.

Five years ago, our churches were deprived of the bread of life to which the manna points forward. During the most intense phase of the COVID pandemic, it wasn't possible for us to receive the bread of the Eucharist alongside one another. There was a fresh realization among many, myself included, of how deeply we valued the sacraments, particularly when being deprived of them. Being accustomed to the regular availability of this great gift of grace had made us take it for granted.

Now we are settled again into the routine of church life, this Feast of Corpus Christi invites us to return spiritually to that wilderness experience; remembering that kindles our gratitude for the food with which God sustains us on our pilgrimage.

Lord Jesus Christ,
we thank you that in this wonderful sacrament
you have given us the memorial of your passion:
grant us so to reverence the sacred mysteries
of your body and blood
that we may know within ourselves
and show forth in our lives
the fruits of your redemption;
for you are alive and reign with the Father
in the unity of the Holy Spirit,
one God, now and for ever.

COLLECT

Reflection by **Michael Ipgrave**   181

Friday 20 June

Job 11

'Know then ...' (v.6)

With the intervention of Zophar the Naamathite, the exchanges between Job and his companions become markedly personal and acerbic. Zophar brusquely criticizes Job's speech for wordiness and goes on to misrepresent him.

Most extraordinary, though, is Zophar's self-confident assurance. He doesn't, like Bildad, appeal to the wisdom of past generations or, like Eliphaz, to a nocturnal vision, but simply presumes to speak in God's name and with insight into God's wisdom. So in verse 6 he brazenly uses the imperative form 'Know!' to inform Job of God's thinking.

I have encountered people like Zophar. Much worse, I know there have been times when I have spoken in the same mode. Faced with somebody's depth of suffering, pain and confusion, it is fatally easy to feel that we must give clear, direct and, if necessary, challenging guidance; and, like Zophar, in looking for the sources of such direction, we turn first to our own instincts and ways of thinking.

For those charged with pastoral care of others, the temptation can be strong to think that, as professional ministers, with thoughts shaped by prayer and wisdom, our perspective will be exactly what others need to hear. But every time I have told somebody else what they need to do in their own suffering I have learned that, like Zophar, I am trying to take the place of God; and, like Zophar, I have been rebuked and told to listen to Job, who speaks truthfully.

COLLECT

Almighty and everlasting God,
you have given us your servants grace,
by the confession of a true faith,
to acknowledge the glory of the eternal Trinity
and in the power of the divine majesty to worship the Unity:
keep us steadfast in this faith,
that we may evermore be defended from all adversities;
through Jesus Christ our Lord.

| *Reflection by* **Michael Ipgrave**

Saturday 21 June

Job 12

'… in a pathless waste' (v.24)

Extreme suffering often focuses sufferers on themselves alone. That is what we have seen from Job thus far, but now he extends his vision to the wider creation and to human society. In both he sees God at work in a way that can only be called destructive.

This is a terrifying account of divine action: God is tearing down, overwhelming, stripping naked, ridiculing, leading astray. In chapter 7, Job parodies Psalm 8; now he bitterly echoes and inverts Psalm 107. Reproducing the Psalmist's experiences of disorientation, but replacing God's restorative interventions with still more violence, Job's vision leads to darkness: the 'pathless waste' recalling the primaeval chaos of Genesis that had to be overcome in God's ordering of creation.

People undergoing traumatic disorientation may, like Job, have a dark and hopeless vision both of their own situation and of the wider world. It can be distressing, sitting alongside somebody suffering in this way, to realize how frightening and hopeless they feel things to be for others as well as themselves. Sometimes this may be delusional, with no relation to reality. But it may also be that the sufferer has a deeper insight into the world's dysfunction, or a stronger empathy with those crushed by it. We cannot simply dismiss Job's disturbing claims about how our world is. Rather, we follow one who knew and confronted the forces of chaos with honesty and clarity – whose last word to the darkness was 'Father!' (Luke 23.46).

Holy God,
faithful and unchanging:
enlarge our minds with the knowledge of your truth,
and draw us more deeply into the mystery of your love,
that we may truly worship you,
Father, Son and Holy Spirit,
one God, now and for ever.

COLLECT

Reflection by **Michael Ipgrave**   183

Monday 23 June

Job 13

'But I would speak to the Almighty' (v.3)

Job, a man bereft, in pain and poverty, endures the 'insights' of his friends Eliphaz, Bildad and Zophar. They effectively tell Job, 'It's all your fault', demonstrating that they had missed out on Pastoral Care 101. It was far better when these three 'worthless physicians' just sat with him in silence (2.13). Their torrents of words threaten to drown Job. He swims up from the flood of their watery arguments, determined. He asserts 'I would speak to the Almighty.'

Job's wisdom is his life raft. 'I desire to argue my case with God.' He turns from his friends to address God directly. His demands are bold and trusting, and show his clear sense of the power and awe of God. He asks that God withdraw his hand far from him, and not let 'dread of you terrify me'. He is asking God to enable their conversation. He wants to talk with God. He tells God the truth he has experienced, without pulling punches. 'What are my sins? What is my wrong? Am I your enemy? Where are you, God?'

Faced with the depth of his sufferings, another person might sink into themselves, but Job cries out to God, he bellows at God, he accuses God. Here is man who roars out his truth 'to the Almighty'. Job is a man of deep faith and refreshing honesty.

COLLECT

O God,
the strength of all those who put their trust in you,
mercifully accept our prayers
and, because through the weakness of our mortal nature
we can do no good thing without you,
grant us the help of your grace,
that in the keeping of your commandments
we may please you both in will and deed;
through Jesus Christ our Lord.

| *Reflection by* **Kate Bruce**

Psalms 50, 149
Ecclesiasticus 48.1-10
or Malachi 3.1-6
Luke 3.1-17

Tuesday 24 June

Birth of John the Baptist

Malachi 3.1-6

'For he is like a refiner's fire and like fullers' soap' (v.2)

The birth of John the Baptist is celebrated six months before we remember the birth of Christ, noting that scripture tells us that John was conceived six months prior to his cousin (Luke 1.36).

A famous altarpiece by the artist Matthias Grünewald at Isenheim in Germany depicts John the Baptist with a disproportionately long index finger, pointing to the crucified Christ. This is John's calling. He prepares the way for and points to Jesus who will baptize with the Holy Spirit and with fire (Luke 3.16).

This reading from Malachi picks up the idea of a messenger who prepares the way, pointing to one who comes with refining purpose and power. This power is compared to fire used in smelting and fullers' soap used to cleanse and whiten dirty sheepskins. The refiner comes to remove the impurities of the human heart.

It's worth holding onto the image of the Lord of hosts who comes with refining judgement as we engage with Job's longing for justice. Malachi points us to the God who bears witness against economic oppressors, the God who sees the widow, the orphan and the alien (v.5). In our readings from Job, we will hear him crying out against numerous injustices on behalf of the poor, children, the enslaved and those in physical distress. Job's longing for justice finds response in Malachi's vision, John's preparation, and Christ's life, death, resurrection and ascension.

COLLECT

Almighty God,
by whose providence your servant John the Baptist
was wonderfully born,
and sent to prepare the way of your Son our Saviour
by the preaching of repentance:
lead us to repent according to his preaching
and, after his example,
constantly to speak the truth, boldly to rebuke vice,
and patiently to suffer for the truth's sake;
through Jesus Christ our Lord.

Reflection by **Kate Bruce**   185

Wednesday 25 June

Psalm **34**
Job 15
Romans 8.1-11

Job 15

'Why does your heart carry you away, and why do your eyes flash?'
(v.12)

Eliphaz the Temanite lacks empathy and imagination. Job has lost his children, seven sons and three daughters, all crushed in a collapsed building; he has endured loathsome sores; he is ruined financially. The life he knew has been wiped off the map (1.13-19). To cap it all his insensitive pal asks why his heart has carried him away and his eyes flash. My eyes would be flashing if I had to listen to Eliphaz's drivel. He accuses Job of turning his spirit against God. Job has done no such thing! He turns to God. He expresses the confusion and pain coming from his broken heart.

Eliphaz's words are dangerous; they sound like wise phrases, but they are cruel and devoid of love. This man is as sympathetic as a house brick. He piles up accusations against Job, saying his talk is unprofitable, his words do no good, his tongue is crafty, and his mouth condemns him. Basically, Eliphaz says, 'Job, just who do you think you are?' Job does not need a theological lecture. He does not need to be condemned for his honesty, or anguish.

Job is a grieving man. If Eliphaz fears Job's questioning means his spirit has turned away from God then Eliphaz does not know Job. What Job needs is love. What he gets is a tedious lecture. What he needs is supportive silence, compassionate presence, and practical care. Worth noting.

COLLECT

O God,
the strength of all those who put their trust in you,
mercifully accept our prayers
and, because through the weakness of our mortal nature
we can do no good thing without you,
grant us the help of your grace,
that in the keeping of your commandments
we may please you both in will and deed;
through Jesus Christ our Lord.

| *Reflection by* **Kate Bruce**

Psalm **37***
Job 16.1 – 17.2
Romans 8.12-17

Thursday 26 June

Job 16.1 – 17.2

'Have windy words no limit?' (16.3)

Poor Job. His 'comforters' send a hurricane of words his way. Job's response is far from windy; he speaks with weight. From his 'deep darkness' he paints a picture of how the God to whom he pours out his tears has become his assailant. It is important we don't mute his words or erase his imagery; they convey the depths of his anguish, and we must attend.

He paints a terrifying image of God as a glowering creature who gnashes his teeth and tears into him, a giant who has snapped him in two and dashed him to pieces, slashing open his innards. His sense of God is confused by his terrible anguish. On one side there is the monster-god and on the other there is the God who 'vouches for' him 'in heaven' and to whom he can pour out his tears.

The unhelpful lectures of his so-called friends open up a doorway through which the undermining spirit can pass, distorting Job's sense of God. These 'miserable comforters', 'scorn him', undermine him, and offer no comfort. The undermining spirit pulls the rug from under Job's feet with the whisper that God hates him and is utterly opposed to him. Yet such is Job's faith that he is able to hold onto a different image of God, the God who sees and receives his 'pure prayer', his witness and advocate.

God of truth,
help us to keep your law of love
and to walk in ways of wisdom,
that we may find true life
in Jesus Christ your Son.

COLLECT

Reflection by **Kate Bruce** | 187

Friday 27 June

Job 17.3-end

'I am like one before whom people spit' (v.6)

Job has become a byword among his people; he is viewed as accursed. People spit before him as a way of warding off evil. 'Stay away from Job; he might be infectious.' Here is a solitary man shunned by his community.

Put yourself in Job's shoes – add to his blinding grief and all-encompassing pain a deep and suffocating loneliness. His profound isolation has existential dimensions. It seems God has locked him out. His friends don't understand him. They seek to reform him with their endless lectures. He is struggling to find hope. Internally he debates with himself in the repeated 'ifs'. If I dwell in death and lie in darkness, if I make darkness and decay my close 'family', if I allow the swirling terror to claim me – where is my hope and who will see it? It's remarkable that he can even dare to speak of hope as he ponders the 'ifs'. Is there a suicidal struggle here? 'If I fold myself into death – where will any hope be?'

If you could step into the narrative and do anything for Job – what would you do? I can't help but think of the actions of the angel with a desolate and suicidal Elijah (1 Kings 19). Elijah is given reassuring physical contact, food, water, and sleep. Not theological lectures, but love earthed in kindness. Who will do that for Job?

COLLECT

O God,
the strength of all those who put their trust in you,
mercifully accept our prayers
and, because through the weakness of our mortal nature
we can do no good thing without you,
grant us the help of your grace,
that in the keeping of your commandments
we may please you both in will and deed;
through Jesus Christ our Lord.

Saturday 28 June

Job 18

'Surely the light of the wicked is put out' (v.5)

Bildad the Shuhite has another go at lecturing Job, in a horrific speech full of passive aggressive fundamentalism. Every time you read 'their', know that Bildad means 'you, Job'. 'You, Job are wicked, which is why light has gone from your life; your strong steps are shortened because you are a bad person; you have tripped into this calamity; you experience this suffering because you don't know God.'

Bildad's simplistic theological arithmetic looks at Job's pain and calculates that Job must be wicked because bad things happen to him. By logical extension, people who experience good things must be faithful. The writer of Psalm 73 wrestled with this, seeing that the wicked do apparently prosper while the good suffer. The cross tells us that the God in flesh suffered horribly. Bildad's maths just don't add up.

That Job speaks to God, even accuses God, from the darkness of his experience is a sign of a much deeper spiritual understanding than Bildad's superficial calculus. Job does know God.

What does Bildad get from his words? He is not touched by Job's crying out for God. He is not open to sharing Job's experience. He is closed to the helplessness of not knowing the answer. What Bildad gets is a sense of smug, superficial, spiritual security. What Job gets is further condemnation, further kicking, and further separation. If Bildad had just sat and wept with Job – then Job might have discerned the divine presence earthed in human flesh beside him.

God of truth,
help us to keep your law of love
and to walk in ways of wisdom,
that we may find true life
in Jesus Christ your Son.

COLLECT

Reflection by **Kate Bruce**

Monday 30 June

Job 19

'For I know that my Redeemer lives' (v.25)

Job boldly states to Bildad that his suffering lies with God. He does not connect God's actions to punishment for his wickedness. He simply sets out what he has experienced of God who 'has put me in the wrong', 'closed his net around me', 'walled up my way' and 'set darkness upon my paths'. Job doesn't try to justify God, but recounts his calamities – the estrangement of his family, his being shunned by the community, and his physical suffering. He simply says it like it is.

Suddenly, remarkably, he takes a different tack. In spite of everything he gives us one of scripture's most compelling and beautiful promises: 'For I know that my redeemer lives, and that at the last he will stand upon the earth, and after my skin has been destroyed, then in my flesh I shall see God.'

Job's name has become synonymous with suffering, but he should be known as a man of profound and awesome faith. He puts at God's feet responsibility for all his calamity. He sits at God's feet awaiting redemption. He does not allow the suffering he has experienced to drive him from God – rather he draws near to God. He continues to exemplify the words he expressed at the start of his suffering, 'The Lord gave, and the Lord has taken away; blessed be the name of the Lord' (1.21). Job's name should be a byword for faith.

COLLECT

Lord, you have taught us
that all our doings without love are nothing worth:
send your Holy Spirit
and pour into our hearts that most excellent gift of love,
the true bond of peace and of all virtues,
without which whoever lives is counted dead before you.
Grant this for your only Son Jesus Christ's sake.

| *Reflection by* **Kate Bruce**

Psalms **48**, 52
Job 21
Romans 9.19-end

Job 21

'... then, after I have spoken, mock on' (v.3)

Job has had enough of the words of his 'comforters'; his complaint is addressed to God, not to them. He wrestles on with the question of why the wicked, far from being thrust into darkness, seem to flourish – growing strong in power, enjoying long years, being materially blessed, and ending with a peaceful death. Job notes that some die in prosperity having known ease and security, and others in bitterness, after a life of suffering.

His comforters offer only 'empty nothings' to him. Job's wrestling with deep questions of suffering and justice are not theoretical. He rebuts their belief that the sins of the adults will be visited on the next generation. He destroys their trite arguments and in return he expects only 'mockery' from them.

Will we mock him? His argument needs to be heard. It is a cry for justice: 'Who declares their way to their face, and who repays them for what they have done?' Job asks us to attend to the cries of those who have known only disease and insecurity. How can we inhabit his call for justice? Especially those of us who are at ease, materialistically well off, living in relative peace? Will we silence Job, ignore or mock him, or listen with him? Are we with the wicked, or with Job? The only place to begin is with God.

Faithful Creator,
whose mercy never fails:
deepen our faithfulness to you
and to your living Word,
Jesus Christ our Lord.

COLLECT

Reflection by **Kate Bruce**   191

Wednesday 2 July

Psalm 119.57-80
Job 22
Romans 10.1-10

Job 22

'If you return to the Almighty, you will be restored' (v.23)

Religious words can be deeply dangerous. At first glance Eliphaz's speech sounds wise. But remember it is addressed to a righteous and good man going through harrowing suffering. Job has never departed from the Almighty – so the instruction to return to God is incredibly undermining.

Job is hemmed in with manipulative advice and false accusations. What does it mean for Eliphaz to tell Job to 'agree with God'? God has not yet expressed a viewpoint in the text. What Eliphaz means is 'agree with me'. He is attempting to silence Job, to stop Job's profound and uncomfortable questions. Religious words can be deeply dangerous.

Taken out of context we would agree with Eliphaz. Surely it is right to 'receive instruction from God', to make God your treasure, and to delight in him. Remember who is being addressed. Job has received instruction from God in the form of deep suffering and he has valued God so highly that he has turned his pain and questions towards God's face, and kept on hanging on.

Eliphaz's words are as smooth as butter, but with destructive intent. Religious words can be deeply dangerous. They can be used to undermine, insinuate and destabilize, while sounding righteous and holy. If our religious words fail to encourage, to draw people to the God who loves, restores and reforms, as God sees fit, then it would be better if our tongues were stopped.

C O L L E C T

Lord, you have taught us
that all our doings without love are nothing worth:
send your Holy Spirit
and pour into our hearts that most excellent gift of love,
the true bond of peace and of all virtues,
without which whoever lives is counted dead before you.
Grant this for your only Son Jesus Christ's sake.

| *Reflection by* **Kate Bruce**

Psalms 92, 146
2 Samuel 15.17-21
or Ecclesiasticus 2
John 11.1-16

Thursday 3 July
Thomas the Apostle

2 Samuel 15.17-21

'... whether for life or for death, there also will your servant be'
(v.21)

Loyalty is to be treasured. Thomas the Apostle is remembered as 'Doubting Thomas' who would not believe in Jesus' resurrection unless he saw it with his own eyes (John 20.24-25). He could also be known as Loyal Thomas. As Jesus journeys to Bethany to raise Lazarus from death, Thomas says to the others 'Let us also go, that we may die with him' (John 11.16). Bethany is just two miles away from Jerusalem, and Thomas is alive to the risk of Jesus' enemies in the region. Loyal Thomas is willing to walk into death with Jesus.

The reading set for today focuses on Ittai the Gittite – another loyal man. David is forced to flee Jerusalem as his son Absalom has risen up against him. Ittai, an outsider, is willing to go into exile with David, even though the king tells him to go back. Ittai responds, 'whether for life or for death, there also will your servant be'.

Ittai's words are reminiscent of Ruth's words to Naomi, 'Where you go, I will go; where you lodge, I will lodge; your people shall be my people, and your God my God. Where you die, I will die, and there I will be buried' (Ruth 1.16-17).

Loyalty binds relationships and holds community together. Would that Job's friends had displayed such loyalty. On this St Thomas Day we remember Loyal Thomas, and with him Loyal Ittai and Loyal Ruth.

Almighty and eternal God,
who, for the firmer foundation of our faith,
allowed your holy apostle Thomas
to doubt the resurrection of your Son
till word and sight convinced him:
grant to us, who have not seen, that we also may believe
and so confess Christ as our Lord and our God;
who is alive and reigns with you,
in the unity of the Holy Spirit,
one God, now and for ever.

COLLECT

Reflection by **Kate Bruce** | 193

Friday 4 July

Psalms **51**, **54**
Job 24
Romans 11.1-12

Job 24

'... his eyes are upon their ways' (v.23)

Job asks why those who know God don't see his judgement. His suffering gives him empathetic insight into the plight of those oppressed by economic injustice, the theft of a child into slavery, and physical distress. He has clear-sighted understanding of the wicked operating under the physical and spiritual cover of darkness. He knows that nothing is hidden from God, 'his eyes are upon their ways'. Where then is God's judgement? Eventually the wicked are swallowed up in death, forgotten by the womb and sweet meat for the worm, but this does not satisfy Job. What of those so rapaciously harmed – the childless woman, the widow and the orphan? Job, who knows powerlessness, stands with those without agency and wrestles with God's apparent lack of active judgement.

He leans into the difficult questions; a voice crying out for justice from the wilderness of suffering. Job's questions are uncomfortable, jarring us out of platitudes. They point forward to Christ who sides with the child, the poor and the marginalized; whose own mother promised that the lowly would be lifted and the hungry filled with good things (Luke 1.52-53). Yet we live in the 'not yet' of Mary's promises. The lowly are placed in detention centres, the hungry starve on the streets, the orphan flees frightened and alone. Like Job, we must cry out in words of prayer and protest, anger and action for the 'poor of the earth'.

COLLECT

Lord, you have taught us
that all our doings without love are nothing worth:
send your Holy Spirit
and pour into our hearts that most excellent gift of love,
the true bond of peace and of all virtues,
without which whoever lives is counted dead before you.
Grant this for your only Son Jesus Christ's sake.

Saturday 5 July

Job 25 – 26

'... how much less a mortal, who is a maggot' (25.6)

Bildad is off again, focusing on God in the heavens, with mighty armies, the source of all light. Then he turns to mortals, who he writes off as 'maggots' and 'worms'.

Job's response might be summarized as 'Thanks so much for helping the little guy.' He asks what spirit has given Bildad his words. It's clearly not one of compassion or empathy. Bildad starts in the wrong place. Answering Job's cries means sitting with Job, not standing a million miles above contradiction. What Job needs is the incarnate God who is alongside, the one he caught a glimpse of earlier (19.25).

Job begins in the smallness of his human experience – as one without power, strength, or wisdom. He starts with a 'maggot-eye' view and looks up. What he describes is 'but a whisper' of the full story of God. Job is a man of humility. What he is able to grasp is breathtaking, whisper or not. He looks to the God who sees into death, who creates from nothing – using words reminiscent of Genesis 1. He describes the God who subdued Rahab – the great sea monster of chaos.

This 'maggot' who has suffered so deeply looks up from his own chaos and perceives the majesty of God. Bildad and company assume the lofty position of their own assumed 'divinity' and look down on Job the worm.

It is Job God commends for having 'spoken right' (42.7).

Faithful Creator,
whose mercy never fails:
deepen our faithfulness to you
and to your living Word,
Jesus Christ our Lord.

COLLECT

Reflection by **Kate Bruce** | 195

Monday 7 July

Job 27

'... my heart does not reproach me for any of my days' (v.6)

It's a bold person who claims to have no secret sins. Who would dare to say they had been morally upright every day of their lives? Never had an unkind thought? A careless act? A tale told so as to come out of it looking good? Most of us would not want our every thought paraded before the world and definitely not brought to our attention by an angry God. On the other hand, we are indignant when wrongly accused and it's natural to strive to justify ourselves.

Job has maintained his righteousness throughout the disasters that have taken place and the accusations of his friends. No, says Job, as long as I have breath left, I will hold fast to my integrity. As for God being angry, Job believes that it is God who has afflicted him and made his soul bitter. Throughout earlier chapters, where his three friends insist that Job must have sinned for him to be suffering so much, he continues to maintain his righteousness. Going further, he boldly states that he will not accept that God is in the right. It is this that makes the book of Job so much more than a straightforward explanation of suffering. It is a thorough-going rebellion against the received view of how the world works.

Is it folly to challenge God in this way? The biblical book of Job gives us permission to express what we really think and feel.

COLLECT

Almighty God,
you have broken the tyranny of sin
and have sent the Spirit of your Son into our hearts
    whereby we call you Father:
give us grace to dedicate our freedom to your service,
that we and all creation may be brought
    to the glorious liberty of the children of God;
through Jesus Christ our Lord.

| *Reflection by* **Liz Hoare**

Tuesday 8 July

Job 28

*'Truly, the fear of the Lord, that is wisdom;
and to depart from evil is understanding' (v.28)*

Who does not want to be wise? Books, courses, podcasts and retreats are just some of the ways people seek out wisdom for living today. Job belongs to the genre of ancient Jewish writing known as wisdom literature. Chapter 28 reflects on the source of wisdom; it forms an interlude in Job's self-defence and poses the fundamental question: 'Where shall wisdom be found?'

It begins with a picture of miners searching the depths of the earth for precious metals. At great risk they delve deep into the dark recesses of the planet for treasure. They know where and how to look, seeing gold where others see only dust. But wisdom is not a commodity to be carved out of the world and held up as a trophy. Just as the miners 'search out to the farthest bound' in their quest for precious ore, so experience teaches that the search for wisdom will be a lifetime's task for those who desire it.

The conclusion of this interlude is that only God knows where wisdom lies. God's own pronouncement that the foundation stone of living wisely is fear of the Lord constitutes the heart of the book of Job. That there is more to add is part of the wrestling of Job with God, which suggests that it may be just the start of unpacking what wisdom is and is not. God, meanwhile, searches out Job, pushing him to the farthest bounds.

God our saviour,
look on this wounded world
in pity and in power;
hold us fast to your promises of peace
won for us by your Son,
our Saviour Jesus Christ.

COLLECT

Reflection by **Liz Hoare** | 197

Wednesday 9 July

Job 29

'... when the friendship of God was upon my tent' (v.4)

In his agony, Job longs for his lost existence, when he was rich, had a family and a relationship with God he saw as friendship. Job, however, does not seem to have esteemed friendship with God as the only, or even the main reason, for his standing in the world. It was also about respect from neighbours; young and old deferred to him, even rulers were impressed. Job's statement 'I put on righteousness and it clothed me' jars, for this righteousness is self-generated. Job has earned his place in the world himself, even though God blessed him.

How much does friendship with God shape our sense of identity in the world and what does it have to do with whether or not we prosper? What do we rely on most for our sense of well-being? Our bank balance? Our ranking in society? Our good reputation? And how much are these down to our own achievement? Perhaps we feel that God is too awesome and powerful to be thought of in such intimate terms as a friend? A true friend is someone who remains steadfast through good times and bad. We feel safe with our dearest friends, who like us for who we are, rather than our economic status or achievements. If we were to reflect on what it means to have a trusted human friend who brings joy to our lives, are there similarities with what we long for where intimacy with God is concerned?

COLLECT

Almighty God,
you have broken the tyranny of sin
and have sent the Spirit of your Son into our hearts
  whereby we call you Father:
give us grace to dedicate our freedom to your service,
that we and all creation may be brought
  to the glorious liberty of the children of God;
through Jesus Christ our Lord.

| *Reflection by* **Liz Hoare**

Thursday 10 July

Job 30

'... you toss me about in the roar of the storm' (v.22)

A Danish TV drama a few years ago, called *Ride upon the Storm*, seemed to allude to God's terrifying power and apparent capriciousness in the lives of a Lutheran pastor and his family. It portrayed vividly how human lives endure huge blows that knock them off their feet and how they cope, or otherwise.

Like a leaf in a whirlwind or a paper boat on the roaring ocean, Job is helpless in the face of God's power. He endures pain in his bones and his skin peels off. His mental anguish is as bad: mocked and humiliated, his mind fills with terrors and his soul pours out. He is the picture of utter dereliction, and it is all God's doing. We might be tempted to think that if only Job would adopt a good Christian attitude and trust God, he would get through this and be OK, but Job is having none of it. He is clear that God is responsible and the worst of it is that he has no redress. We might tone down our language, but behind the question 'Why?' may lurk a deep grievance that the God we are told is love has betrayed us. Job waited for light, but only darkness came. His experience is not reconcilable with the God he thought he knew. Job invites us to reconsider our images of God and be open to a wilder, more mysterious, uncontrollable divinity whose ways are not ours.

COLLECT

God our saviour,
look on this wounded world
in pity and in power;
hold us fast to your promises of peace
won for us by your Son,
our Saviour Jesus Christ.

Friday 11 July

Psalm **55**
Job 31
Romans 13.8-end

Job 31

'O that I had one to hear me! (Here is my signature! Let the Almighty answer me!)' (v.35)

It's not supposed to be like this. Isn't God meant to be our advocate? The heart of the problem, as Job sees it, is that God isn't listening. He is convinced of the rightness of his cause. His final speech is a catalogue of sins that he could have committed, but insists he has not. He hasn't indulged in lust or deceit; his treatment of people in his service, the poor, the widow and the orphan, are all exemplary. He hasn't relied on his wealth, nor been tempted to worship idols, and hasn't gloated when his enemies are ruined. Indeed, he has no secret sins at all, as he would explain if only God would grant a hearing in the heavenly court, but Job's self-justification appears to fall on deaf ears.

One of the desert fathers commented on how we weigh ourselves down with the heavy burden of self-justification. It's heavy because it never ends, and we bear it all alone. Jesus talked of taking up the cross, which sounds a heavy burden indeed, but also said that his yoke was easy and his burden light (Matthew 11.30). Unlike Job, we may be sure that we have an advocate in heaven who has borne the burden for us. As we follow the costly way of learning to die to self, we find the truth of Jesus' words that set us free from the weight of justifying ourselves to God or to anyone else.

COLLECT

Almighty God,
you have broken the tyranny of sin
and have sent the Spirit of your Son into our hearts
    whereby we call you Father:
give us grace to dedicate our freedom to your service,
that we and all creation may be brought
    to the glorious liberty of the children of God;
through Jesus Christ our Lord.

| *Reflection by* **Liz Hoare**

Saturday 12 July

Job 32

'Now Elihu had waited to speak' (v.4)

The book group I attend has members who love to share their insights into the latest good read – it makes for a great discussion. But there is one who always holds back until others have spoken. She is a good listener: she chooses her words with care, and we are always the richer for her contributions.

Elihu begins well. He has listened to Job's three friends and deferred to them as his elders, who in his culture command respect. He also attributes understanding to the breath of God's Spirit in a person, breath and spirit being interchangeable words in Hebrew. Waiting for a space to jump in with a pre-prepared speech, rather than listening carefully to others so that we enable the conversation to move forward, does not build relationships of trust. Elihu's promising start is sadly not sustained; he declares that he is bursting to have his say, but his being 'full of words' has little more to offer than his seniors.

Our society is less generous with giving older people space to share their experiences and possible wisdom gained. The passage of years brings experience and the chance to reflect on events both personal and more widely in ways that may enrich younger generations. Age does not guarantee wisdom of course, as Job's friends demonstrate. That said, many can testify to having been formed through the influence of wise grandparents or an older mentor. Do we know an older person who would appreciate being included more in our communities?

God our saviour,
look on this wounded world
in pity and in power;
hold us fast to your promises of peace
won for us by your Son,
our Saviour Jesus Christ.

COLLECT

Reflection by **Liz Hoare** | 201

Monday 14 July

Psalms **80**, 82
Job 33
Romans 14.13-end

Job 33

'I have found a ransom' (v.24)

Elihu now sets himself up as God's defender. There's something ironic in his asserting God's omnipotence and freedom to do as he pleases. God is righteous and fair, insists the young advocate and no one is righteous in his sight. If he afflicts someone, it's to warn them against sin.

Paired with Romans in the lectionary, these readings from Job offer interesting commentary on what makes for true righteousness. Elihu refers to an angel, a mediator, who is instrumental in saving a person from the pit. Like Paul writing to the young church in Rome, Elihu is confident of God's justice and righteousness and, like Paul, he recognizes that God alone can restore relationship. There the similarity ends, for Paul has met the Saviour who said of himself that he came to serve and to give his life as a ransom for many (Matthew 20.28). Jesus is the one, says Paul, who went down into the pit on our behalf, confronting death itself and defeating it. God raised him to life again. Without understanding the finer points of atonement theories, countless believers have found joy and freedom in trusting that God, through Christ, has set them free with now no condemnation to fear.

The relationship with God, which Elihu can only imagine from a respectful distance, has been restored. 'Ransomed, healed, restored, forgiven, / who like me his praise should sing?' The recognition that we are in constant need of forgiveness and restoration is present in this remarkable chapter too.

COLLECT

O God, the protector of all who trust in you,
without whom nothing is strong, nothing is holy:
increase and multiply upon us your mercy;
that with you as our ruler and guide
we may so pass through things temporal
that we lose not our hold on things eternal;
grant this, heavenly Father,
for our Lord Jesus Christ's sake.

| *Reflection by* **Liz Hoare**

Job 38

'Who is this that darkens counsel without knowledge?' (v.1)

We can almost hear the thunderous drum roll as God's voice looms out of the whirlwind and takes centre stage. It's notable that most of Job consists of dialogue and debate within which we find deep wisdom and glaring foolishness. We find ourselves drawn into process of discerning what is wisdom and what is not. Job does his fair share of asking questions, but now the tables are turned, and he is in the dock, being interrogated by God.

Job is taken to the beginning of creation, the creation cursed in his misery, to demonstrate beyond doubt that he has uttered words without knowledge. He was not there to see the earth's wondrous foundations being laid, the depths of the oceans we know to be miles deep, the source of light and darkness and the wonders of the heavenly bodies. All is displayed in beautiful poetic form, another key aspect of the book's style. So much more can be conveyed with poetry than straight prose and we are invited to experience the same wonder that Genesis itself suggests as we contemplate the majesty of the created world.

God's question could be aimed at all human efforts to gain knowledge and thereby power. We possess knowledge in profusion, but lack the wisdom to use it well. We covet the kind of knowledge that brings power to those who possess it. Indeed, regarding knowledge as a commodity to be owned rather than shared is one of humanity's greatest failings.

Gracious Father,
by the obedience of Jesus
you brought salvation to our wayward world:
draw us into harmony with your will,
that we may find all things restored in him,
our Saviour Jesus Christ.

COLLECT

Reflection by **Liz Hoare** | 203

Wednesday 16 July

Job 39

'Is the wild ox willing to serve you?' (v.9)

An eagle soaring in the sky, a horse galloping across the heath or a river sparkling in the sunlight as it races through the landscape do not depend on us being witnesses to such wonders for them to exist. Everything in creation exists for its own sake, with a freedom and intrinsic value in God's sight that humans have frequently lost sight of. The result is an attitude which sees the world existing to serve humankind. From plundering the planet's minerals, to chopping down forests, to scouring the seas for diminishing supplies of fish, we have put ourselves and our needs and wants first. It's only recently that we have been forced to contemplate earth devoid of humans. We have begun to realize that everything is connected and not everything exists merely for our flourishing.

Again, the poetry of these passages renders its wonders so vividly. We are invited to join God in revelling in creation's zest, abundance and uncontainability. Job has related everything to his own condition, for this is what suffering does; it shrinks our horizon until all we see is our pain. While we sympathize with Job in his loss and misery, we are also invited to continue our own search for wisdom.

These passages stand as a stern rebuke to conceiving of creation in terms of human utility, control or even comprehensibility. God has created the world not even for his personal use, but for its own sake. Creation has a dignity, beauty, mystery and freedom of its own.

COLLECT	O God, the protector of all who trust in you, without whom nothing is strong, nothing is holy: increase and multiply upon us your mercy; that with you as our ruler and guide we may so pass through things temporal that we lose not our hold on things eternal; grant this, heavenly Father, for our Lord Jesus Christ's sake.

| *Reflection by* **Liz Hoare**

Thursday 17 July

Job 40

'Then the Lord answered Job out of the whirlwind' (v.6)

If Job was hoping that things would calm down after God's explosive burst out of the whirlwind, he was to be disappointed. After a brief exchange, when Job acknowledges his littleness, God continues the bombardment of his helpless challenger. It's hard not to see in this encounter a gnat contemplating being crushed by a terrifying giant of an elephant. Indeed, the chapter ends with just the creature who might fulfil such a role: the creature with limbs like bars of iron, Behemoth. Well might Job tremble, while God seems to be enjoying his display of might without apology.

Elijah might have found God in a still small voice, but not Job. Is it that God neither accuses Job of wickedness nor explains himself that enables him to let go and yield to God's mysterious ways? We are given no packaged explanation of suffering or of where wisdom is to be found. But there is suffering aplenty in evidence and much seeking after wisdom to digest. God is vindicated because he said that Job had not closed his mind to God, despite everything. Of course, Job knew nothing of the conversations between God and Satan at the outset of his sequence of catastrophes. He did not know that God had insisted on Job's righteousness, nor that this confidence in him would remain at the end. We do not know the mind of God, but he is for us and is faithful.

COLLECT

Gracious Father,
by the obedience of Jesus
you brought salvation to our wayward world:
draw us into harmony with your will,
that we may find all things restored in him,
our Saviour Jesus Christ.

Friday 18 July

Psalms **88** (95)
Job 41
Romans 16.1-16

Job 41

'Can you draw out Leviathan with a fish-hook?' (v.1)

'Why is the Bible more entertaining and instructive than any other book?' asked William Blake in a letter of 1799. He answered his own question: 'because it is addressed to the imagination which is spiritual sensation.' The book of Job is particularly vivid in this respect, and Blake, in 1826, published 22 illustrations for it. Behemoth and Leviathan feature in one of them, the latter a strange and fearsome creature having a whole chapter to himself. Is it a crocodile as some think, or is it something otherworldly like one of Katherine Rundell's 'impossible creatures' from her acclaimed eponymous children's book? Is God enjoying a joke at Job's expense?

As we continue to discover new species, especially in the unexplored depths of the ocean, we are reminded that there is much about creation that remains a mystery. It is full of wonders and, despite the damage done by humans, refuses to be tamed. Catch a sea monster with a fish-hook? Of course not, but it seizes our imaginations to consider the work of God's hands. God loves variety, difference and superabundance, and whether it's a flea or a sea monster, humans are humbled before its majesty. The only proper response is worship. Is there anything in the natural world that brings you to your knees, either literally or metaphorically? It may be the vastness of the Milky Way streaking across the sky or as small as the song of a blackbird at dusk.

COLLECT

O God, the protector of all who trust in you,
without whom nothing is strong, nothing is holy:
increase and multiply upon us your mercy;
that with you as our ruler and guide
we may so pass through things temporal
that we lose not our hold on things eternal;
grant this, heavenly Father,
for our Lord Jesus Christ's sake.

| *Reflection by* **Liz Hoare**

Job 42

'... now my eyes see you' (v.5)

There may be no denial of Job's trauma and no attempt to explain, but through a pedagogy of question and response, God has been revealed to Job in a new way, opening his eyes to who he is, to elicit humble testimony to God's greatness. Job has engaged in lament and thereby discovered something of God's greatness, but also that God has remained in relationship with him.

Is this a fairytale ending that is too good to be true? Arguments about how the beginning and end of the book relate to the dialogues in the middle notwithstanding, why should Job not emerge from his terrible ordeal with a life that is blessed? Job's restored fortunes do not negate the story of suffering and despair between chapters 1 and 42. Job is not the same. There are subtle differences between the two scenarios, suggesting that Job is not simply returning to the status quo. Likewise, our images of God need constant revision in the light of experience. Job's struggles to understand why such catastrophes had happened to him must remain a mystery. Yet he could still state 'I have seen you.'

I have a friend who loves to exclaim, 'The best is yet to come.' He says it when things turn out well, and when they don't. Such glimpses of God as Job received have been given to us in a fresh way in Jesus, who told his disciples that those who had seen him had seen the Father also. We still see through a glass darkly, but one day we will indeed see him face to face.

Gracious Father,
by the obedience of Jesus
you brought salvation to our wayward world:
draw us into harmony with your will,
that we may find all things restored in him,
our Saviour Jesus Christ.

COLLECT

Reflection by **Liz Hoare** | 207

Monday 21 July

2 Corinthians 1.1-14

' ... even as you are our boast' (v.14)

One of the things I give thanks for is that I have not ever had to minister to or worship in a church that is in such a parlous state ethically as was the church in Corinth. We read of the shocking things that were happening there in Paul's first letter to them. It grieved Paul terribly and yet he continued to have faith in them. In these verses we learn something of how, apart from worrying about them, he had experienced 'terrible affliction in Asia' to the point where he was 'so utterly unbearably crushed that he despaired of life itself'.

And yet. And yet. He keeps faith and retains hope, in and through the love of God in Jesus. He retains hope in this motley group of former ne'er-do-wells in Corinth and speaks of them being his boast on the day of the Lord Jesus. Elsewhere he tells the Romans that he is convinced that 'nothing in all creation will be able to separate us from the love of God that is in Christ Jesus our Lord' (Romans 8.39).

In this passage we see that these were not cheap words. We could do no better than to pray that we will be given strength and grace to keep faith, whatever terrible things life might throw at us.

COLLECT

Almighty and everlasting God,
by whose Spirit the whole body of the Church
    is governed and sanctified:
hear our prayer which we offer for all your faithful people,
that in their vocation and ministry
they may serve you in holiness and truth
to the glory of your name;
through our Lord and Saviour Jesus Christ.

| *Reflection by* **John Inge**

Psalms 30, 32, 150
I Samuel 16.14-end
Luke 8.1-3

Tuesday 22 July
Mary Magdalene

Luke 8.1-3

'The twelve were with him, as well as some women' (vv.1-2)

One of my favourite cartoons shows a group of men talking to a group of women outside the empty tomb. The caption reads, 'OK. Thank you, ladies: we'll take it from here.' Not only were Mary Magdalene and her companions the first witnesses to the resurrection; they were also, as we are reminded in this passage, central to Jesus' life and ministry, in a way that was ground-breakingly countercultural at the time.

Maybe it was too much for Christians in the centuries that followed. It was once said to me that, although Paul believed what he wrote to the Galatians – that 'in Christ there is no longer Jew or Greek, there is no longer slave or free, there is no longer male and female' (Galatians 3.28) – he concentrated his attention on the first. It wasn't until the nineteenth century that the second was finally tackled, and we are still grappling with the third.

Sexism remains a terrible blight in our society and women continue to be treated appallingly across the world. As Christians, we should follow the teaching and example of Jesus and do everything in our power to expunge it. May this passage reinforce our determination to do that, through prayer and action.

COLLECT

Almighty God,
whose Son restored Mary Magdalene
to health of mind and body
and called her to be a witness to his resurrection:
forgive our sins and heal us by your grace,
that we may serve you in the power of his risen life;
who is alive and reigns with you,
in the unity of the Holy Spirit,
one God, now and for ever.

Reflection by **John Inge**   209

Wednesday 23 July

2 Corinthians 2.5-end

'For we are the aroma of Christ to God' (v.15)

It is fascinating to me that St Paul speaks of spreading through us the fragrance that comes from knowing Christ (v.14). Smell is perhaps the most evocative of the senses. A smell can provoke my memory to take me back immediately into a situation that happened years ago, much more thoroughly than sight or sound.

There is something primal about smell. Smells can be offensive and repugnant – which can have survival value preventing us from, say, eating food that is off. And the opposite: smells can be attractive and alluring. The perfume industry does not exist just to make the world smell more pleasant, it relies on the fact that a person who smells nice is more likely to attract a potential mate than one who smells repugnant.

But the fragrance of which Paul speaks is not applied by a vaporizer. He lights on his image having written about forgiveness, 'What I have forgiven, if I have forgiven anything, has been for your sake in the presence of Christ' (v.10). It is by showing forgiveness that Christians exude the attractive fragrance that can act like a pheromone, drawing others to Christ, drawing them in procession from death to life.

COLLECT

Almighty and everlasting God,
by whose Spirit the whole body of the Church
    is governed and sanctified:
hear our prayer which we offer for all your faithful people,
that in their vocation and ministry
they may serve you in holiness and truth
to the glory of your name;
through our Lord and Saviour Jesus Christ.

| *Reflection by* **John Inge**

Thursday 24 July

2 Corinthians 3

'You yourselves are our letter, written on our hearts' (v.2)

St Paul is immensely, and rather touchingly, committed to the Christians in Corinth whose behaviour he had found it necessary to rebuke very strongly in his first letter to them. That commitment shines out of this letter in many places but nowhere more than here where he expresses his love for them in the beautiful image of them being a letter written on his heart, a letter from God written 'not with ink but by the Spirit, written not on tablets of stone, but on the tablets of human hearts'.

He is remembering the words of the prophet Jeremiah, 'But this is the covenant that I will make with the house of Israel after those days, says the Lord: I will put my law within them, and I will write it on their hearts; and I will be their God, and they shall be my people.' (Jeremiah 31.33). Unlike tablets of stone, the human heart is a living organism, responsive, adaptable and – most of all – loving. Paul had rebuked the Corinthians not for breaking the rules so much as for a lack of love for one another. Now he commends them that they are indeed living by the only law that matters, the law of love.

Almighty God,
send down upon your Church
the riches of your Spirit,
and kindle in all who minister the gospel
your countless gifts of grace;
through Jesus Christ our Lord.

COLLECT

Reflection by **John Inge** | 211

Friday 25 July

James the Apostle

Psalms 7, 29, 117
2 Kings 1.9-15
Luke 9.46-56

Luke 9.46-56

'... for the least among all of you is the greatest' (v.48)

Interpreting the Scriptures can require an exercise in archaeology: the reader has to dig down through the layers of the intervening centuries to get to the bedrock of the original meaning. Take a simple example, the word 'child'. This word has connotations and resonances deposited over the years that can obscure the meaning, such as the idea that a child is innocent or humble.

There is no consensus among biblical scholars about the place of children in Jesus' day, but there is wide acceptance that a child then had no status in society. Indeed, there are those who believe that children were of such little value that child sacrifice was still being practised, if not in Israel, then among the surrounding tribes. So, when Jesus takes the child to his side and speaks of 'the least among you', it would seem that he knew that they would think of the child as practically worthless. It's quite a shock that he identifies himself with this non-person.

Similarly in Matthew 25, Jesus tells his disciples that whenever they feed the hungry, clothe the naked or visit someone in prison, then it is he whom they are serving. And of course, he goes on to be the sacrifice, the Suffering Servant who is counted as nothing. What greater contrast could there be between greatest and least?

COLLECT

Merciful God,
whose holy apostle Saint James,
leaving his father and all that he had,
was obedient to the calling of your Son Jesus Christ
and followed him even to death:
help us, forsaking the false attractions of the world,
to be ready at all times to answer your call without delay;
through Jesus Christ our Lord.

| *Reflection by* **John Inge**

Saturday 26 July

2 Corinthians 5

'… he made him to be sin who knew no sin' (v.21)

Yesterday we saw Jesus taking a child to his side as an example of 'the least' and identifying himself with the child, who was of no worth. It was almost the most extreme of contrasts between greatest and least. Almost, because Paul gives a yet more extreme expression of contrast, extreme almost to being blasphemous: the Christ, the Son of God, the divine sinless one, is somehow transformed by God into the essence of sin itself.

God becoming human is mystery enough; God becoming sin goes beyond all human – and I am sure Paul would add 'angelic' – reasoning. Yet for Paul, human wisdom is folly: he knows Christ crucified, and Paul's expression here surely reflects his profound meditation on the cross of Christ. As Gregory Nazianzus would write some three hundred years after Paul, 'what is not assumed is not healed'. Jesus takes the full weight of human sinfulness on himself. He does so of his own free will. He will bear the full cost of this when he utters his words of abandonment on the cross: 'My God, my God, why have you forsaken me?'

There is absolutely no sin that is beyond the redemptive power of God in Jesus; this same Jesus who became sin was raised gloriously from the dead. 'He made him to be sin who knew no sin' expresses a mysterious yet reassuring hope.

COLLECT

Almighty and everlasting God,
by whose Spirit the whole body of the Church
is governed and sanctified:
hear our prayer which we offer for all your faithful people,
that in their vocation and ministry
they may serve you in holiness and truth
to the glory of your name;
through our Lord and Saviour Jesus Christ.

Reflection by **John Inge** | 213

Monday 28 July

2 Corinthians 6.1 – 7.1

'... as servants of God we have commended ourselves in every way: through great endurance, in afflictions' (6.4,5)

In the meeting I was attending, the representative from the mission agency was giving a slide presentation of the work of the agency in some of the poorest parts of the world. One sequence of slides showed images of people scavenging on the enormous rubbish heaps that are to be found in or near some of the big cities in Africa, India and South America, eking out a living from whatever they could salvage. The speaker had a prepared speech, but suddenly he stopped and put the slide show into reverse. 'I have just noticed something,' he said. 'Just look again at these slides – see how many of these people are smiling and laughing.'

World poverty is an evil scandal. The fact that so many millions of lives are blighted by hunger, preventable disease, lack of sanitation – the list of deprivations is long – while others live in luxury or at least considerable comfort is a terrible injustice which calls for action. But wealth on its own does not equal happiness, and the slide presentation showed that joy can blossom in the most unpromising circumstances. Those people on the rubbish heaps were working together, looking out for and encouraging each other, a tight-knit community. Paul was no stranger to affliction, hardship and suffering. But he had a community, a purpose and above all a faith that gave him hope and sustained him through all his tribulations.

COLLECT

Merciful God,
you have prepared for those who love you
such good things as pass our understanding:
pour into our hearts such love toward you
that we, loving you in all things and above all things,
may obtain your promises,
which exceed all that we can desire;
through Jesus Christ our Lord.

| *Reflection by* **John Inge**

Psalms **132**, 133
Ezekiel 11.14-end
2 Corinthians 7.2-end

Tuesday 29 July

2 Corinthians 7.2-end

'God, who consoles the downcast ...' (vv.7-8)

I once read an article by a parachutist whose 'chute had failed to open. Plot spoiler – you will have deduced that she survived. She was badly injured, but had landed on some trees, which saved her life. In the article she described her feelings once she realized that the parachute had failed to open. Uppermost was, understandably, fear. And she said her greatest fear was the feeling of being totally alone. Of all the things she might have been dreading – horrific injury, pain, dying, death – none was worse than the sense of utter loneliness.

Now, I know there are times when I want to be on my own; and I know there are people who prefer to be on their own most of the time. But I suspect that there are moments in most people's lives when loneliness provokes dread. In his earlier correspondence with the church in Corinth, Paul had admonished them. It had clearly pained him to do so, and it seems he was worried that his relationship with them had broken down irretrievably. To console someone means to comfort them in distress. Paul clearly felt distress about the situation, so he is consoled on two counts, first that the Corinthians had mended their ways, secondly that he was back in friendship and fellowship with them: he no longer felt alone. 'Perfect love casts out fear' (1 John 4.18).

Creator God,
you made us all in your image:
may we discern you in all that we see,
and serve you in all that we do;
through Jesus Christ our Lord.

COLLECT

Wednesday 30 July

2 Corinthians 8.1-15

'The one who had much did not have too much, and the one who had little did not have too little.' (v.15)

Paul is appealing for generosity. As part of his appeal, he reminds the Corinthians of the story of the Israelites in the desert. He quotes – or rather, he slightly misquotes – Exodus 16.17-18. Exodus recounts the story of the manna, which God provided and instructed the Israelites to collect each day. 'The Israelites did so, some gathering more, some less. But when they measured it with an omer, those who gathered much had nothing over, and those who gathered little had no shortage; they gathered as much as each of them needed.'

The point in Exodus is the miraculous equalization of the amounts collected. Paul is concerned here to emphasize that all the Israelites had enough, all were provided for, therefore the more fortunate should give to the less so. But in making this reference, he is surely also reminding them of God's generous providence: 'they gathered as much as each of them needed', no one was in need. In appealing to the Corinthians to be generous, Paul is inviting them to take stock of what they have, to realize how well off they really are; he is suggesting that the Church, the new Israel, should resemble the old Israel in that resources should be distributed to ensure that everyone had enough; and he is encouraging them to see that generosity is a divine quality.

COLLECT

Merciful God,
you have prepared for those who love you
such good things as pass our understanding:
pour into our hearts such love toward you
that we, loving you in all things and above all things,
may obtain your promises,
which exceed all that we can desire;
through Jesus Christ our Lord.

| *Reflection by* **John Inge**

Psalms **143**, 146
Ezekiel 12.17-end
2 Corinthians 8.16 – 9.5

Thursday 31 July

2 Corinthians 8.16 – 9.5

'... for we intend to do what is right not only in the Lord's sight but also in the sight of others' (8.21)

Paul's conversion was so dramatic that it could equally be called the inversion of Paul – his whole world was turned upside down. But none of his Pharisaic learning was lost: he was steeped in his Jewish scripture, so much so that he draws on them almost unconsciously. When he speaks of intending to do what is right in the sight of God and in the sight of others, whether deliberately or not he is referring to the book of Proverbs: 'Do not let loyalty and faithfulness forsake you; bind them round your neck, write them on the tablet of your heart. So you will find favour and good repute' (Proverbs 3.3-4).

Paul is concerned with his reputation. Yes, his main concern is always to obey God's will, to do what is right 'in the Lord's sight', but he sees also the need to do what is right in the sight of others. He understands that this can be problematic: if others do not like what he is doing and saying, they may not hold him in high repute. But he hopes his loyalty and faithfulness to God will shine through. As Jesus said, 'Let your light shine before others, that they may see your good deeds and glorify your Father in heaven' (Matthew 5.16). He is concerned for his reputation not because he wants people to like him, but because he seeks credibility as an ambassador for Christ and so bring others to faith.

COLLECT

Creator God,
you made us all in your image:
may we discern you in all that we see,
and serve you in all that we do;
through Jesus Christ our Lord.

Reflection by **John Inge**   217

Friday 1 August

2 Corinthians 9.6-end

'As it is written, "He scatters abroad, he gives to the poor;
his righteousness endures for ever."' (v.9)

Here Paul is quoting Psalm 112 verse 9. Yet again he is appealing to the Corinthians to be generous in giving (they seem to have needed some convincing). He has done so by speaking of fairness, of a just distribution of resources. Justice is a matter of human relations, of ordering the Church with compassion and equity. Here his appeal is subtly different.

It is not simply a matter of generosity, it is about righteousness, being in right relation, not with people, but with God. Psalm 112 opens, 'Praise the Lord! Happy are those who fear the Lord, who greatly delight in his commandments. Their descendants will be mighty in the land; the generation of the upright will be blessed.' Being in right relation with God brings blessing, first to the person who seeks to live a righteous life. If the Corinthians respond positively to Paul's call for generosity, then they too will find happiness, and this happiness will be evident to others. So righteousness and generosity are evangelical qualities. As we saw with the 'fragrance' of forgiveness, so also righteous and generous living will spread the aroma of Christ and draw others to faith.

COLLECT

Merciful God,
you have prepared for those who love you
such good things as pass our understanding:
pour into our hearts such love toward you
that we, loving you in all things and above all things,
may obtain your promises,
which exceed all that we can desire;
through Jesus Christ our Lord.

Psalm 147
Ezekiel 14.1-11
2 Corinthians 10

Saturday 2 August

2 Corinthians 10

'His letters are weighty and strong, but his bodily presence is weak, and his speech contemptible' (v.10)

If I were to be given the opportunity to invite six saints of the Christian Church to dinner, would Paul be on my list? He can be awkward, dogmatic, boastful, apparently misogynistic, and his detractors in Corinth regarded his 'bodily presence' as 'weak' and his 'speech contemptible' – and I don't think that when they said 'his letters are weighty and strong' they were aiming to pay him a compliment. Yet when we see Paul as he is described in the Acts of the Apostles, his bodily presence seems far from weak, and his speech can be both eloquent and powerful.

It would seem that his detractors are just being rude about him. And as for his letters, yes, they can be weighty and strong, but he is striving to put into words mysteries that are beyond human understanding. Archbishop Rowan Williams has spoken of sometimes having to 'wrestle an idea to the ground' – a wonderful and rather comic image indicating the effort required in the struggle to find the right expression. Paul is undoubtedly an intellectual heavyweight with a highly subtle and creative brain. In my experience such people are not always very good at small talk, but they are always worth listening to.

I think maybe I would invite him to dinner.

Creator God,
you made us all in your image:
may we discern you in all that we see,
and serve you in all that we do;
through Jesus Christ our Lord.

COLLECT

Monday 4 August

2 Corinthians 11.1-15

'... bear with me in a little foolishness' (v.1)

Here we encounter a very human Paul. We can hear his hurt, because he's been made to feel foolish, threaded through the passage. We understand the hints of sarcasm and scorn because we've all been there: feeling let down, betrayed even, by those to whom we have given much and for whom we care most deeply. It is much harder to cope with being hurt by those you love.

As Paul desires those he is writing to in Corinth to be formed by Christ, he also desires that for himself. Jesus knew what it was to be misunderstood, to be let down, betrayed, by those he'd given most to and loved most closely. And Paul knows that Jesus chose not to respond with self-justification, rejection or anger but to persist in clothing those who hurt him with a mantle of mercy, woven from love.

We can identify with Paul wanting to follow Jesus' example and respond in love despite his hurt. We recognize the real struggle it is to live up to that expectation under such provocation. Like Paul we too sometimes lash out in defensive self-justification when we feel humiliated and disregarded.

We can see that the thread of Paul's love for those who disagree with him and disregard his guidance is stretched very thin – but it doesn't break. In the end, Paul can cope with being made to feel foolish because Christ chose to be a fool for him.

COLLECT

Lord of all power and might,
the author and giver of all good things:
graft in our hearts the love of your name,
increase in us true religion,
nourish us with all goodness,
and of your great mercy keep us in the same;
through Jesus Christ our Lord.

| *Reflection by* **Libby Lane**

Psalms **5**, 6 (8)
Ezekiel 18.1-20
2 Corinthians 11.16-end

2 Corinthians 11.16-end

'If I must boast ...' (v.30)

Paul seems here not so much to be writing a letter as speaking to himself. The accusations of weakness, of lack of authority and substance from others resonate with the insecurities he carries in himself.

Paul had given up so much for Jesus and his Church. But that means little to the church in Corinth. So, although he knows it is not God's way, he parades his credentials, as much for himself as for his readers. He lays out what might count as grounds for respect in the sight of others. And in doing so he remembers where his real assurance lies and the secure foundation upon which he now bases his life

We will have our own lists of connections and experiences, qualities and achievements that give us a sense of who we are and what we're worth. When we feel undermined, we too are tempted to parade those external markers that might earn us respect.

Like Paul, though, we are followers of Jesus. A choice has been made, but it was not ours. Like Paul, we are chosen – not because of any gifts and capacities we may have, nor, in fact, despite whatever failings and weaknesses we carry. It is a choice not earned by strength nor grudgingly given out of pity, but a free expression of unconditional love: may we never boast of anything except the cross of our Lord Jesus Christ.

Generous God,
you give us gifts and make them grow:
though our faith is small as mustard seed,
make it grow to your glory
and the flourishing of your kingdom;
through Jesus Christ our Lord.

COLLECT

Wednesday 6 August
Transfiguration of Our Lord

Psalms 27, 150
Ecclesiasticus 48.1-10
or 1 Kings 19.1-16
1 John 3.1-3

1 John 3.1-3
'... we are God's children now' (v.2)

The Feast of the Transfiguration reminds us to wonder that God's glory is fully revealed in Jesus. The letter of John speaks of the wonder that such glory is shared with us in love. Look how beautiful this gift of love is, he writes: this jewel of good news.

That we are children of God is spoken of with awe but also with deep assurance. This is infinitely precious but real and tangible, something that is within our grasp now. Our striving for the future is possible only because we are beloved in the present.

Our experiences of being family will be varied. Our relationships with our own parents, being parents ourselves – or not – will not always have been all good all the time. And for some of us that experience will have been very difficult and painful.

Those things impact us profoundly but need not prevent or distort the gift of knowing ourselves beloved of God – precious children, made whole in a love that is perfect even though we cannot be until the promise is fulfilled and we see God face to face.

That purity and perfection is beyond our grasp, at the very reaches of our yearning. But it depends not on what we don't yet know or haven't yet achieved but in what is ours already: we are God's children *now*. Let's abide awhile in the wonder of being so beloved.

COLLECT

Father in heaven,
whose Son Jesus Christ was wonderfully transfigured
before chosen witnesses upon the holy mountain,
and spoke of the exodus he would accomplish at Jerusalem:
give us strength so to hear his voice and bear our cross
that in the world to come we may see him as he is;
who is alive and reigns with you,
in the unity of the Holy Spirit,
one God, now and for ever.

| *Reflection by* **Libby Lane**

Thursday 7 August

2 Corinthians 13

'Do you not realize that Jesus Christ is in you?' (v.5)

As Paul draws this letter to a close, he returns to what lies at the heart of his witness: the call to serve a crucified God in the person of Jesus Christ.

Through the twists and turns of the letters recorded in scripture, we realize his relationship with the church in Corinth is not fixed but evolving and interdependent. We have evidence of various visits back and forth, of correspondence to and fro. Paul's relationship with them and his place among them is contested and necessarily negotiated.

Shaped by the living presence of Jesus Christ in and among them, they are discovering what the dynamics of power mean in Christian community. It is hard and they clearly do not always get it right. Seeking to be faithful to Jesus' example, Paul is learning to exercise restraint as he inhabits a position of leadership and works out, in real time and through real situations, the shifting parameters of organizational and relational authority and responsibility.

These letters give us a glimpse into the lives of ordinary people in a changing world and developing Church trying to work out how to live as those with Christ in them. Their struggle gives me hope. Perhaps despite our divisions and disputes and dissensions, the grace of the Lord Jesus, the love of God and the communion of the Holy Spirit will be with us too.

Lord of all power and might,
the author and giver of all good things:
graft in our hearts the love of your name,
increase in us true religion,
nourish us with all goodness,
and of your great mercy keep us in the same;
through Jesus Christ our Lord.

COLLECT

Reflection by **Libby Lane** | 223

Friday 8 August

James 1.1-11

'... that you may be mature and complete, lacking in nothing' (v.4)

From the outset, the letter of James is a call to repentance. In addressing the letter to 'the twelve tribes in the dispersion' the author is exhorting the reader to repent. Dispersion was understood to represent God's punishment for Israel's failure to fulfil their side of the covenant. Diaspora letters were sent by Jeremiah, for example, in the expectation that repentance would bring restoration and homecoming.

James is writing to the 'new Israel' and calling them to repentance. Neglect of the poor, preferential treatment of the rich and powerful, gossip and hypocrisy, failure to put faith into action will each be challenged. But such temptations are for James an opportunity for blessing, for such testing can be a route to completion, a means to becoming those who lack nothing.

Here James identifies the lack in those whose instability means they are unable to receive all that God offers and the lack of those whose worldly riches lead to misplaced trust in their own resources and not in God. James longs for his readers, who inevitably face trials and temptations, to resist such testing that appeals to whatever is lacking in us by growing reliance on the completion given ungrudgingly only by our generous God.

Let's heed James' exhortation and journey towards maturity, facing with honesty and humility those things that most appeal to our insecurities and selfish desires, asking God to meet our needs and bring us to completion in Christ.

T	Lord of all power and might,
C	the author and giver of all good things:
E	graft in our hearts the love of your name,
L	increase in us true religion,
L	nourish us with all goodness,
O	and of your great mercy keep us in the same;
C	through Jesus Christ our Lord.

| *Reflection by* **Libby Lane**

Psalms 20, 21, **23**
Ezekiel 24.15-end
James 1.12-end

Saturday 9 August

James 1.12-end

'… being not hearers who forget but doers who act' (v.25)

James' letter is as provocative now as it was when it was written. To live the way James exhorts us to is, many would say, unrealistic. To be characterized by meekness, some have always said, is to be taken advantage of and to lose out. A more realistic and satisfying approach to life, we are often told, is to assume that our opinion is what matters, that we should fight for what we want, that we should go our own way. Perhaps it is time that Christian idealism got real?

James writes that, contrary to popular opinion, it is God's unchanging way that is subversively, transformatively real. Such life-giving reality relies on honest self-reflection and deep listening, and is demonstrated in wise speaking, great patience and compassionate action.

The meekness that James advocates is not about being a doormat but is strength channelled by kindness which extends care to the excluded and overlooked. Such meekness is not at the beck and call of popularity or prosperity but guided by the unchanging light-filled grace of God. Such meekness is both honest and humble. It means we can take a good long look at ourselves with sober judgement – without deceiving ourselves – knowing ourselves fallen but beloved. It means we do not forget to do good because we know not to rely on ourselves but on God whose service is perfect freedom.

Generous God,
you give us gifts and make them grow:
though our faith is small as mustard seed,
make it grow to your glory
and the flourishing of your kingdom;
through Jesus Christ our Lord.

COLLECT

Monday 11 August

Psalms 27, **30**
Ezekiel 28.1-19
James 2.1-13

James 2.1-13

'You do well if you ... fulfil the royal law' (v.8)

It seems contradictory to name an injunction of such revolutionary equality the 'royal law'. James is exhorting God's people to eschew all favouritism and to love every neighbour, regardless of social or any other status, as they love themselves. That hardly seems to equate with an image of royalty whose expected practice was redolent with self-aggrandizement, ostentation, and preferential treatment.

James, by contrast, condemns behaviour that is self-serving or that passes judgement. His illustration of such offensive behaviour is wonderfully evocative and immediate. He takes us into an easily recognized and understood situation that presents the choices we face every day, an example of how we make judgements that are contrary to God's Kingdom.

It is the law of that kingdom and its gracious king that James holds up as the mirror before us. How can we say we believe in the One who, en route to being raised to God's right hand, gave up equality with God and the glory of heaven to become a servant for our sake, obedient unto death – even death on a cross, and yet still behave without mercy to those around us?

When our choices and behaviour dishonour the poorest, we dishonour the king who chooses those least among us to be heirs of his kingdom and puts an end to the injustice of self-serving pretension. His law is the royal law of liberty and his service is perfect freedom.

COLLECT

Almighty Lord and everlasting God,
we beseech you to direct, sanctify and govern
    both our hearts and bodies
in the ways of your laws
    and the works of your commandments;
that through your most mighty protection, both here and ever,
we may be preserved in body and soul;
through our Lord and Saviour Jesus Christ.

226 | *Reflection by* **Libby Lane**

Psalms 32, **36**
Ezekiel 33.1-20
James 2.14-end

Tuesday 12 August

James 2.14-end

'... what is the good of that? (v.16)

There's a Bob Dylan song that asks: 'What good am I if I know and don't do, if I see and don't say, if I look right through you?' It's a powerful question that James first asks in this letter: What is the good of pious words, even if they arise out of deeply held belief, if they don't lead to merciful action?

James doesn't pull any punches: such faith he says is dead. James contends that a faith that is not demonstrated in just and generous action is no faith at all. He shockingly aligns those who believe but don't translate that belief into practical, merciful action with demons. That's quite an assertion.

The examples that James offers as illustrations of living faith could not be more different. Abraham is a founding hero in the story of Israel, the one from whom God's people descend. Rahab is a foreign prostitute. James makes them equivalent examples counted as righteous, justified by God as their actions demonstrated their faith. For James actions of self-giving service to God and actions of service to God's people are counted the same.

James echoes Ezekiel's powerful imagery of the valley of the dry bones which, even when brought together with sinews and flesh so they had the appearance of living beings, were dead without the wind, the breath, the Spirit of God (Ezekiel 37.1-14). So professed faith, without the life-giving breath, the Spirit of enlivening good works, is dead.

Lord God,
your Son left the riches of heaven
and became poor for our sake:
when we prosper save us from pride,
when we are needy save us from despair,
that we may trust in you alone;
through Jesus Christ our Lord.

COLLECT

Reflection by **Libby Lane** | 227

Wednesday 13 August

Psalm **34**
Ezekiel 33.21-end
James 3

James 3

'Does a spring pour forth ... both brackish and fresh water?' (v.11)

James urges his readers, those he first wrote to and us reading many centuries later, to guard our hearts. With vibrant imagery of forest fires, taming wild animals and springs of water, James illustrates that we guard what lies within us by having a care for what comes out of us. In doing so he may be recalling Jesus' teaching, at the heart of the kingdom he came to proclaim, that it is not what goes into us that determines who we are, but what comes out of us.

James urges particular caution to those whose exercise of faithful service is offered through speaking, those with a teaching ministry. He recognizes that words have particular power and that those gifted in the public use of them face particular temptations to abuse that power. It is so easy for words spoken and written to cause such damage when they could be used for good. Words can be easily used to undermine and tear down rather than offer support and build up.

How we use our words, in public or in private, in speech or in writing, in person or online, is a real test of the integrity and maturity of our faith. If our words betray bitter envy and selfish ambition, God still has much work to do in us. A godly life is wisely gentle in words as well as gently merciful in action.

COLLECT

Almighty Lord and everlasting God,
we beseech you to direct, sanctify and govern
    both our hearts and bodies
in the ways of your laws
    and the works of your commandments;
that through your most mighty protection, both here and ever,
we may be preserved in body and soul;
through our Lord and Saviour Jesus Christ.

| *Reflection by* **Libby Lane**

Psalm **37***
Ezekiel 34.1-16
James 4.1-12

Thursday 14 August

James 4.1-12

'Draw near to God and he will draw near to you' (v.8)

The letter of James is attention-grabbingly immediate. He insists we pay attention by writing about what is right in front of us and demands action in the present moment. What he has to say is urgent.

But here, at the heart of his letter, is an invitation to peace: a space made for still, quiet encounter with God.

This invitation and promise sets the rest of the letter in the context of eternity. It allows the recognition that we are works in progress and that it is OK to fail and to fall. Although James seems a hard task-master, his expectations revolve around this merciful premise: God is not finished with us yet.

The beautiful tableau conjured up by this invitation to intimate loving encounter gives us hope. As we recognize our need to lament and mourn and weep because we fall short so often, we need not fall into despair. The invitation into God's embrace is never withdrawn. We can return again, and again, and again. And we will have to. And each time we come in sorrow and penitence for our sin and the sin of the world, needing to humble ourselves before the Lord, we are lifted up and put back on our feet and sent on our way, the Way, to continue our journey of being transformed into the likeness of Christ.

COLLECT

Lord God,
your Son left the riches of heaven
and became poor for our sake:
when we prosper save us from pride,
when we are needy save us from despair,
that we may trust in you alone;
through Jesus Christ our Lord.

Friday 15 August
The Blessed Virgin Mary

Psalms 98, 138, 147.1-12
Isaiah 7.10-15
Luke 11.27-28

Luke 11.27-28

'... a woman in the crowd raised her voice' (v.27)

In Luke's Gospel, women are given space to use their voices and be heard. Luke records the voices and words of women that other accounts have been deaf to or have chosen to silence. In Luke's Gospel, women are drivers of the narrative and agents of change. Again and again, according to Luke, Jesus heard women and was changed by them.

The voice of this unnamed woman is raised amidst contention and opposition. The hostile environment does not prevent her from recognizing Jesus nor inhibit her from intervening. Her words are both an encouragement to Jesus and provide an opportunity for him to invite others to share his work.

In his response, I don't think Jesus is disagreeing with the woman. Rather he is expanding her revelation to include others. According to both declarations, Mary is blessed: as *theotokos* – the one who bore the Christ – and as one who heard God's word and obeyed it.

Blessed also, by Jesus' affirmation, is the woman who raised her voice. She alone among that crowd, as they listened to the words of Jesus, heard the word of God in him and obeyed the call to give testimony. I hope she realized that blessing upon her.

We can learn from her. By making space and time to bless Jesus in the midst of our difficult situations we too may open up possibilities to discover a fresh perspective from unexpected sources, and receive blessing ourselves.

COLLECT

Almighty God,
who looked upon the lowliness of the Blessed Virgin Mary
and chose her to be the mother of your only Son:
grant that we who are redeemed by his blood
may share with her in the glory of your eternal kingdom;
through Jesus Christ our Lord.

Psalms 41, **42**, 43
Ezekiel 36.16-36
James 5.7-end

Saturday 16 August

James 5.7-end

'... prayer ... is powerful and effective' (v.16)

There is an internal contradiction in the Christian teaching and practice of prayer. The prayer of faith makes a difference: the sick will be healed, sins will be forgiven, need will be met. In answering prayer, God shows mercy and compassion. And, be patient: like a farmer waiting for crops to grow, learn to wait and endure even through suffering, for in that will we discover God's mercy and compassion.

James faces this conundrum squarely. I'm not sure he seeks to resolve it, but he sets it out. I expect we all hold this same tension in our practice and experience of prayer. We may have known ourselves or have rejoiced with others when prayers have been answered and God has been seen and felt to be at work. And we will have known or shared with others long costly times of persistent prayer that seem not to yield visible noticeable result, or experience seasons when prayer itself seems impossible and God seems far away.

James recognizes and honours both experiences and holds them as examples of godly faithfulness. According to James we are to pray with a humble patience that does not test God or set demands – and to know God in the waiting. And we are to pray in expectation, longing for divine action – and to know God in the transformation.

Almighty Lord and everlasting God,
we beseech you to direct, sanctify and govern
both our hearts and bodies
in the ways of your laws
and the works of your commandments;
that through your most mighty protection, both here and ever,
we may be preserved in body and soul;
through our Lord and Saviour Jesus Christ.

COLLECT

Reflection by **Libby Lane** | 231

Monday 18 August

Psalm **44**
Ezekiel 37.1-14
Mark 1.1-13

Mark 1.1-13

'The beginning of the good news of Jesus Christ ...' (v.1)

Perhaps the most famous opening sentence in English literature is found in Jane Austen's *Pride and Prejudice*. 'It is a truth universally acknowledged, that a single man in possession of a good fortune, must be in want of a wife.' You are left in no doubt about the nature of the story. The author's dry humour is compelling. You want to read on.

How does Mark's opening line to his Gospel compare? Authors don't usually tell us they are beginning their story. It's self-evident. Mark is too good a storyteller to have made such an elementary mistake. Surely, he wants us to hear an echo of Genesis – 'In the beginning when God created the heavens and the earth' (Genesis 1.1). This story is one of a new creation redeemed in Jesus Christ. Mark's use of the word 'beginning' may refer not just to his written Gospel but to a story which will unfold across space and time.

With this strong focus on beginning, it may seem surprising there's no birth narrative. But Mark is anxious to get on and tell us about the ministry of Jesus. Within a few verses Jesus is baptized by John. There's no time to waste in telling this 'good news'. The urgency continues throughout the whole of Mark's Gospel.

At the beginning of another day in our lives, what urgency do we experience, especially in telling 'the good news of Jesus Christ'?

COLLECT

Almighty God,
who sent your Holy Spirit
to be the life and light of your Church:
open our hearts to the riches of your grace,
that we may bring forth the fruit of the Spirit
in love and joy and peace;
through Jesus Christ our Lord.

| *Reflection by* **Graham James**

Psalms **48**, 52
Ezekiel 37.15-end
Mark 1.14-20

Tuesday 19 August

Mark 1.14-20

'And immediately they left their nets' (v.18)

The urgency in Mark's Gospel is sustained with the calling of the first disciples. There must have been something compelling about Jesus because Simon and Andrew immediately left their nets and their livelihood. James and John are called 'immediately' too. There's no time to waste. But we do not hear what Zebedee thought when Jesus removed his workforce – and his family – from him.

Around four decades have passed between these events and Mark writing them down. Christians told and retold the stories they knew about Jesus, but no one had previously written a connected narrative. The urgency in Mark's account suggests he did not think God would tolerate the world as it was much longer. Many scholars think he wrote after the fall of Jerusalem and the destruction of the Temple in AD 70. These events shocked Jews, and caused Christians, who were waiting anyway for the Kingdom of God to come, to believe it must have been imminent.

We are well placed to understand why events in Mark's world might have prompted him to write his Gospel with such urgency. Events in our world may seem equally cataclysmic. Climate change, migration and the refugee crisis, corrupt governments and despotic rulers – such things mean the need to bring hope is urgent. Mark's response was not to despair but to trust in the good news of Jesus Christ as the transforming agency within human history. Is that our response as well to the world today?

COLLECT

Gracious Father,
revive your Church in our day,
and make her holy, strong and faithful,
for your glory's sake
in Jesus Christ our Lord.

Wednesday 20 August

Psalm 119.57-80
Ezekiel 39.21-end
Mark 1.21-28

Mark 1.21-28

'... he taught them as one having authority' (v.22)

We live in an age of superlatives. The advertising industry exhausts itself trying to find fresh adjectives for whatever we are being sold. 'Amazing' or 'astonishing' (the words favoured by Mark here to describe the teaching of Jesus) are frequently employed. I once heard a vintage wine described as 'having authority'. My mind immediately recalled Jesus teaching 'as one having authority'. It wasn't what the advertiser intended, but I doubt many people would have been theologically distracted!

Jesus is teaching in the synagogue at Capernaum. Mark tells us nothing of the content of what he says but focuses instead on the reaction of the congregation. They sense that this teacher is different and unlike the scribes they usually heard. Even the demons recognize the authority of Jesus. It's 'an unclean spirit' who declares Jesus is 'the holy one of God', a recognition of the supreme spiritual power Jesus possessed.

Mark is setting the stage for a major conflict. Despite Jesus being astonishing and amazing, there is no honeymoon period with the religious authorities at the time. They are soon on the alert to the danger posed by this popular wandering rabbi. There will be conflict too with the evil which convulses and torments the lives of so many people. In this out of the way synagogue in Galilee, Mark describes the beginning of a conflict which is both local and cosmic. It's one which is not finished even yet.

COLLECT

Almighty God,
who sent your Holy Spirit
to be the life and light of your Church:
open our hearts to the riches of your grace,
that we may bring forth the fruit of the Spirit
in love and joy and peace;
through Jesus Christ our Lord.

Psalms 56, **57** (63*)
Ezekiel 43.1-12
Mark 1.29-end

Thursday 21 August

Mark 1.29-end
'... there he prayed' (v.35)

The first day in the public ministry of Jesus, as recorded by Mark, cannot be said to lack activity. Jesus has taught in the synagogue, he's cast out an evil spirit from a disturbed man, he's healed Simon's mother-in-law of a fever, and later that evening 'cured many who were sick'. It's been quite a day. Having earned a good night's sleep, Jesus cuts it short and finds an isolated place to pray. He's away so long that in the morning the disciples go searching for him. They want him to come back because a crowd has gathered. He's popular. Jesus doesn't do as they ask (this will be a repeated pattern), and travels on elsewhere instead.

Despite the urgency and almost unrelenting activity, Mark wants us to realize Jesus is not relying on himself alone. The contemplative side of Jesus is not divorced from his active ministry. He prays. He needs to spend time with his heavenly Father. To use today's jargon, he needs space.

Among the many criticisms I've heard of Church leaders over the years I cannot recall anyone saying they did not think they prayed enough. It's usually something done (or left undone) that gives cause for complaint. And yet it may well be prayer that's most neglected.

When drawing up a 'to do' list of activities for today, would prayer appear on our list?

Gracious Father,
revive your Church in our day,
and make her holy, strong and faithful,
for your glory's sake
in Jesus Christ our Lord.

COLLECT

Reflection by **Graham James** | 235

Friday 22 August

Psalms **51**, 54
Ezekiel 44.4-16
Mark 2.1-12

Mark 2.1-12

'When Jesus saw their faith ...' (v.5)

The paralysed man is blessed – in his four friends. They ensure an encounter with Jesus, lowering their friend through the roof when the crush of the crowd is too great to permit any other access. Their action was sufficiently arresting for Jesus to be impressed. He sees their faith – the faith of these friends – and the man is healed. Jesus even forgives the man's sins (without a confession, let it be noted) which would restore him to society. The scribes don't like that. Jesus is demonstrating a greater authority than theirs.

It's our faith, rather than the faith of those for whom we pray, which is at the heart of our intercessions. It's our faith that God hears our prayers that prompts us to pray for conflict zones, and those oppressed by poverty, want or cruelty, and our planet in its fragility, for those we love. We may not always know precisely what we are praying for, but presenting the people and situations on our minds before God is prayer in itself.

I once ordained a young deacon whose parents were perplexed because they had no Christian faith and couldn't understand their son's vocation. Then I met his maternal grandmother. 'I've been praying for him every day since he was born,' she said, 'but I never knew what for until now.' Let's be open to the unexpected in our prayers today.

COLLECT

> Almighty God,
> who sent your Holy Spirit
> to be the life and light of your Church:
> open our hearts to the riches of your grace,
> that we may bring forth the fruit of the Spirit
> in love and joy and peace;
> through Jesus Christ our Lord.

Psalm **68**
Ezekiel 47.1-12
Mark 2.13-22

Saturday 23 August

Mark 2.13-22
'Follow me ...' (v.14)

Having called four fishermen to be his disciples, Jesus now adds Levi (frequently identified with Matthew) to their number. A tax-collector for the Roman occupiers of Palestine, he was a controversial choice. Collaborators with a foreign enemy are never popular. In this period of occupation by a foreign power, the scribes were keen to ensure stricter observance of purity laws in Judaism, so it's no surprise Jesus is criticized for mixing with sinners. They think him scarcely fit to be a rabbi let alone the Messiah.

Mark is keen to make this point but does not tell us anything about why Levi should have abandoned his lucrative life so instantly. Like the fishermen before him, he answers the call of Jesus immediately, and leaves his old life behind. Mark has nothing to say about the drawing power of the personality of Jesus. Nor does he comment on his vocations policy. There's no job description, no training, no selection process for a Christian disciple. It's a contrast with vocational discernment in all the Churches today.

Perhaps that's the point. Jesus is recruiting disciples. There are no qualifications. No one deserves to be a disciple of Christ. All are called. Indiscriminately. Two thousand years later it's not always apparent the Church has yet understood this, or the radical nature of answering the call, 'Follow me'. It's a repeated call to which even the most established disciple needs to respond to afresh.

Gracious Father,
revive your Church in our day,
and make her holy, strong and faithful,
for your glory's sake
in Jesus Christ our Lord.

COLLECT

Monday 25 August

Psalm **71**
Proverbs 1.1-19
Mark 2.23 – 3.6

Mark 2.23 – 3.6

'... lord even of the sabbath' (2.28)

The Pharisees have had a bad press over the years, especially in Christian circles. 'Pharisaical' has become a term to describe self-serving and hypocritical people. It's unfair since most Pharisees did practice what they preached. They thought Judaism had become too fixated on the Temple and ritual demands and that the Jewish law should apply to ordinary life, including agriculture. But the law lay heaviest on those with least resources. The poor found it burdensome to observe rules about what should or should not be planted, let alone that fields should be left fallow in the sabbath year (every seventh year), good agricultural practice though that was. It's hard to follow best practice when you're hungry.

The carefree way the disciples of Jesus ignored sabbath rules by plucking grains in the cornfields seems almost provocative. Jesus defends them because they were hungry and in need, just as David was when he took the Bread of the Presence to feed his soldiers (1 Samuel 21). Finding a clever precedent was bound to annoy his opponents further.

The conflict grows between Jesus and the Pharisees. It's a dispute between a religion where the law of God (with its restrictions) is applied in fine detail, against one in which God puts supplying the needs of his people first rather than rigid observance of divine law. This tension in understanding between Jesus and the Pharisees has not gone away. Where do you see it played out in the world today, including within the Church?

COLLECT

> Let your merciful ears, O Lord,
> be open to the prayers of your humble servants;
> and that they may obtain their petitions
> make them to ask such things as shall please you;
> through Jesus Christ our Lord.

| *Reflection by* **Graham James**

Tuesday 26 August

Mark 3.7-19*a*

'And he appointed twelve ...' (v.14)

It cannot have been an accident that Jesus 'appointed twelve, whom he also named apostles'. Mark is so keen that we do not miss the significance of the number that he repeats it two verses later – 'so he appointed the twelve'.

Wherever one looks in antiquity the number twelve possesses a cosmic symbolism. There were twelve major gods in the Greek pantheon. The twelve lunar months in a solar year lead to the twelve months in our calendar. The twelve tribes of Israel would have been uppermost in Mark's mind, and perhaps also the appointment by Joshua of twelve men to lead the way as the people of Israel crossed the Jordan into the promised land (Joshua 4). God was doing a new thing in Jesus, but was fulfilling past promises too.

Unlike Joshua's twelve, the names of the twelve apostles are recorded. '"I have called you by name; you are mine" says the Lord' (Isaiah 43.1). Those words echo through this account. There's accountability in recording names too. The last name is 'Judas Iscariot, who betrayed him'. This is no sanitized list.

It will not be the apostles alone who are called by name in the Church. Every Christian is called by name at their baptism. Our identity is enfolded in the identity of Jesus. Mark's passing comment about Judas is a warning of the accountability we all carry when we are called by Jesus Christ.

Lord of heaven and earth,
as Jesus taught his disciples to be persistent in prayer,
give us patience and courage never to lose hope,
but always to bring our prayers before you;
through Jesus Christ our Lord.

COLLECT

Wednesday 27 August

Mark 3.19*b*-end

'He has gone out of his mind' (v.21)

When we face serious opposition, a dispute at work or some other major difficulty, the love and support of our family is frequently crucial to our mental and emotional health. Mark has already shown how Jesus faced serious opposition from the Pharisees and the scribes. They believed Jesus was possessed: 'He has Beelzebul, and by the ruler of the demons he casts out demons.' Others tell Jesus' family that 'he has gone out of his mind'.

It's not surprising that his mother Mary and his brothers and sisters are worried and concerned for him. Their attitude is sometimes linked with what we hear in John 7.5 – 'For not even his brothers believed in him' – so it's assumed Mark thinks Jesus faced conflict with his family too.

I wonder. Mary may well have been perplexed by Jesus, but when you trace her appearances in the Gospels, she is constantly vigilant and loving towards her son. She's there at the foot of the cross, and present when the first believers wait for the promised Holy Spirit. Some of his brothers may not have believed in Jesus, but the tenderness of Mary is consistent.

Many families two thousand years ago would have avoided contact with a son whom others thought possessed or out of his mind. Mary and his family have not cast Jesus out but seek to embrace him still, whatever others might say.

COLLECT

Let your merciful ears, O Lord,
be open to the prayers of your humble servants;
and that they may obtain their petitions
make them to ask such things as shall please you;
through Jesus Christ our Lord.

| *Reflection by* **Graham James**

Thursday 28 August

Mark 4.1-20

'Listen!' (v.3)

Mark is well into his Gospel before he gives us some examples of what Jesus taught, and why large crowds were drawn to him. 'Listen!' is not a plea for silence so that Jesus can be heard, although that would surely be necessary. Nor is it a throwaway line. There's an echo here of the formula Jews used in their daily prayers, 'Hear, O Israel, the Lord is our God, the Lord is one.' Then as he concludes telling the parable of the sower, Jesus says 'let anyone with ears to hear listen!' His opening word is his last one too.

Anyone can hear the parables without understanding them, as Jesus points out to the twelve. 'Listen' must be about more than hearing. It is, famously, the first word in the Rule of St Benedict – 'Listen, O my son, to the teachings of your master, and turn to them with the ear of your heart.'

Benedict understands listening to be the disposition of the faithful disciple. Those who live under his rule are expected to be constantly listening, both in communal and individual prayer, and attentively to the rest of the community and abbot, and also to the guests and the sick.

Attentive listening does not seem to be fashionable in the contemporary world. Perhaps it never was. That's why Jesus challenges us to 'Listen!' To whom or to what will you be listening attentively today?

Lord of heaven and earth,
as Jesus taught his disciples to be persistent in prayer,
give us patience and courage never to lose hope,
but always to bring our prayers before you;
through Jesus Christ our Lord.

COLLECT

Reflection by **Graham James** | 241

Friday 29 August

Psalm 55*
Proverbs 3.27 – 4.19
Mark 4.21-34

Mark 4.21-34

'... he did not speak to them except in parables' (v.34)

Mark gives us several brief parables in this passage. He does not interpret them, although he does say Jesus 'explained everything in private to his disciples'. There's at least a possibility that Mark himself did not have an interpretation.

That has not prevented Christian preachers and evangelists interpreting the parables ever since, sometimes in contradictory ways. Think of the parable of the mustard seed, for example. The image is arresting. A mustard seed is tiny, and yet in first-century Palestine the plant which sprang from it could be so big (perhaps six feet or more) that it may be called a tree.

What, then, is the application or interpretation? The ministry of Jesus, despite drawing crowds, takes place in a remote and largely unvisited part of the Roman Empire. It seems a small thing compared with the salvation of the whole human race. Is this parable assuring us of eventual spectacular growth? And does the growth of the seed represent the expansion of the Church, or the eventual redemption of all humanity? Or perhaps Jesus is telling the crowds rather cryptically that his small movement will become more powerful than the Roman Empire and its puppet rulers in Palestine? Or is it all these things? For that may be the point of the parables – they are the word of God living and active, speaking to us even 2,000 years later. What do you hear today?

COLLECT

Let your merciful ears, O Lord,
be open to the prayers of your humble servants;
and that they may obtain their petitions
make them to ask such things as shall please you;
through Jesus Christ our Lord.

| *Reflection by* **Graham James**

Saturday 30 August

Mark 4.35-end

'He ... said to the sea, "Peace! Be still!"' (v.39)

Twice in this brief passage Mark refers to the Galilean lake as a 'sea'. Yet he calls it a 'lake' at the beginning of chapter 5 so he is using 'sea' deliberately here. Mark writes with an eye to how readers will interpret the healings, teaching and events in the ministry of Jesus. This nature miracle follows his comments about the parabolic teaching of Jesus. Perhaps there's a parable here as well.

A great storm at sea brings to mind the story of Jonah. But it is Psalm 107 that most faithfully prefigures this miracle. At risk of drowning in a storm, the people of God 'cried to the Lord in their distress' and 'he made the storm be still, and the waves of the sea were hushed'. Who but the Messiah would do that on the 'sea' of Galilee?

There is safety in the boat with Jesus, even in a great storm. This would have been a compelling narrative for believers when the early Church suffered persecution. It was a stormy, unpredictable life for many Christians. They would have been encouraged to stay together in the boat (the Church) and trust in the ultimate protection of Jesus.

The relevance of this story remains in our own age when Christians continue to be persecuted in many parts of the world, for whom other believers more secure in the boat should surely pray.

Lord of heaven and earth,
as Jesus taught his disciples to be persistent in prayer,
give us patience and courage never to lose hope,
but always to bring our prayers before you;
through Jesus Christ our Lord.

COLLECT

Reflection by **Graham James** | 243

Monday 1 September

Mark 5.1-20

'... clothed and in his right mind' (v.15)

This account of a chronically ill man and his 'demons' sounds strange – unacceptable, even – to the modern ear; it would be told very differently in a twenty-first-century context. Despite the archaic language, however, the description of his mental and physical distress rings true, as does the isolation it imposed upon him.

I love the phrase 'clothed and in his right mind'. No longer chasing relentlessly terrifying thoughts round and round his head, no longer raving and using his own strength to hurt himself, now he sits, bathed and dressed, calm and serene, and engaging in daily conversation. The healing Jesus brought was more than just the absence of illness. It was the re-making of his life, the restoration of his dignity, and his successful reintegration into the community. Healing, in God's scheme, is not just about mending broken things , but about re-creating our lives, so that – whatever our mental make-up may be – we are able to live our everyday lives in ways that benefit us and those around us.

The last detail is easy to miss: his healing was life-changing in one sense, but this did not transfer into a new, 'superstar' life on the road with Jesus. The idea of 'life-changing' experiences can be over-sold. Sometimes the most transformative healing is not to move to a new place, but to be able to inhabit fully the life we already have.

COLLECT

O God, you declare your almighty power
most chiefly in showing mercy and pity:
mercifully grant to us such a measure of your grace,
that we, running the way of your commandments,
may receive your gracious promises,
and be made partakers of your heavenly treasure;
through Jesus Christ our Lord.

Reflection by **Maggi Dawn**

Psalms 87, **89.1-18**
Proverbs 8.22-end
Mark 5.21-34

Tuesday 2 September

Mark 5.21-34

'She had heard about Jesus, and came up behind him' (v.27)

Two stories are interwoven here as Jairus, a religious leader and an important and respected man, approaches Jesus directly with a desperate request to heal his daughter. On the way to Jairus' home, a marginalized woman – a nameless social outcast – reaches out to Jesus indirectly, doing her best to receive healing without being seen. Both stories revolve around physical healing. But making Jairus wait while Jesus stopped to pay attention to the woman shifts the focus to Jesus' rejection of public opinion over class and social status. He did not need to stop in order to heal the woman; she had already been healed. But giving her precedence over Jairus was doubly significant, for it was precisely the religious culture that Jairus represented that was the source of her status as an outcast.

The woman was accustomed to people turning their backs on her; for Jesus, it was not enough for her to see his back, he would not leave until they had spoken face to face. As well as health instead of sickness, he gave her peace in place of fear, and respect instead of shame. Again, we see that God's healing is more than the absence of illness. He brought her out from the shadows, and healed her soul as well as her body.

God of glory,
the end of our searching,
help us to lay aside
all that prevents us from seeking your kingdom,
and to give all that we have
to gain the pearl beyond all price,
through our Saviour Jesus Christ.

COLLECT

Wednesday 3 September

Psalm 119.105-128
Proverbs 9
Mark 5.35-end

Mark 5.35-end

'Talitha cum' (v.41)

This is, on one level, a story of an extraordinary event – a child brought back from the brink of death. But Mark threads through his account a series of small, everyday details. The woman in yesterday's reading had been ill for twelve years; Jairus' daughter was twelve years old. Yesterday's healing took place in a crowded street; in today's episode, Jesus dismisses the noisy crowds twice before he heals the girl. They weep and wail, they laugh and sneer, but he sweeps past all of that, and takes just three disciples and the girl's parents into the room with him.

Mark's Gospel is written in Greek, but just a few times he recorded Jesus' words in the vernacular language of Aramaic. In this conversation with a young girl, removing the formality from the narrative adds a note of tenderness. And as well as being written in the vernacular, the words themselves are informal and familiar words – something to the effect of, 'my little lamb, get up' (also, perhaps, linking the story to the idea of Jesus as the Shepherd of the sheep in Mark 6.34).

Once again, Mark shows Jesus not only delivering physical healing, but responding to the individual in front of him. For this child, there is no drama, no crowd, no formal language, but privacy, kindness, and affectionate words she can understand and trust.

COLLECT

O God, you declare your almighty power
most chiefly in showing mercy and pity:
mercifully grant to us such a measure of your grace,
that we, running the way of your commandments,
may receive your gracious promises,
and be made partakers of your heavenly treasure;
through Jesus Christ our Lord.

Psalms 90, **92**
Proverbs 10.1-12
Mark 6.1-13

Thursday 4 September

Mark 6.1-13

'... as you leave, shake off the dust' (v.11)

Analysis of this story often revolves around the symbolism of shaking off the dust, emphasizing the 'testimony against' those who would not receive the gospel. But the phrase can also speak directly to the one who is walking away. Not everything we attempt goes well; not every project we undertake is a success, and – even when we feel profoundly called by God – not everything we offer is received. There are times when, metaphorically speaking, you find yourself with the door closed in your face. Sometimes, the right thing to do may be to fight back, and kick the doors down. But sometimes the best thing for all concerned is simply to move on, and find an open door.

When that is the case, I find this phrase really liberating. If life gives you a closed door that is never going to open, there is no point bloodying your fists trying to beat it down. But if you walk away, it is so difficult not to take with you either some guilt (should I have tried harder?) or some grinding resentment (they have ruined my life or my plans with their obtuseness...). A firmly closed door is often reason enough to walk away. But leave the dust behind. Shake off the guilt, the disappointment, the resentment. And then go find another door, this time one that is open.

God of glory,
the end of our searching,
help us to lay aside
all that prevents us from seeking your kingdom,
and to give all that we have
to gain the pearl beyond all price,
through our Saviour Jesus Christ.

COLLECT

Friday 5 September

Mark 6.14-29

'Ask me for whatever you wish, and I will give it' (v.22)

Herod heard rumours that Jesus was, in fact, John the Baptist raised from the dead, and was filled with fear. Mark then uses a flashback technique to fill in the backstory. What had happened before, to make Herod so afraid?

Before all of this, Herod had known John, and there was something about him that he had liked, despite John's habit of challenging Herod on his integrity and ethics. So Herod protected John from his enemies by putting him in the safest place he knew – in prison. From there the story rolled out tragically, trapping Herod in a maze of his own making. He wanted to protect John, and to keep his marriage sweet, and to appear as a great benefactor, and – having made rash promises in public – never be seen to renege on his own word. Herod, then, was a man in constant conflict with himself, easily provoked to the fear of being overthrown, or of being made to look foolish or weak. A guilty conscience, and a mind absorbed in self-interest, makes it impossible to see clearly, or make good decisions.

John and Jesus both modelled a way of using their own power to empower others; in so doing they each lost their own lives, but brought life to other people. Herod, though, wielded his power mainly to protect himself and his own interests. And ultimately, he brought a lot of death and destruction.

COLLECT

O God, you declare your almighty power
most chiefly in showing mercy and pity:
mercifully grant to us such a measure of your grace,
that we, running the way of your commandments,
may receive your gracious promises,
and be made partakers of your heavenly treasure;
through Jesus Christ our Lord.

| *Reflection by* **Maggi Dawn**

Saturday 6 September

Mark 6.30-44

*'And they went away in the boat to a deserted place
by themselves' (v.32)*

This is an iconic story, of a picnic-for-one that becomes a feast for thousands. But right before the great miracle comes a moment of challenge for the disciples. For days on end, they had worked through the crowds, with all their noisy demands, and their desperate need for Jesus' teaching and his healing powers. Now, they were rowing across the water to get away from it all, a precious day off to relax and put their feet up. You can practically feel the sigh of relief as they pull up the oars and wade ashore. Peace at last. Except, there was another crowd waiting on the beach.

We don't know how the disciples felt – weary, dismayed, cross, or ready to help? We do know that Jesus looked at this multitude of faces, and all he felt was compassion. They looked like lost sheep – and as any shepherd or farmer will tell you, there is nothing more lost than a lost sheep. And all those plans for a well-earned break were put on hold.

It is true that – following the way of Christ – we do need to take care of ourselves. There is nothing holy or commendable about being so burned out that we can barely function. But there will be times when we need flexibility in the moment. Perhaps we will be best guided by developing the gift of compassion.

God of glory,
the end of our searching,
help us to lay aside
all that prevents us from seeking your kingdom,
and to give all that we have
to gain the pearl beyond all price,
through our Saviour Jesus Christ.

COLLECT

Reflection by **Maggi Dawn** | 249

Monday 8 September

Mark 6.45-end

'Then he got into the boat with them and the wind ceased' (v.51)

The contrast between the calm and the storm occurs twice in this short passage. First, they sail through a fierce storm, the wind and the waves beating against them, until Jesus steps into the boat, and chaos gives way to calm. But as soon as they moor the boat and step ashore, another kind of storm awaits them: complete chaos breaks out as the people 'rush about the whole region' bringing queues of sick people to be healed.

In *The Peace of Wild Things*, the poet Wendell Berry names the distress that can build up as we face social chaos, pressure of work, personal anxieties, and worries about the state of the world. He writes about getting up in the middle of a sleepless night to go out and find a peaceful spot in the natural world, where he lies down among the 'wild things, who do not tax their lives with forethought of grief'. Sometimes the solution to dealing with stress is to reduce the pressure, but sometimes it is enough simply to discover sufficient inner calm to be able to withstand the pressure.

When Jesus walked across the water and calmed the wind and waves, it was regarded as a miracle. Perhaps the greater miracle was that, in the process, the disciples discovered enough stillness in their souls to handle the chaos they met shortly afterwards.

COLLECT

Almighty and everlasting God,
you are always more ready to hear than we to pray
and to give more than either we desire or deserve:
pour down upon us the abundance of your mercy,
forgiving us those things of which our conscience is afraid
and giving us those good things which we are not worthy to ask
but through the merits and mediation
of Jesus Christ our Lord.

Psalm **106*** (*or* 103)
Proverbs 15.18-end
Mark 7.1-13

Tuesday 9 September

Mark 7.1-13

'... making void the word of God through your tradition' (v.13)

Jesus speaks with the very best, the most religiously observant people, the people who uphold tradition, who ensure that things are done properly and done well. They know and love every detail of canon law, every rubric of the liturgy, and it matters enormously to them that it is done correctly. Why, then, does Jesus not appreciate their devotion to religious service?

As the twentieth-century composer Igor Stravinsky pointed out, 'A real tradition is not the relic of a past that is irretrievably gone; it is a living force that animates and informs the present.' Traditions are supposed to live and grow with us, being life-forming. Jesus' quibble with these upstanding religious people was, I think, that they had slipped into treating rules and institutions as more important than people, so that they were no longer a true 'tradition', merely a stifling habit. Traditions and institutions are supposed to enhance and develop the life of a community, and enable people to grow and develop. But to remain alive, they have to exist to serve the people, and not the other way around.

Jesus' words are startling but true: the very traditions that are supposed to help us draw close to God can, if we turn them into rules that must be obeyed for their own sake, become mere traditionalism, giving us all the appearance of religious devotees while, in fact, we are far from God.

God of constant mercy,
who sent your Son to save us:
remind us of your goodness,
increase your grace within us,
that our thankfulness may grow,
through Jesus Christ our Lord.

COLLECT

Wednesday 10 September

Mark 7.14-23

'... the things that come out are what defile' (v.15)

Purity laws revolve around external and physical concerns: what you eat, what or whom you touch, who you speak to. Religions have always produced purity codes: from dietary restrictions and limits on physical intimacy to extreme exclusion from mainstream society. But the modern world has invented and reinvented its own purity codes: what is deemed a healthy or sustainable diet, a correct amount of exercise, attitudes to recycling, organic farming, sustainable energy, and so on. All of these are based on habits that are reasonable, and beneficial to society and to the individual. In their origins, so were most religious purity codes.

But the distinction Jesus made was this: that it is possible to have a near-perfect lifestyle, whether for religious or secular reasons, yet still have emotional and social habits that are quite destructive. Ironically, purity codes can even amplify those habits. The most observant religious person can be viciously unkind to someone they deem spiritually or morally inferior. Equally, so can someone with admirable habits in some form of sustainable eating be judgemental, as can devotees of ecological protection. The point is that if, in the process of achieving an excellent lifestyle, we judge, condemn, mock, or exclude those who are less excellent, then what merit does it hold?

Jesus, undoubtedly, would praise any effort to make a better world materially or ecologically, but he was looking at what comes out of our mouths and hearts: if we cannot treat our fellow human beings with kindness and compassion, then what is it for?

COLLECT

Almighty and everlasting God,
you are always more ready to hear than we to pray
and to give more than either we desire or deserve:
pour down upon us the abundance of your mercy,
forgiving us those things of which our conscience is afraid
and giving us those good things which we are not worthy to ask
but through the merits and mediation
of Jesus Christ our Lord.

| *Reflection by* **Maggi Dawn**

Psalms 113, **115**
Proverbs 20.1-22
Mark 7.24-30

Thursday 11 September

Mark 7.24-30

'But she answered him' (v.28)

This is a curious moment in the Gospel, where Jesus seems to be somewhat offhand and rude to a woman who asks for his help (is he really calling her a 'dog'?), but she refuses to be put off by his insult and changes his mind, seemingly through her quick-witted reply.

Reading the Bible, it is understandable that we dredge every story for its depth of meaning, and especially if a story is hard to understand, we look for hidden meanings. Surely, we think, Jesus must have been saying something profound, so what are the layers we are missing? But it is equally possible that Jesus was tired, focused on the task at hand, and regarded this woman as a distraction from what he was supposed to be doing. And what shifts the gears is not so much a deep hidden meaning, but humour. Maybe he warmed to her daring to answer him back, to her refusal to accept his being short with her. Maybe her dark humour caught his attention. Maybe he even laughed out loud.

We don't know for sure. But it might not be a bad idea to be open to the notion that, if Jesus wept now and again, he probably also laughed when he heard a good joke. And a good joke can sometimes be more effective in changing the course of a conversation than deep theological analysis.

God of constant mercy,
who sent your Son to save us:
remind us of your goodness,
increase your grace within us,
that our thankfulness may grow,
through Jesus Christ our Lord.

COLLECT

Reflection by **Maggi Dawn** | 253

Friday 12 September

Mark 7.31-end

'... he sighed and said to him, "Ephphatha"' (v.34)

According to other Gospel accounts, Jesus varied the way he carried out healings: sometimes simply by speaking a few words, and sometimes with more elaborate rituals, such as using mud and spit (John 9.6-7), the laying on of hands (Luke 13.10-13), or even by doing nothing at all (Mark 5.27). This might be because the Evangelists wanted to be clear that his healings were purely through the power of God, and not techniques, spells, or incantations.

More than the other Gospel writers, Mark records Jesus' exact words in Aramaic, possibly because he heard them from Simon Peter. And here, after touching the man's ears, and praying to heaven, he breathes just one word: 'Ephphatha', This can be translated as 'be opened', but words conjure meaning from how they sound as well as from their etymology, and this word sounds like a deep sigh, a lamentation not only for the immediate suffering of this man, but also for the plight of the world he was meeting every day. The need of the man before him was to see and hear physically. But Jesus seems to feel even more depth of sorrow for those who had no physical needs, and yet failed to hear or communicate with God. Perhaps, sometimes, we are so wrapped up in our concern for physical needs and abilities that we fail to notice our own lack of emotional or spiritual awareness.

COLLECT

Almighty and everlasting God,
you are always more ready to hear than we to pray
and to give more than either we desire or deserve:
pour down upon us the abundance of your mercy,
forgiving us those things of which our conscience is afraid
and giving us those good things which we are not worthy to ask
but through the merits and mediation
of Jesus Christ our Lord.

Saturday 13 September

Mark 8.1-10

'... there was again a great crowd without anything to eat' (v.1)

In chapter 6, we read Mark's account of Jesus feeding 5,000. Now he tells an almost identical story. Even if it did happen twice, why would Mark relate both versions, given that they are so similar? The differences are subtle. But numbers are rarely incidental in the biblical narratives, and the way the people and loaves and leftovers are counted may hint at layers of meaning we might easily miss. The earlier account (Mark 6.30-44) took place near Bethsaida, near Galilee, and the numbers are five and twelve – five thousand men, five loaves, twelve baskets of leftovers. This might allude to the five books of the Law (Genesis-Deuteronomy), and the twelve tribes of Israel, indicating that as Jesus fed the people, he was both the fulfilment of the Law and the one promised to Israel.

This second version counts in sevens and fours: seven loaves, seven baskets, four thousand people. The number seven symbolizes perfection and completeness, and also recalls the seven days of creation. The whole of creation, in its completeness, includes the Gentiles, and we know that this second occurrence of the miracle took place when Jesus was in the region of Decapolis – a Gentile area (7.31). Perhaps, then, Mark thought both versions of the story needed telling to demonstrate that Christ's message and ministry was for the whole world. 'We who are many are one body, for we all partake of the one bread' (1 Corinthians 10.17).

God of constant mercy,
who sent your Son to save us:
remind us of your goodness,
increase your grace within us,
that our thankfulness may grow,
through Jesus Christ our Lord.

COLLECT

Reflection by **Maggi Dawn** | 255

Monday 15 September

Psalms 123, 124, 125, **126**
Proverbs 25.1-14
Mark 8.11-21

Mark 8.11-21

'... they had only one loaf with them in the boat' (v.14)

How does Mark want us to understand the one loaf in the boat? Is it a reference to Jesus, the nourishment of life, who is with them as they sail along? Is it an encouragement to see that there is only one unifying bread sufficient for everyone, Jew and Gentile? Is it an early eucharistic reference to the solitary but faithful one whose love remains even when the disciples are forgetful or fearful? Whatever was in Mark's mind as he shaped this story, we find Jesus sighing with frustration at the Pharisees wanting proof of who he is, and his own followers not comprehending the generosity and reach of the good news he is sharing.

In fact, Jesus describes his disciples as if they were the idols mentioned in Psalm 115, having eyes that can't see and ears that can't hear. It is a challenge to us in today's Church to ask whether, like those disciples, we have ended up being the very opposite of what Jesus in his first sermon identifies as a true sign of his kingdom – the recovery of sight (Luke 4.18). Do we similarly contradict Jesus' signs of release and the end of oppression? It is perhaps not too difficult to imagine Jesus listening in on a parish meeting or some disputing synod, still asking 'Do you not yet understand?' (v.21). Mark challenges the Christian community more than once in his Gospel, as he reminds them that the insiders often prove obtuse while the outsiders get it.

COLLECT | Almighty God,
who called your Church to bear witness
that you were in Christ reconciling the world to yourself:
help us to proclaim the good news of your love,
that all who hear it may be drawn to you;
through him who was lifted up on the cross,
and reigns with you in the unity of the Holy Spirit,
one God, now and for ever.

Tuesday 16 September

Mark 8.22-26

'Can you see anything?' (v.23)

A blind friend of mine once complained to me that she was fed up with Christians using her disability as a metaphor for their spiritual conversions. There is no getting away from the fact that, for Mark, this story is connected to the next he will relate, about Peter's confession of faith. In this healing of a nameless man defined by his blindness, there are two stages. First, Jesus takes the man by the hand and gently leads him out of the noisy and nosey village. To be able to make significant change in lives, we first need to recognize that where there is a crowd there is often untruth and ungenerous pressure. After hands have been laid, and spittle used like an ointment, the man ends up seeing people, like many of us do today, as if they were trees – wooden, inhuman, useable.

The healing finally allows the man to see clearly and to embrace the gift that people really are. You sense that his life and relationships will now look very different. He will be able to lead people by the hand as well now. Many a spiritual director has asked the question, 'Can you see anything?' Spiritual health is found in the ability to stay amazed and stay grateful, and to bring about a world in which all are free to do this.

Almighty God,
you search us and know us:
may we rely on you in strength
and rest on you in weakness,
now and in all our days;
through Jesus Christ our Lord.

COLLECT

Wednesday 17 September

Psalm **119.153-end**
Proverbs 26.12-end
Mark 8.27 – 9.1

Mark 8.27 – 9.1

'... what will it profit them to gain the whole world?' (8.36)

Right at the centre of Mark's Gospel, Peter proclaims that Jesus is the Messiah. As is often the case with Peter, he is both right and wrong. Where he misunderstands this time is in regard to the nature of Messiahship as embodied in Jesus. It is not in being a popular wonderworker or a political saviour – both short-term projects – that forms his Messiahship. Instead, Jesus has patiently to teach Peter and the others that his vocation is one of crucified love, showing the world the reach and depth of God's tenderness and cherishing of the world, as well as God's challenge to it.

Jesus then teaches that his apprentices similarly have to choose the way of costly love. Nothing else can break the cycles of self-destruction that human beings create or get trapped in. This means recognizing that all the complex 'devices and desires', as the old prayer book puts it, of the human heart need honestly confronting and setting aside. The one primary call to our life is to be realistic and courageous ambassadors of love's potential, as shown in Jesus Christ. He asks his disciples what they can give in return for their life. They have been given the gift of their being. In response they are now to give back their gift of becoming, shaping their lives with the example of their friend.

COLLECT

Almighty God,
who called your Church to bear witness
that you were in Christ reconciling the world to yourself:
help us to proclaim the good news of your love,
that all who hear it may be drawn to you;
through him who was lifted up on the cross,
and reigns with you in the unity of the Holy Spirit,
one God, now and for ever.

| *Reflection by* **Mark Oakley**

Psalms **143**, 146
Proverbs 27.1-22
Mark 9.2-13

Thursday 18 September

Mark 9.2-13

'... listen to him!' (v.7)

Although we know the focus of this story as the 'transfiguration', Mark actually calls it a 'metamorphosis'. It appears to be a confirmation for the closest disciples of what emerged in the conversation we read about yesterday. Elijah is present as the one who acted as forerunner to the Messiah, and Moses predicted the coming of a prophet like himself (Deuteronomy 18.15). The white clothes, so difficult to make and maintain in the local terrain, are a sign of high status, their luminosity recalling the time when Moses' face shone brightly because he had been talking with God (Exodus 34.29-35).

Mark tells us that the same voice is heard as was heard at Jesus' baptism. Jesus is called the 'Beloved' again, and those present are asked to listen to him. After the first voice was heard, Jesus was 'thrown' into the wilderness (Mark 1.12). He has to hold to the voice from heaven as so many other voices came at him, trying to erode his sense of calling and confidence in God. Here, in a similar way, a voice is heard that will need remembering, as the dark and painful days of the passion and death of Jesus begin. Jesus talks to his disciples about the Messiah rising from the dead, teaching them that the suffering that awaits is not some forlorn tragedy but the necessary path to a distilled, awakened and renewed life.

Almighty God,
you search us and know us:
may we rely on you in strength
and rest on you in weakness,
now and in all our days;
through Jesus Christ our Lord.

COLLECT

Friday 19 September

Psalms 142, **144**
Proverbs 30.1-9, 24-31
Mark 9.14-29

Mark 9.14-29

'… only through prayer' (v.29)

The story of the healing of the epileptic child is rather long. The first half focuses on the disciples' failure of faith; the second on the faith of the child's father which, even as he admits his unbelief, feels more alive and expectant than the docile faith of Jesus' close friends that can't generate what is needed. The Gospels are full of stories of Jesus finding a lack of faith where it should be and a lot of faith where it is not presumed to be. Jesus here speaks out about a 'faithless generation', and in a private house he tells his perplexed friends that healing can only be done through prayer, that is, not through spectacle, self-assurance or power games.

We can be in danger of reading this story and rather ignoring the boy himself. Everyone is talking over him, and we are listening in on them. He is clearly distressed and frightened by a condition that recurs. He is not able to speak, and gets injured by the ferocity of his convulsions. Jesus does here exactly what he did to the blind man. He takes him by the hand. This is an image that the metaphysical poet George Herbert returns to many times in his poems, saying of Jesus in his poem *Easter*:

> 'Who takes thee by the hand, that thou likewise
> With him mayst rise.'

After Jesus talking of the Son of Man's rising in yesterday's reading, perhaps in this story we see intimations of the relief and joy that this resurrected love brings to human hearts.

COLLECT

Almighty God,
who called your Church to bear witness
that you were in Christ reconciling the world to yourself:
help us to proclaim the good news of your love,
that all who hear it may be drawn to you;
through him who was lifted up on the cross,
and reigns with you in the unity of the Holy Spirit,
one God, now and for ever.

| *Reflection by* **Mark Oakley**

Psalm 147
Proverbs 31.10-end
Mark 9.30-37

Saturday 20 September

Mark 9.30-37

'What were you arguing about?' (v.33)

It's true to say that many of our arguments are about greatness, who has the most power, who should have the most money, and who ranks higher in social status. It isn't surprising, then, that the disciples are discovered having such an argument among themselves, even though Jesus has been recently teaching them about love and its necessary sacrifices. This time, he places a child in front of them to communicate what is required of us to understand what it is we are committed to in following Jesus. It's easy to go native and still believe we are disciples of Jesus, whereas our words and life together give us away. We can easily lose our convictions and identity as Christians by replicating the world's obsessions.

Jesus shows here that the heart of the human problem is the problem of the human heart. He is teaching them that greatness lies in a servant's soul not a master's power. To be a servant is not to serve people's wants and so become some sort of doormat. It is to serve their needs and therefore become a channel of hope for them. We have also to learn to see our own needs, and be able to receive from others for our own strength and healing, just as the child knows that there are so many things in life that he or she cannot do alone. Pride is all about display. Service is about connection and growth.

Almighty God,
you search us and know us:
may we rely on you in strength
and rest on you in weakness,
now and in all our days;
through Jesus Christ our Lord.

COLLECT

Monday 22 September

Psalms 1, 2, 3
Wisdom 1
or 1 Chronicles. 10.1 – 11.9
Mark 9.38-end

Mark 9.38-end

'Whoever is not against us is for us' (v.40)

One may well get a sight of life in the early Church from this reading. We get a glimpse of divisions between people both of whom are saying they are doing work in the name of Jesus. We find warnings against letting people stumble in their faith, an alert not to lose the distinct flavour of faith, and a request to live in peace with one another. It could all have been written last week, it is so recognizable to Christians! What we can also see is that, for Mark, Jesus has an open and generous understanding of who might be defined as a member of the Church. It isn't a place where we fit in. It is a place in which we belong.

Today's reading also shows us something of the preacher Jesus was. He is persistently figurative in the Gospels, and here we see the hyperbole he uses to stress the point that nothing is more important than the life of faith, the pulse of the human spirit. The word 'hell' here is, in the Greek, 'Gehenna', a valley near Jerusalem used as a rubbish dump which became a symbol for the place of the future destruction of the wicked. When Jesus says that everyone will 'be salted with fire', is he saying that all will experience difficulties, but the fire must be seen as a purification process which results in a distilled and stronger faith, the salt in us, making us more empathetic and able to live together better?

COLLECT

Almighty God,
whose only Son has opened for us
a new and living way into your presence:
give us pure hearts and steadfast wills
to worship you in spirit and in truth;
through Jesus Christ our Lord.

| *Reflection by* **Mark Oakley**

Psalms **5**, 6 (8)
Wisdom 2
or I Chronicles 13
Mark 10.1-16

Tuesday 23 September

Mark 10.1-16

'... do not stop them' (v.14)

We live in a world where, on the whole, children are treated well and held in high esteem. Safeguarding processes are agreed to be crucial. Charities like the UK's 'Children in Need' raise millions of pounds even when families are struggling to keep paying their own bills. The killing or harm of children is considered the greatest outrage of all. In the ancient world, however, children were of the lowest status and perhaps this is what Jesus is getting at when he tells his disciples not only to receive them but to be like them. He is not asking them to be sweet or innocent or naive. He is asking them to be willing to be poor, dispossessed, having no rights or held in no esteem, and to be open enough to welcome such folk into their fellowship.

As regards divorce, Jesus seems clear about the ideal – a permanent, faithful and stable union of hearts and lives. What Christians have struggled with ever since is how this ideal relates to the realities of an imperfect world. For some societies, we are asking how it applies to those who find themselves in love with someone of the same sex. What is clear is that Jesus condemns a casual or cruel approach to relationships. He sees both partners as equals. This is surely his belief in the ideal, that love reflects God and should be preserved whenever possible. We are left to pray and discern as to what we do when it isn't.

Merciful God,
your Son came to save us
and bore our sins on the cross:
may we trust in your mercy
and know your love,
rejoicing in the righteousness
that is ours through Jesus Christ our Lord.

COLLECT

Reflection by **Mark Oakley** | 263

Wednesday 24 September

Mark 10.17-31

'When he heard this, he was shocked ...' (v.22)

When the actor Alec McCowen performed the whole Gospel of St Mark from memory around theatres in the 1970s and 1980s, it was during this story that the audience started to shift uncomfortably in their seats. Having had an ice cream in the interval after the transfiguration, they were now hearing that money, and our attitude to it, is a spiritual problem. They were hearing that following Christ is not about increasing but decreasing, and an acknowledgment that the best things in life are never things. Instead, they are values and truths that shape us rather than possess us.

We can often fail to notice the remark that when the man told Jesus that he had kept all the commandments, Jesus 'loved him'. In other words, he wasn't out to have a go at him because he was rich, he wasn't a self-righteous critic making himself feel better and hide his envy. It was because he loved him that he was asking him to reconsider his life and see whether he was able to walk away, for the sake of freedom and peace with God, from everything that gave him stability and power. The kingdom is a topsy-turvy place, where the first end up last, and where children, the poor and overlooked, hold the key.

COLLECT

Almighty God,
whose only Son has opened for us
a new and living way into your presence:
give us pure hearts and steadfast wills
to worship you in spirit and in truth;
through Jesus Christ our Lord.

| *Reflection by* **Mark Oakley**

Thursday 25 September

Psalms 14, **15**, 16
Wisdom 4.7-end
or 1 Chronicles 17
Mark 10.32-34

Mark 10.32-34

'... those who followed were afraid' (v.32)

We are told that Jesus was walking ahead and that those who followed were afraid. Why? Is it because they feel they are getting deeper into something they don't quite understand? Or that it all feels more demanding than they imagined it would be? After all, Jesus' teachings have been non-negotiable and challenging of late. Or is it because they sense that Jesus is walking towards Jerusalem and inevitable conflict and, maybe, worse? Are they too caught up with Jesus to get out unscathed?

Jesus privately takes his disciples aside and predicts what is to happen to him in more detail than usual. He is spelling out the cost to himself and, by implication, to those who are journeying alongside him. We have another prediction of resurrection, here, too. It is a faint, unimaginable mention of something hopeful but, surely, unbelievable to them as they tried to hear him out. Perhaps they were afraid that Jesus was losing a sense of reality and that they were wasting their time? Whatever they were afraid of, fear remains an enemy of Christian faith. Time and again, the scriptures tell us not to be afraid and to set our sights on the promised land of who we might become – if we allow Jesus to walk ahead.

Merciful God,
your Son came to save us
and bore our sins on the cross:
may we trust in your mercy
and know your love,
rejoicing in the righteousness
that is ours through Jesus Christ our Lord.

COLLECT

Friday 26 September

Psalms 17, **19**
Wisdom 5.1–16
or I Chronicles 21.1 – 22.1
Mark 10.35-45

Mark 10.35-45

'What is it you want me to do for you?' (v.36)

It looks as if the disciples are still having arguments about status. James and John ask for positions of glory and Jesus replies by asking them a question as to whether they can undergo suffering and a flood of catastrophes, symbolized by a cup and baptism. Their misunderstanding of Jesus' teaching continues as they ask to sit on the left and right of Jesus in his glory. What we later find is that those on his left and right are actually the criminals being crucified with him.

Jesus again spells out the importance of service. Maybe he senses their fear about the future and realizes that when love and care start to falter, possession and control begin to take over. He needs to wean them off the ways of worldly competition in which we build ourselves up in order to look down on others. He redefines greatness as something that is seen in our better self and not in our *curriculum vitae*. He then reveals that this is not just an abstract teaching but that he is exemplifying it in his own living and loving. Not only must they remember this. They must re-member him, be his body and his witness in the world, known for their love and patient attention towards those who need friendship and their dignity to be reclaimed.

COLLECT

Almighty God,
whose only Son has opened for us
a new and living way into your presence:
give us pure hearts and steadfast wills
to worship you in spirit and in truth;
through Jesus Christ our Lord.

| *Reflection by* **Mark Oakley**

Psalms 20, 21, **23**
Wisdom 5.17 – 6.11
or 1 Chronicles 22.2-end
Mark 10.46-end

Saturday 27 September

Mark 10.46-end

'Take heart; get up, he is calling you' (v.49)

We come to the end of a long section (beginning at 8.22) in which Jesus teaches about discipleship. The section began with the healing of a blind man and now ends with this story about Bartimaeus. The miracle is due to his faith, which is said to have 'saved' him. This evokes the sense that salvation here is much deeper and more significant than having restored eyesight. He sees who Jesus is, and he sees that he must follow him. We are told that he does this by following Jesus 'on the way'. He has become a disciple, with both clarity of sight and the insight of faith.

Bartimaeus' faith, in which he springs up, chucks his cloak away, and transparently tells Jesus what he needs, is in such contrast to the disciples we have recently been reading about. Although in private being patiently taught about the vitality of faith and its translation into loving service, they still find themselves falling back into arguments about who's better, who's in and who's out. The heart is resistant to change. Our fears imprison us in the status quo that somehow works for us, but yet isn't us fully alive. The question of Jesus resonates now as it did then, 'What is it you want me to do for you?'. Faith is needed to face the question and faith is needed to enable the answer to become a reality, full of grace and truth.

COLLECT

Merciful God,
your Son came to save us
and bore our sins on the cross:
may we trust in your mercy
and know your love,
rejoicing in the righteousness
that is ours through Jesus Christ our Lord.

Reflection by **Mark Oakley** | 267

Monday 29 September
Michael and All Angels

Psalms 34, 150
Tobit 12.6-end *or* Daniel 12.1-4
Acts 12.1-11

Acts 12.1-11

'... suddenly the angel left him. Then Peter came to himself'
(vv. 10-11)

The Bible is rich with examples of human encounter with God's angels – literally, in Hebrew, God's 'messengers' – and the communications from God which they bring in words or actions. Often, as in this passage, it is only with hindsight that they, their message, and its implications are recognized.

In her poem 'Saint Peter and the Angel', Denise Levertov focuses on that point where the angel leaves Peter, and he finds himself coming to his senses, recognizing not only that this was no dream, but that he is now free to pursue whatever unimaginable path God might set before him. She describes his realization that he could hear his own footsteps as being more frightening than either arrest or chained captivity, as he becomes aware that he himself must take responsibility for living into this new, unexpected liberty, becoming the one who must unlock – as if he himself were the key – the terrifyingly unknowable prospect of freedom and joy that might lie ahead.

Powerful experiences of God's love for, and engagement with, us are not given for us to dwell on, comforting though it may be to look back on them. They are to inspire, encourage and equip us to go forwards confident in him, however daunted we may be by circumstances or our own capacity. Are we open to grasping in both hands such invitations to our 'next terrors of freedom and joy'?

COLLECT

Everlasting God,
you have ordained and constituted
    the ministries of angels and mortals in a wonderful order:
grant that as your holy angels always serve you in heaven,
so, at your command,
they may help and defend us on earth;
through Jesus Christ our Lord.

| *Reflection by* **Sarah Rowland Jones**

Psalms 32, **36**
Wisdom 7.1-14
or I Chronicles 28.11-end
Mark 11.12-26

Tuesday 30 September

Mark 11.12-26

'Jesus answered them, "Have faith in God."' (v.22)

Mark's Gospel sets Jesus' cleansing of the Temple within an account of the fruitless fig tree. He curses it, and it is later found withered. Some commentators suggest this deliberately provides a context for us to interpret his actions in the Temple.

Only the previous day the crowd had shouted 'Hosanna! Blessed is the one who comes in the name of the Lord!' This might have appeared very promising: recognition of his messiahship. But would that promise deliver? We're invited to ponder that question alongside the fig tree. Even if it was early in season, a tree in leaf was likely to have fruit. Yet the promise suggested by those leaves literally bore nothing.

Jesus had yearned – had been hungry for – the Jewish people, under its spiritual leaders, to bear the first-fruits of the coming kingdom. Yet despite his preaching, teaching and the signs of his ministry, not only did they not recognize him, but they had allowed the focus of the Temple to be diverted from worship to commerce. Some suggest that this business had only recently been brought into the 'court of the Gentiles', where it impeded, rather than enabled, the prayer of 'all the nations'. The obvious conclusion is that fruitless promise leads only to withering.

Peter is shocked, and we may well feel daunted. But Jesus reassures, 'Have faith in God.' When we persist in faith, and in prayer, we shall see the kingdom's fruit.

God, who in generous mercy sent the Holy Spirit
upon your Church in the burning fire of your love:
grant that your people may be fervent
in the fellowship of the gospel
that, always abiding in you,
they may be found steadfast in faith and active in service;
through Jesus Christ our Lord.

COLLECT

Reflection by **Sarah Rowland Jones** | 269

Wednesday 1 October

Psalm **34**
Wisdom 7.15 – 8.4
or 1 Chronicles 29.1-9
Mark 11.27-end

Mark 11.27-end

'By what authority …?' (v.28)

As holy week in Jerusalem unfolds, Jesus is assailed by a raft of questions. But few are designed to elicit helpful answers or valuable information. They are more like the trick questions and 'gotcha' traps that today we too often find laid in the political sphere. Mind you, even where questions are reasonable, many politicians have a knack of answering the questions that they would have liked to be asked instead!

Jesus is alert to all this, avoiding and subverting the highly pointed question with his own, which unmasks their devious motivation. Listeners then, as today, are able to put two and two together and draw their own conclusions: both John and Jesus had the authority of heaven, but these religious leaders were not prepared to acknowledge either of them.

I find myself challenged by this passage to own up to those times when I don't use straight language. It's generally because I'm engaging with things I don't find palatable, or because I know asking a neutral question will bring an answer I don't want to hear. But truthfulness sets us free – for it follows the way of Jesus, who embodies ultimate truth. When assailed by temptation to speak deviously, I need to have courage to take refuge under his authority, believing that, however uncomfortable I may find it, this is the route to finding his redemptive path through territory I find challenging.

COLLECT

God, who in generous mercy sent the Holy Spirit
  upon your Church in the burning fire of your love:
grant that your people may be fervent
in the fellowship of the gospel
that, always abiding in you,
they may be found steadfast in faith and active in service;
through Jesus Christ our Lord.

| *Reflection by* **Sarah Rowland Jones**

Psalm **37***
Wisdom 8.5-18
or I Chronicles 29.10-20
Mark 12.1-12

Thursday 2 October

Mark 12.1-12

'The stone that the builders rejected has become the cornerstone'
(v.10)

Yesterday's questioning was designed to back Jesus into a corner. Today he does much the same to his questioners, in what the Gospel describes as a parable. Yet usually parables open up, rather than close down, and listeners are invited to enter into the story and find their own place within it; often there is no single interpretation that must be drawn. But it seems all alike recognize that here Jesus is making a barely veiled criticism of the chief priests, scribes and elders.

Nonetheless, this passage still challenges us with shifting interpretation in the quote from Psalm 118.22-23. Through God's marvellous redemptive action, what was rejected may become crucially important. While the verse is most completely fulfilled in Jesus Christ, it illustrates a persistent thread in the wider weaving of salvation into our lives.

How often have we written off some possibility, situation or even individual, perhaps through negligence, ignorance or because it was just more convenient for us – and yet have later come to realize that we had misconstrued a channel of God's rich gifts to us? How often have we discovered with hindsight that some unwelcome development, which may even have challenged our faith, later by grace brought us into a deeper experience of God, or healing, or trust, that we had never anticipated. What other 'stumbling-blocks' might we still need to re-engage with, to discover they are the Lord's gift of stepping stones?

Lord God,
defend your Church from all false teaching
and give to your people knowledge of your truth,
that we may enjoy eternal life
in Jesus Christ our Lord.

COLLECT

Reflection by **Sarah Rowland Jones** |

Friday 3 October

Psalm **31**
Wisdom 8.21 – end of 9
or 1 Chronicles 29.21-end
Mark 12.13-17

Mark 12.13-17

'Should we ... should we not?' (v.15)

If a broad question doesn't provide an effective trap, then why not try a binary one: yes or no? This or that? But such questions are rarely appropriate or useful, and their real objectives are often only thinly disguised at best. We can almost hear Jesus' exasperation as he responds.

I saw a Facebook meme recently that said, 'Don't listen to the person with all the right answers, but the person with all the right questions.' The best questions are those that keep us learning and growing, that are designed to build up rather than put down. Jesus' questions, like his parables, so often open up fresh territory of faith, inviting us to explore and discover.

So also does his answer given here, which Christians have debated for 2,000 years. What *does* Jesus mean by 'render unto Caesar ... and unto God,' as we traditionally know his words? Perhaps we need to go back to the previous question, and ask ourselves who is 'the emperor' for us today – whether as individuals or as a society and culture.

The genius of Jesus' perplexing response is that all his followers, now as then, are invited to engage afresh with every change in context – for the nature of secular power and influence, and their relationship with Christianity, always vary over time and place. So who, now, is Caesar for me? How might I be rendering to false gods?

COLLECT

God, who in generous mercy sent the Holy Spirit
    upon your Church in the burning fire of your love:
grant that your people may be fervent
in the fellowship of the gospel
that, always abiding in you,
they may be found steadfast in faith and active in service;
through Jesus Christ our Lord.

| *Reflection by* **Sarah Rowland Jones**

Psalms 41, **42**, 43
Wisdom 10.15 – 11.10
or 2 Chronicles 1.1-13
Mark 12.18-27

Saturday 4 October

Mark 12.18-27

'Some Sadducees … came to him and asked him a question' (v.18)

Here's another loaded question, but rather than aiming at Jesus, the Sadducees seem to be trying to get one up on their rival co-religionists. It's another effort at argument winning, this time taking aim at the Pharisees who believed in the afterlife. May God give us grace to avoid such behaviour within the body of Christ!

Jesus is having none of this point scoring. But he will engage with the important underlying issue, the matter of the dead being raised. And so he responds to their question by pointing them in a more profitable direction. 'Have you not read…?' The clear answer then follows.

Sometimes we have genuine questions to ask of Jesus. Sometimes life unfolds in perplexing ways, and 'Why?' echoes loudly inside our heads. Sometimes we find teachings of the Church confusing or hard to fathom, or even accept. Sometimes we wonder how to apply Scripture to our own circumstances. Sometimes we have difficult decisions to take, or can't see the path ahead.

We know from the questioning, even arguing, of the Psalmist that we too are invited to voice our confusions through prayer. We should not be afraid to ask about what sincerely troubles or bewilders us. We might not get an immediate straight answer – but we can be confident Jesus will bring us the answers we need, even if he has to get us asking better questions along the way. What is perplexing you?

Lord God,
defend your Church from all false teaching
and give to your people knowledge of your truth,
that we may enjoy eternal life
in Jesus Christ our Lord.

COLLECT

Monday 6 October

Psalm **44**
Wisdom 11.21 – 12.2
or 2 Chronicles 2.1-16
Mark 12.28-34

Mark 12.28-34

'... seeing that Jesus answered them well, he asked' (v.28)

Finally we have a good question! It is asked by someone who has recognized the wisdom of how Jesus had responded to all that was thrown at him. This scribe is genuinely desiring to know Jesus' answer. And his straight question receives a straight, and generous, response.

I return endlessly to these words of Jesus' answer, finding them such a rich touchstone for life's choices. They affirm that to be human is to have emotional, spiritual, intellectual (or cognitive), and physical capacity for living in love with God. (I find it helpful to think of the last as encompassing both our embodiment, and our agency and resources.) Further, humanity best walks closely with God in the flourishing that he intends, when we are also in loving relationship with others. None of us is wholly self-determining regardless of anyone else, nor should our distinct, God-given, individuality be consumed or denied by our mutual belonging.

Therefore, I often find myself asking whether a particular option might enrich or impoverish my or others' capacity for growing in godly love, shared with him and his world in each of these dimensions: the affective and cognitive, spiritual and material, individual and communal. It's also illuminating beyond the Church: for example in deciding to oppose the closure of libraries, which impoverishes the minds particularly of those who most need such access. What decisions do you have before you which might benefit from pondering from these perspectives?

COLLECT
O Lord, we beseech you mercifully to hear the prayers
    of your people who call upon you;
and grant that they may both perceive and know
    what things they ought to do,
and also may have grace and power faithfully to fulfil them;
through Jesus Christ our Lord.

| *Reflection by* **Sarah Rowland Jones**

Psalms **48**, 52
Wisdom 12.12-21
or 2 Chronicles 3
Mark 12.35-end

Tuesday 7 October

Mark 12.35-end

'... she out of her poverty has put in everything' (v.44)

Jesus now takes the initiative, posing a question that is something of a riddle. I wonder if he's having fun teasing the religious leaders, who both used riddles in their own teaching, yet also strove to classify theology and the practices of the life of faith. I doubt they enjoyed being wrong-footed, though the crowd was delighted.

But time and again, we can also find ourselves wrong-footed. C.S.Lewis famously wrote in his Narnia books that the Christ-like Aslan 'is not a tame lion'. God cannot be systematized nor pinned down so we can feel safe and comfortable. It can be tempting to put our trust in theology, or liturgical practices, or the structures of the Church – all able to bring us gratifyingly close to the Lord for whom we yearn, yet simultaneously keeping us at a nice safe distance from his disconcerting awesomeness and unpredictability.

But these will never truly satisfy. Instead we must learn from the poor widow. She's not caught up in the world's preoccupations of riches, power and status – central to Jesus' own temptations, and which endlessly re-echo in our lives, with their mirages of false security. Freed from their seductive call, because they all lie so far beyond her grasp, she is able to put radical trust in her God, sharing her everything with him, in true liberty of life. She has riches others cannot comprehend.

COLLECT

Lord of creation,
whose glory is around and within us:
open our eyes to your wonders,
that we may serve you with reverence
and know your peace at our lives' end,
through Jesus Christ our Lord.

Wednesday 8 October

Psalm 119.57-80
Wisdom 13.1-9
or 2 Chronicles 5
Mark 13.1-13

Mark 13.1-13

'... the one who endures to the end will be saved' (v. 13)

'Tell us, when...?' asks Jesus' inner circle of disciples. It's another misplaced question. It reflects how, on the eve of the crucifixion, his closest friends still fail to understand the nature of his messiahship and kingdom.

We should not be too hard on them. We also may struggle to make sense of God's promises and how they are being fulfilled, given the moral ambiguities of so much of life, to say nothing of the downright tragedies that permeate human history. But it's not just a question of knowing how to interpret these words. Even if we had complete understanding of Jesus' response, we would still have no control over the events he describes.

The deeper message is that it is only safe to trust in God. The Psalmist, for example, tells us not to rely on chariots or horses – military might (Psalm 20.7); and Mark's Gospel has already warned against trusting religious practices (Mark 7.1ff.) or money (Mark 10.21). Now, not spiritual insight, nor interpreting signs, nor even family are reliable. Not that any are intrinsically bad for us, unless we expect them to rescue us when life is most challenging. In the final analysis, only Jesus remains. We will find that he is the one who is always there for us, if we endure to the end – in Greek, *telos*, which also means ultimate 'goal'. Our end truly lies in Christ.

COLLECT

O Lord, we beseech you mercifully to hear the prayers
of your people who call upon you;
and grant that they may both perceive and know
what things they ought to do,
and also may have grace and power faithfully to fulfil them;
through Jesus Christ our Lord.

| *Reflection by* **Sarah Rowland Jones**

Psalms 56, **57** (63*)
Wisdom 16.15 – 17.1
or 2 Chronicles 6.1-21
Mark 13.14-23

Thursday 9 October

Mark 13.14-23

'But be alert; I have already told you everything' (v. 23)

The 'desolating sacrilege', a phrase derived from the book of Daniel, harks back to a pagan altar set up in the Temple by Antiochus IV in 168 BC, which was among the catalysts of the successful Jewish Maccabean revolt against their Greek overlords. The Gospel's first readers would have known how terrible those times had nonetheless been for the local population.

Threats against the city persisted. Scholars suggest this passage may refer to the Emperor Caligula's abortive plan of 40 AD to set up his own statue in the Temple, or to events prior to the Temple's destruction in 70 AD (debate continues as to whether this Gospel was written before or after this date). Note also that, unlike the far longer parallel passage in Matthew's Gospel, here we have no explicit reference to Jesus' return at the end of the age.

So it seems we're expected to understand this chapter as applying historically – even if we, who employ understatement to emphasize a point, can find it hard to navigate the overstatement and hyperbole that is more typical of semitic languages, such as the Aramaic which Jesus spoke, and is reflected here in Greek.

The underlying message woven through these vivid images is that Jesus Christ's salvation will triumph over human conflict, and his hope over false narratives. Though this world may be shaken in every age, by word and action Jesus has taught that he is always our firm foundation.

COLLECT

Lord of creation,
whose glory is around and within us:
open our eyes to your wonders,
that we may serve you with reverence
and know your peace at our lives' end,
through Jesus Christ our Lord.

Reflection by **Sarah Rowland Jones** | 277

Friday 10 October

Mark.13.24-31

'... but my words will not pass away' (v.31)

It is worth looking back to the passage in Daniel 7 quoted here. When the Son of Man comes in the clouds in Daniel's vision, he is not coming to earth. Rather, Daniel sees him being brought before 'the Ancient of Days', almighty God. He is then given 'dominion and glory and kingship' so 'all peoples, nations, and languages should serve him'. His is 'an everlasting dominion that shall not pass away, and his kingship is one that shall never be destroyed'.

And if we look forward to Mark 14.62, we find Jesus uses these words to answer the High Priest's question, 'Are you the Messiah, the Son of the Blessed One?' 'I am' he responds, then quotes the same verse. He implies he will be at the right hand of God, exercising the fullness of that dominion, glory and kingship. This the High Priest will see, if not personally, then through the accounts of the resurrection and all that follows.

The great power and glory of the resurrection, the coming of the Holy Spirit, and the birth of the Church did indeed all take place during the generation of Jesus' disciples. They remain with us, as does the fullness of Jesus' teaching. Wherever we recognize that Jesus reigns, we should expect to experience the fruit of his kingdom – as surely as the leaves of the fig tree promise a harvest of fruit.

COLLECT

O Lord, we beseech you mercifully to hear the prayers
of your people who call upon you;
and grant that they may both perceive and know
what things they ought to do,
and also may have grace and power faithfully to fulfil them;
through Jesus Christ our Lord.

| *Reflection by* **Sarah Rowland Jones**

Psalm **68**
Wisdom 19
or 2 Chronicles 7
Mark 13.32-end

Saturday 11 October

Mark 13.32-end

'And what I say to you I say to all: Keep awake' (v.37)

This has been a challenging chapter to read. It has made more sense taken at face value – hyperbole and vivid linguistic imagery notwithstanding – rather than trying to read it through an assumed lens of 'the second coming', or *parousia*, a word that appears in other Gospels, but not here.

For it seems that Mark's Gospel intends to give us advice for the here and now. When Jesus said 'this must take place' in verse 7, it was not so much a prediction of what will unfold, as an assertion of the necessity of his victory over sin and death in and through the trials and tribulations of history. This is the battleground on which his victory is played out.

We are called to be part of this drama, not merely spectators. God works out his purposes, inviting us to be caught up in the tremendous momentum of his redemptive engagement with humanity and all creation. None of us can predict or control when and how Christ's reign comes. But, as my late husband and I found through his terminal illness, our determination to keep on trusting that he would work for good, even in what at times seemed the most hopeless of circumstances, opened our eyes to glimpses of his glory and dominion persistently penetrating our daily reality. Through refusing temptation to despair, we were caught up in Christ's victory, for this life, and for the life to come.

> Lord of creation,
> whose glory is around and within us:
> open our eyes to your wonders,
> that we may serve you with reverence
> and know your peace at our lives' end,
> through Jesus Christ our Lord.

COLLECT

Reflection by **Sarah Rowland Jones** | 279

Monday 13 October

Mark 14.1-11

'For you always have the poor with you' (v.7)

Six of Mark's sixteen chapters describe the events of the last week of Christ's life, beginning in chapter 11 with the triumphal entry into Jerusalem, and ending with the 'terror and amazement' of the disciples outside the empty tomb. Today we begin to read chapter 14, which describes the penultimate two days of Jesus' earthly life. While most of the chapter deals with the events of what we would now call Maundy Thursday, the first few verses are set the previous day, and have things to say about money, and about response.

Jesus' assertion that 'you always have the poor with you, and you can show kindness to them whenever you wish' is a realistic though depressing commentary on the world. The juxtaposition between the actions of the woman and the actions of 'some' (among whom we might reasonably number Judas) is the important thing. The woman's response to meeting the Christ is to respond with outrageous generosity, as illogical as that generosity might seem. Judas' response is to seek financial reward in exchange for betrayal. We can use the gifts we have been given for worship or for personal gain. We can respond to the presence of Christ in our lives with joyful abandon, or with fear and plots to evade his gaze. The choice is ours.

COLLECT

Almighty God,
you have made us for yourself,
and our hearts are restless till they find their rest in you:
pour your love into our hearts and draw us to yourself,
and so bring us at last to your heavenly city
where we shall see you face to face;
through Jesus Christ our Lord.

| *Reflection by* **Tom Clammer**

Tuesday 14 October

Mark 14.12-25

'... a man carrying a jar of water will meet you' (v.13)

There is much that is unclear about the opening verses of today's reading. They can be read simply as Jesus having made careful arrangements around his dinner plans with people in Jerusalem. In that reading the 'man carrying a jar of water' and the 'owner of the house' have been pre-briefed by Jesus, and all that the disciples are doing is completing a transaction. In another reading something more mysterious is happening, and both of these characters, who never appear again, and never say a word, are in some sense fulfilling a supernatural destiny. Both readings are legitimate, and there is really no way of knowing which might be the historically more accurate.

Either way, two characters appear today who seemed to be integral to the unfolding of the story of Maundy Thursday, each playing their part in the inevitable journey of our Lord towards the cross, though neither of them has a name, and they disappear from the story as quickly as they appear. We might be moved, today, to remember that, as unfeted as our own ministry and service might seem to be, we are all exactly where God has placed us, to play our part in the outworking of his mysterious plans.

Gracious God,
you call us to fullness of life:
deliver us from unbelief
and banish our anxieties
with the liberating love of Jesus Christ our Lord.

COLLECT

Reflection by **Tom Clammer** | 281

Wednesday 15 October

Mark 14.26-42

'Even though all become deserters, I will not' (v.29)

Reading this section of the chapter can feel horribly familiar to any of us who have let down a friend, or promised to do something at which we subsequently failed. The response of Peter and the other disciples is at the same time completely familiar to us, and rather harrowing. Most, if not all, of us have made promises that we have broken, and most, if not all, of us have underestimated how difficult some things that are asked of us might be.

We, of course, read this passage with the benefit of knowing the ending. We know that the threefold denial of Peter finds its redemption, at least according to St John, in Jesus' threefold commissioning of Peter: 'feed my lambs, feed my sheep (John 21.15-19) which we read back in May. It is not wrong to aspire to 'attempt great things for God', as the lectern in Westminster Abbey proclaims. We may well sometimes feel that our faith is bullet-proof. Today's reading reminds us that it is not always so, that we cannot always know in advance the moments that will test our faith the most and, most importantly, that our redemption is not contingent on our 'success'.

COLLECT

Almighty God,
you have made us for yourself,
and our hearts are restless till they find their rest in you:
pour your love into our hearts and draw us to yourself,
and so bring us at last to your heavenly city
where we shall see you face to face;
through Jesus Christ our Lord.

| *Reflection by* **Tom Clammer**

Psalm **78.1-39***
1 Maccabees 2.1-28
or 2 Chronicles 13.1 – 14.1
Mark 14.43-52

Mark 14.43-52

'... he went up to him at once ... and kissed him' (v.45)

One the most famous examples of the adoption of this part of the passion narrative by popular culture is when Bob Dylan, choosing to play an electric rather than an acoustic guitar, was heckled by a member of his audience at a concert in 1966. The angry man simply shouted, 'Judas!'

Judas' kiss in the Garden of Gethsemane, a signal to the soldiers by which he would identify Jesus, has entered into history as the epitome of betrayal. The world hates a 'Judas'.

This part of the story is among the most chilling, because we recognize ourselves very clearly, either in Judas himself – those moments where we have actively betrayed – but probably more so in the rest of the group who flee into the night. One popular theory is that the man who runs off naked is the author, Mark, himself.

Christ, in the midst of this, is calm and resigned. He bears the betrayal and abandonment, knowing the deeper contours of the scripture, which tell a story that is leading not only to the high priest's audience chamber, but to a garden and an empty tomb. Most of us, when we betray, do so because we have forgotten that. Praise God that he has not forgotten.

Gracious God,
you call us to fullness of life:
deliver us from unbelief
and banish our anxieties
with the liberating love of Jesus Christ our Lord.

COLLECT

Reflection by **Tom Clammer** | 283

Friday 17 October

Psalm **55**
1 Maccabees 2.29-48
or 2 Chronicles 14.2-end
Mark 14.53-65

Mark 14.53-65

'But he was silent and did not answer' (v.61)

Because of the intervention of the Feast of Luke the Evangelist tomorrow, we will not read the closing verses of chapter 14, so you might want to take the time either now or later on to read those final eight verses. They matter to the story because what we find in these accounts of the events of the night of Jesus' betrayal is all sorts of people saying all sorts of things, while Christ remains largely silent. Lots of 'testimony' is given, some of it apparently 'false', and lots of it contradictory. In those verses that we will miss tomorrow, we find Peter outside by the fire being challenged by the servant girl, and he is motivated out of fear, embarrassment, or a sense of self-preservation to deny that he knows Jesus.

Jesus, however, remains silent, not engaging in the games and posturing. When he does speak, he quotes words from the prophet Daniel, with which the high priest would have been familiar.

We might reflect today on how we use our gift of language, on our natural instincts when we engage in conversation, and whether there are moments when we use the gift of communication to be unnecessarily combative, manipulative, or cowardly. And we might thank God for the words of scripture, and commit once again to giving them primacy in our lives.

COLLECT

Almighty God,
you have made us for yourself,
and our hearts are restless till they find their rest in you:
pour your love into our hearts and draw us to yourself,
and so bring us at last to your heavenly city
where we shall see you face to face;
through Jesus Christ our Lord.

Saturday 18 October
Luke the Evangelist

Luke 1.1-4

'... so that you may know the truth concerning the things about which you have been instructed' (v.4)

Today is the Feast of Luke the Evangelist, and intriguingly we are given not one of the action-packed sections of his Gospel, nor one of the great parables. We are given these first four verses, which effectively form a prologue. They are concise, and scholars tell us that they conform broadly to the standard form of the time. The intriguing figure of Theophilus appears, for one of only two occasions, the other being the opening of Acts, or 'Luke II' as it is sometimes called (v.1). We learn that Luke was not himself an eyewitness to the events he describes. We learn that he is a diligent investigator. We learn that both Luke and Theophilus believe that there is important truth here.

This is such a striking passage, and utterly unlike the openings of the other three canonical Gospels. As we celebrate St Luke today, and give thanks to God for those who transmitted the stories of faith to us, why not find some time today to read the opening passages of the other three Gospels, and wonder at how very different in style, and yet united in purpose, are the glorious Gospel texts.

Almighty God,
you called Luke the physician,
whose praise is in the gospel,
to be an evangelist and physician of the soul:
by the grace of the Spirit
and through the wholesome medicine of the gospel,
give your Church the same love and power to heal;
through Jesus Christ our Lord.

COLLECT

Reflection by **Tom Clammer** | 285

Monday 20 October

Psalms **80**, 82
I Maccabees 3.1-26
or 2 Chronicles 17.1-12
Mark 15.1-15

Mark 15.1-15

*'Pilate, wishing to satisfy the crowd, after flogging
Jesus, handed him over to be crucified' (v.15)*

The trial of Jesus was a miscarriage of justice. The evidence was rigged, contradictory and offered by false witnesses. The defendant was deemed to have condemned himself, though by law this was not admissible as evidence. The outcome was pre-determined. A criminal was released in exchange for the innocent. Crowds were manipulated and the verdict was forced upon a weak and ineffectual Roman governor. The death of Jesus was the work of supposedly devout, godly people. There is a dark side to believing. When the stakes are high and our deepest securities are threatened, religious people may not fight any more fairly than anyone else. When a religion puts its own God on trial and kills him, you know something is terribly wrong. Our goodness, our understanding of holiness, our certainties about our rightness, need as much conversion as our badness.

The novelist Graham Greene suggested there are three positive marks of authentic believers. Firstly, they have an uneasy conscience. That leaves them less likely to collude with atrocities (great or small). Secondly, they identify with all humanity, the whole mix of it, and so are unlikely to be seduced into political or religious extremism. Thirdly, the believer has a certain capacity for disloyalty to the authorities and powers. They will not be found 'just obeying orders'.

Believers are not immune from collusion, jealousy and extremism. But we may pray for their constraining and redeeming.

COLLECT

Almighty and everlasting God,
increase in us your gift of faith
that, forsaking what lies behind
and reaching out to that which is before,
we may run the way of your commandments
and win the crown of everlasting joy;
through Jesus Christ our Lord.

| *Reflection by* **David Runcorn**

Psalms 87, **89.1-18**
1 Maccabees 3.27-41
or 2 Chronicles 18.1-27
Mark 15.16-32

Mark 15.16-32

'And they crucified him' (v.24)

Crucifixions were public spectacles. Brutal beyond imagining, they were intended to intimidate and deter. So they took place by the busy cross roads leading to and from the city, probably on the edge of one of the quarries there. Golgotha may have gained its name after a rejected piece of rock that bore some resemblance to a human skull. It was the Passover festival in Jerusalem. Those roads would have been crowded with travellers, traders and impromptu gatherings – a bustling, holiday atmosphere. The crucifixion, shame and pain of Jesus was there for all to see and mock.

One of the crowd is named. Simon, father of Alexander and Rufus. This detail suggests that his sons were known in the early Christian community. He is 'coming in from the country'. Quite what that means is unclear. Cyrene was 850 miles away on the North African coast. We learn from another account that the mocking title on the cross was written in three languages. All worlds meet at this place. They still do.

And here comes the execution procession. Three that we know of. One of them has been so badly beaten he keeps stumbling and falling under the load of his cross. A passer-by is forced to carry his cross for him. And so it is that in a scene of otherwise relentless, loveless violence, there is a moment in which Jesus is cared for.

God, our judge and saviour,
teach us to be open to your truth
and to trust in your love,
that we may live each day
with confidence in the salvation which is given
through Jesus Christ our Lord.

COLLECT

Reflection by **David Runcorn** | 287

Wednesday 22 October

Mark 15.33-41

'My God, my God, why have you forsaken me?' (v.34)

Jesus' cry from the cross is the first verse of Psalm 22. There is a tradition in the Jewish faith that to speak the first line is to evoke the whole psalm. Perhaps Jesus was reciting this psalm, as strength and consciousness allowed. It is the anguished song of one persecuted, despised, feeling far from the care and comfort of God. The psalmist reminds God he has delivered past generations when they call upon him. In utter forsakenness he casts himself on the God he has known since he was born. He has no one else to turn to.

> 'Do not be far from me,
>   for trouble is near
>   and there is no one to help.' (Psalm 22.11)

The psalmist's physical agony could well describe crucifixion. 'All my bones are out of joint ... my tongue sticks to my jaw ... my hands and feet have shrivelled' (vv.14-16). The psalm includes a scene familiar at executions, as the soldiers divide up the victim's belongings: 'for my clothing they cast lots' (v.18).

But as so often in the psalms, the despair turns to praise and he even calls watchers to faith. He speaks with hope that 'the earth shall remember and turn to the Lord' (v.27). His sings of a world of justice and mercy, where all now abandoned shall 'proclaim his deliverance to a people yet unborn' (v.31).

This place is a beginning and not an end.

COLLECT

Almighty and everlasting God,
increase in us your gift of faith
that, forsaking what lies behind
and reaching out to that which is before,
we may run the way of your commandments
and win the crown of everlasting joy;
through Jesus Christ our Lord.

Psalms 90, 92
I Maccabees 4.1-25
or 2 Chronicles 20.1-23
Mark 15.42-end

Thursday 23 October

Mark 15.42-end

'Mary Magdalene and Mary the mother of Joses saw where the body was laid' (v.47)

Every detail in this part of the Good Friday story was verifiable. Joseph of Arimathea was a prominent member of Jerusalem high society and the governing authorities. His approach to Pilate for the body of Jesus was very public. He went 'boldly'. It would have taken great courage. Death by crucifixion was usually long and lingering. That Pilate checks Jesus is indeed already dead is understandable.

We know from other accounts that Joseph had given his own tomb for the body of Jesus. Its location would therefore have been well known. That such a respected figure had made such a personal gift to a man condemned for blasphemy and executed as a common criminal would have been notorious news, discussed endlessly in the small and intense world of Jerusalem society.

One particular detail would not have been made up. Women are named as witnesses. The word of a woman was not accepted in Jewish law. Nevertheless, they are about to replace men at the centre of the drama that follows.

The scene is set. But first the world must rest. It is the sabbath, even for Jesus – 'who at this evening hour lay in the tomb and so hallowed the grave to be a bed of hope for all who put their trust in you' (from the service of Night Prayer).

God, our judge and saviour,
teach us to be open to your truth
and to trust in your love,
that we may live each day
with confidence in the salvation which is given
through Jesus Christ our Lord.

COLLECT

Reflection by **David Runcorn** | 289

Friday 24 October

Psalms **88** (95)
I Maccabees 4.26-35
or 2 Chronicles 22.10 – end of 23
Mark 16.1-8

Mark 16.1-8

*'Do not be alarmed; you are looking for Jesus of Nazareth,
who was crucified. He has been raised' (v.6)*

The work of burial was unfinished. The women were unable to complete the rituals of anointing before the sabbath began. They have honoured the day of rest but can hardly get to the tomb quickly enough, without even a plan in place for gaining access to the body when they get there. But something had happened in the night. First light reveals an open and empty tomb. The body of Jesus gone. An angel tells them what has happened, with a message from Jesus, and instructs them to share this. But for the moment this is just too much. Speechless and overwhelmed, they flee in terror.

There is something very authentic and honest about this scene. They would have been grief-stricken and emotionally exhausted after the events of the previous days. Today we might be speaking of post-traumatic stress. The narrative attaches no blame to them for their reaction and their silence.

And there, abruptly, the original Gospel of Mark ends. Theories abound. Mark never finished it for whatever reason. The earliest scroll was damaged or torn and Mark's conclusion lost. Mark intended this to be the end. The truth is, we simply do not know.

But one effect of this unfinished story is that the ending is left to us. We have our own response of faith to make.

COLLECT

Almighty and everlasting God,
increase in us your gift of faith
that, forsaking what lies behind
and reaching out to that which is before,
we may run the way of your commandments
and win the crown of everlasting joy;
through Jesus Christ our Lord.

| *Reflection by* **David Runcorn**

Psalms 96, **97**, 100
1 Maccabees 4.36-end
or 2 Chronicles 24.1-22
Mark 16.9-end

Saturday 25 October

Mark 16.9-end

'Go into all the world and proclaim the good news' (v.15)

The lack of a positive conclusion to Mark's Gospel was a problem to the early Church. Ending the Gospel with women running away in terror and telling no one is hardly 'good news' and begs the question as to how word of the resurrection ever spread in the first place. Attempts were made to supply a suitable conclusion. Two versions found a place in the New Testament, though neither really 'works'. They are often placed in brackets, expressing a general reticence. Neither bear any resemblance to Mark's familiar writing style. The first is unnumbered and is a brief, rather formal statement. The second is a collection of short accounts, and fragments of teaching including some dramatic faith assertions.

The join onto the end of the main text is clumsy. Mary Magdalene was central in chapter 15 but is introduced here as if for the first time. She is given prominent and positive place, however, and the (male) disciples are rebuked by Jesus not just for their lack of faith, as in other accounts, but more specifically that 'they had not believed those who saw him after he had risen'. That is the women – whose testimony was true, and to be believed.

To these fragments and stories of faith in the crucified, risen, and ascended Lord, we add our own.

God, our judge and saviour,
teach us to be open to your truth
and to trust in your love,
that we may live each day
with confidence in the salvation which is given
through Jesus Christ our Lord.

COLLECT

Reflection by **David Runcorn** | 291

Monday 27 October

Psalms **98**, 99, 101
1 Maccabees 6.1-17
or 2 Chronicles 26.1-21
John 13.1-11

John 13.1-11

'Unless I wash you, you have no share with me' (v.8)

This week we revisit some of Jesus' parting words and actions before his arrest, trial and crucifixion. We are back at the Passover. Jesus, assuming the role of a servant, washes the feet of his disciples. He washes them all, including those who will betray or deny him, those who will fail to keep watch; those who will run away. All receive the same intimate, humble and loving care from Jesus. Peter is horrified by Jesus' servant-shaped actions. But once Jesus explains that they signify belonging, Peter asks to be drenched from head to toe. He wants to belong to Jesus with every fibre of his being.

Later, Jesus will ask his disciples and us to imitate his gestures of servanthood. But before the Spirit empowers us to do that, we need to accept Jesus serving us, even though it may feel too intimate or undeserved. Imagine Jesus kneeling and washing your feet, holding your body with his loving hands, knowing exactly the journeys your feet have been on, and how the calluses, bumps, bruises and chilblains of life have happened. Accepting Jesus ministering to us in this way means receiving him with an open, trusting heart, like a child or a partner. Here we find love – deep, strong, and true. Being washed and held in this love we learn to serve, not by our own efforts, but in the strength, love and humility of God, modelled for us in Jesus.

COLLECT

Blessed Lord,
who caused all holy Scriptures to be written for our learning:
help us so to hear them,
to read, mark, learn and inwardly digest them
that, through patience, and the comfort of your holy word,
we may embrace and for ever hold fast
the hope of everlasting life,
which you have given us in our Saviour Jesus Christ.

| *Reflection by* **Catherine Williams**

Psalms 116, 117
Wisdom 5.1-16
or Isaiah 45.18-end
Luke 6.12-16

Tuesday 28 October
Simon and Jude, Apostles

Luke 6.12-16

'... he called his disciples and chose twelve of them' (v.13)

Today the Church celebrates Simon and Jude. We know little about these two apostles who are tenth and eleventh out of twelve on Luke's list. Simon is described as a zealot, a politically-minded Jewish nationalist. Jude is identified by his family relationships; he is the son of James. When researching Simon and Jude you will quickly find that they are almost always defined by who they are not before the commentator gets round to saying who they are and what they may have done. Simon is not Simon Peter, and Jude (or Judas) is not *that* Judas – the one who betrayed Jesus.

There is a good precedent for being defined by who we are not. When questioned by the religious authorities, John the Baptist established that he was not the Messiah, Elijah, or a prophet, before indicating his role in pointing the way to Jesus. Sometimes we have to journey through finding out who we are not before we can enter with confidence into who God is calling us to be and become. That adventure of discovery can be a painful one as the person we thought we were is reworked by the Spirit who enables space for our true self to blossom and flourish. God knows who we are becoming, but sometimes we need some convincing. Simon and Jude were called and chosen by Jesus, to witness to him throughout their lives. We are called and chosen to do the same.

COLLECT

Almighty God,
who built your Church upon the foundation
of the apostles and prophets,
with Jesus Christ himself as the chief cornerstone:
so join us together in unity of spirit by their doctrine,
that we may be made a holy temple acceptable to you;
through Jesus Christ our Lord.

Wednesday 29 October

Psalms 110, 111, 112
1 Maccabees 7.1-20
or 2 Chronicles 29.1-19
John 13.21-30

John 13.21-30

'Lord, who is it?' (v.25)

Did you ever experience one of those days at school when your teacher said someone in the class had done some terrible thing, and no one was going to lunch until the culprit was found? I used to shrink in my seat trying not to be seen. And though I was usually innocent, I often thought it might be me who had broken some petty rule. The tense atmosphere made us all feel guilty. I sense the disciples squirming as Jesus says one of them will betray him. They need to know who it is, so Peter gets the one closest to Jesus to ask: 'Lord, who is it?' Even then they don't realize that the one Jesus sends out into the night is being drawn into a perilous betrayal by Satan, the deceiver. This scene is especially heart-breaking because Judas is one of God's own. Called, chosen, trained and loved by Jesus, Judas is used by evil forces to try to snuff out the light.

Betrayals from inside the family, Church, friendship groups, workplaces, charities or political parties are the hardest to bear because we think we know and trust each other, and have often shared much together. I wonder how Jesus felt as he realized that no amount of love and care could keep Judas from betraying him. We're reminded that even those closest to Jesus can be tempted into betrayal. But let's remember too that betrayal is not the end of the story.

COLLECT

Blessed Lord,
who caused all holy Scriptures to be written for our learning:
help us so to hear them,
to read, mark, learn and inwardly digest them
that, through patience, and the comfort of your holy word,
we may embrace and for ever hold fast
the hope of everlasting life,
which you have given us in our Saviour Jesus Christ.

Psalms 113, 115
1 Maccabees 7.21-end
or 2 Chronicles 29.20-end
John 13.31-end

Thursday 30 October

John 13.31-end

'I will lay down my life for you' (v.37)

Jesus' new commandment seems so simple. It's very straightforward. We are to love one another. Jesus loves each of us, and in turn, we are to reflect that love to each other. He loves us first and we pass it on – rather like a relay race. So why are we often so terrible at it? Regularly we drop the baton of God's love and get into all manner of disputes and battles – falling out with each other, creating factions and spreading discord. When people look at the Church do they see God's love in action? Sometimes – but sadly not always.

Simon Peter's interaction with Jesus in this passage gives a clue to the problem. Peter wants to lay down his life for Jesus. In time he will do so, though not before his triple denial, restoration and encounter with the Spirit. Peter has jumped the gun – he's got above himself. It is Jesus who will lay down his life first, not just for Peter, but for the entire cosmos. Jesus' sacrifice will set the pattern for all subsequent sacrifices.

Maybe we struggle to love others as Jesus loves us because we have yet to embrace the enormity of being fully loved by God. That must come first. When we love in our own strength we fail. It is the reflection of God's love through us that enables the sacrifice of ego necessary for the flourishing of true love among God's people.

Merciful God,
teach us to be faithful in change and uncertainty,
that trusting in your word
and obeying your will
we may enter the unfailing joy of Jesus Christ our Lord.

COLLECT

Reflection by **Catherine Williams** | 295

Friday 31 October

Psalm 139
I Maccabees 9.1-22
or 2 Chronicles 30
John 14.1-14

John 14.1-14

'I will come again and will take you to myself' (v.3)

Sitting with a newly bereaved man, helping plan his mum's funeral, he suddenly turned to me and said: 'How did she get there – to heaven I mean?' I could see that he was deeply troubled by this and I paused to ponder my response. In the space, he added: 'She found it difficult to go new places on her own, she would have been so scared if she had to go alone.' Using this passage, I reassured him that Jesus promises to come and take us to be where he is. The man visibly relaxed. 'That's good', he said: 'She loved Jesus. She would have felt safe with him.' Our planning took a life-giving turn as we engaged more deeply with Jesus: the way, the truth and the life.

Both Thomas and Philip ask questions of Jesus which open up rich new seams in their experience and understanding of God. Thomas asks for clarity about the direction of travel. Philip asks for a vision of God. Jesus indicates that both these requests will be fulfilled by believing in him. It's good to question. Being curious and seeking truth opens new insight, and can take us to a deeper place in our relationship with God.

On this All Hallows Eve when our thoughts turn to both the living and the dead, what's the question you really want to ask Jesus? Ask it and be open to his answer.

COLLECT

Blessed Lord,
who caused all holy Scriptures to be written for our learning:
help us so to hear them,
to read, mark, learn and inwardly digest them
that, through patience, and the comfort of your holy word,
we may embrace and for ever hold fast
the hope of everlasting life,
which you have given us in our Saviour Jesus Christ.

| *Reflection by* **Catherine Williams**

Psalms 15, 84, 149
Isaiah 35.1-9
Luke 9.18-27

Saturday 1 November
All Saints' Day

Luke 9.18-27

'But who do you say that I am?' (v.20)

The disciples came up with a variety of answers when Jesus asked them what people were saying about him. If we went out with a camera today and filmed people answering the question, 'Who is Jesus?' we'd get a diversity of answers too, some more palatable than others. Some would be wildly inaccurate, some spot on, and some responses we wouldn't dare broadcast! Jesus follows up his generic question with a personal one: 'But who do *you* say that I am?' It's heartening that Peter, who often gets things spectacularly wrong, gets it right this time. Whatever, we think about Jesus, and however much we've learnt about him from others, there comes a point in our journey of faith when we're asked to nail our colours to the mast and make a personal commitment to Christ, 'the Messiah of God'. And that doesn't just happen once. Over and over again Jesus calls us deeper into relationship with him by whispering: 'But who do *you* say that I am?'

Today is All Saints' Day. All God's people are saints, connected within the body of Christ throughout time and eternity. We are connected to those who have gone before, those alive here and now and those yet to be born. Though we are one body of saintly believers each of us still needs to answer Jesus' question for ourselves: 'But who do *you* say that I am?'

Almighty God,
you have knit together your elect
in one communion and fellowship
in the mystical body of your Son Christ our Lord:
grant us grace so to follow your blessed saints
in all virtuous and godly living
that we may come to those inexpressible joys
that you have prepared for those who truly love you;
through Jesus Christ our Lord.

COLLECT

Monday 3 November

Psalms **2**, 146 *or* 123, 124, 125, **126**
Isaiah 1.1-20
Matthew 1.18-end

Isaiah 1.1-20

'Come now, let us argue it out' (v.18)

It would be nice to think that when I get into an argument, I'm not arguing so that I can win, but so that the truth may win. Sadly, I'm not always sure that's the case. We often have a lot of misplaced pride on the line when we get into arguments. When Isaiah speaks for God, however, we may be sure that God's pride isn't at stake. God wants truth to prevail.

As ever when the prophet speaks there's good news and bad news. The bad news is that both personally and in their worship the people of Judah and Jerusalem are making a serious mess of things. The good news is that if they cease to do evil and learn to do good, they will be utterly forgiven and become 'like snow'.

Arguing with God could seem to be a somewhat one-sided activity, though there's plenty of precedent for it in the Psalms, for example. We're unlikely to win, but the beauty is that God invites us to be completely open and honest when we pray. As we're won over by the gracious logic of God's love, we find a deeper release and freedom in the truth then revealed to us. The lovely thing is to be respected and trusted enough to argue.

Perhaps this is how we might approach all our reading of Scripture. To read the Bible is to enter a conversation with God in which we are all committed to unearthing the truth and living it fully for the sake of the world.

COLLECT

Almighty and eternal God,
you have kindled the flame of love in the hearts of the saints:
grant to us the same faith and power of love,
that, as we rejoice in their triumphs,
we may be sustained by their example and fellowship;
through Jesus Christ our Lord.

Psalms **5**, 147.1-12 *or* **132**, 133
Isaiah 1.21-end
Matthew 2.1-15

Tuesday 4 November

Isaiah 1.21-end

'Afterwards you shall be called the city of righteousness' (v.26)

Isaiah likes to employ colourful language when he's in full flow. Jerusalem has become a whore; she houses murderers; everyone loves a bribe. Christians tend to use more moderate language today but global society is beset by similar faults. Greed, violence, unbridled capitalism, corruption in high places, the damage done to individuals on social media – it's all familiar territory.

Isaiah is only bearing witness to human frailty and the ubiquity of sin. However, he also points beyond such chaos to a future when the holy city will be put to rights, and justice and righteousness will win the day. The golden thread of hope is never far from Isaiah's thought, no matter how dire his warnings of judgement.

At the wedding of Prince Harry and Meghan Markle, Michael Curry, the Presiding Bishop of the Episcopal Church in the United States, used a powerful image in his sermon. He threw out a challenge to 'imagine a world where love is the way; imagine families where love is the way; imagine nations where love is the way; imagine commerce where love is the way; imagine international relations where love is the way ...' It sounds very much like the Kingdom of God.

Isaiah had something like the same vision. Perhaps we can too.

God of glory,
touch our lips with the fire of your Spirit,
that we with all creation
may rejoice to sing your praise;
through Jesus Christ our Lord.

COLLECT

Reflection by **John Pritchard**   299

Wednesday 5 November

Psalms **9**, 147.13-end
or **119.153-end**
Isaiah 2.1-11
Matthew 2.16-end

Isaiah 2.1-11

'... nation shall not lift up sword against nation' (v.4)

Once more Isaiah offers a beautiful vision of a world at peace, beyond the corruptions and violence of the age. We love the familiar words of this passage but we don't seem to have a clue how to achieve the goal. The American General Omar Bradley said, 'We have grasped the mystery of the atom and rejected the Sermon on the Mount. Ours is a world of nuclear giants and ethical infants. We know more about war than we know about peace, more about killing than we know about living.'

The nature of warfare has changed so that now we all live in a warzone. The poet Ben Okri said that war now takes place in people's minds and hearts and dreams. If that's the case then that's where the healing of these distortions must take place as well. There's a continuous line that runs from our violent hearts to our violent world. Christians believe in a gospel of reconciliation that flows from the restored brokenness of the cross and resurrection. It's in the world's wounds that peacemakers act as children of God.

In one major conflict an 11-year-old child raised his hand at school and asked, 'Sir, which side is Jesus on?' We need the confidence to answer, 'God is on everyone's side. So what shall we do about it?'

COLLECT

Almighty and eternal God,
you have kindled the flame of love in the hearts of the saints:
grant to us the same faith and power of love,
that, as we rejoice in their triumphs,
we may be sustained by their example and fellowship;
through Jesus Christ our Lord.

| *Reflection by* **John Pritchard**

Thursday 6 November

Isaiah 2.12-end

'... the Lord of hosts has a day' (v.12)

There seems to be a deep human longing for a special day when our ship comes in, when we win the lottery, when today's troubles are past and the sun will shine on us forever. And Isaiah longs for it too. Indeed he predicts it. Against every imaginable rival the glory of the Lord will rise 'to terrify the earth' (vv.19, 21). The day of the Lord became a regular feature of prophetic writing when enemies would be routed and righteousness revealed.

Inasmuch as we might associate this day with the last judgement it might seem something to fear. I'm not too keen for my misdeeds, mis-thoughts and misjudgements to be exposed to scrutiny. But inasmuch as we might instead associate this day with the new creation inaugurated by the resurrection it becomes a time of radiant hope. I'm content to leave that day with the Lord who revealed his lavish, extravagant love in the person and work of Jesus.

In the meantime, there's more than enough to be done to make the world more peaceful, just and kind. Civil rights leader Martin Luther King said, 'We are now faced with the fact that tomorrow is today. We are confronted with the fierce urgency of now.' Or, in the words of martyred theologian Dietrich Bonhoeffer, 'Make up your mind and come out into the tempest of living.' Today is the day.

God of glory,
touch our lips with the fire of your Spirit,
that we with all creation
may rejoice to sing your praise;
through Jesus Christ our Lord.

COLLECT

Reflection by **John Pritchard** | 301

Friday 7 November

Psalms **16**, 149 *or* 142, **144**
Isaiah 3.1-15
Matthew 4.1-11

Isaiah 3.1-15

'It is you who have devoured the vineyard' (v.14)

Isaiah is describing a society in a state of collapse. The usual structures, norms and values no longer apply and it's the leaders who must take most of the blame. In the West, where democracy is under increasing strain, it's also leaders in public and Church life who get blamed for the malaise.

The truth of course is more complex. In our climate emergency, for example, we all have to hear the challenge that it is we who have devoured the vineyard. We are all the perpetrators of over-consumption and selfishness in relation to an environment that has been ravished and exploited. Most of us reading these words are among the richest few percent of the world's population and consuming the largest proportions of its natural resources. It could be said that the Lord has risen 'to argue his case' (v.13) for many years now. We know the score. What is it that holds the world back from the massive shift in global policies in relation to climate and the environment that we clearly need? We know the answer: the short-term self-interest of every human group.

We need a new starting point. The playwright David Hare once said, 'Make up your mind, you Christians. Either the gospel is true, which changes everything and you're forced totally to reconstruct the model of the universe you carry in your head, or it's fantasy and changes nothing.'

We believe the first. Let's act on it.

COLLECT

Almighty and eternal God,
you have kindled the flame of love in the hearts of the saints:
grant to us the same faith and power of love,
that, as we rejoice in their triumphs,
we may be sustained by their example and fellowship;
through Jesus Christ our Lord.

| *Reflection by* **John Pritchard**

Psalms **18.31-end**, 150 *or* **147**   **Saturday 8 November**
Isaiah 4.2 – 5.7
Matthew 4.12-22

Isaiah 4.2 – 5.7

'... judge between me and my vineyard' (5.3)

In the seventeenth century, an Irish clergyman called Nahum Tate wrote happy endings for Shakespeare's tragedies so that, for example, in his version of King Lear the king is restored to his throne, Cordelia recovers, and she and Edgar go on to marry happily – and that's how King Lear was performed until 1843.

It could look as if the chapter 4 section of today's reading is that kind of 'correction', a happy-ever-after ending after the judgement and doom-like predictions of the prophet's main message. However, the strands of tragedy and triumph are both part of Isaiah's message. There are promises of a glorious future alongside the constant dire warnings. Prophets don't so much *fore-tell* the future as *forth-tell* the present; they lay out the consequences of contemporary policies and behaviours.

That remains one of the Church's responsibilities under God – to offer society the plumbline or straight-measure of God's truth as far as we are able to discern it from scripture, tradition, and reason. It means that the Church's leaders will always be blamed for 'being political' or rather, 'being political on the wrong side'. The reality was well described by Archbishop Desmond Tutu when he said, 'I am puzzled about which Bible people are reading when they suggest that religion and politics don't mix.' Christians have to stay faithful both to the golden future of the new creation and to the serious implications of human folly.

And to speak of both.

God of glory,
touch our lips with the fire of your Spirit,
that we with all creation
may rejoice to sing your praise;
through Jesus Christ our Lord.

COLLECT

Reflection by **John Pritchard** | **303**

Monday 10 November

Psalms 19, **20** *or* 1, 2, 3
Isaiah 5.8-24
Matthew 4.23 – 5.12

Isaiah 5.8-24

'But the Lord of hosts is exalted by justice' (v.16)

In the classic TV series *Dad's Army,* Private Frazer was well known for his frequent lament, 'We're doomed.' Many conversations today over a drink or around a table or while watching the news revolve around the same theme. There are so many problems facing our angry world and its damaged fabric. Isaiah wasn't slow to point out the shortcomings of Judah and Jerusalem either. Pride, selfishness, drunkenness, injustice – all these point to the inevitability of God's judgement. When good is called evil and evil good it is obvious that such a society is doomed.

It's tempting for people of faith, inspired by the prophets, to adopt a similar high tone today and to condemn racketeering (v.8), selfish consumption (vv.11, 12), corruption (v.23) and a host of other social evils. The effect, however, is rarely edifying and the result is that people become resistant to the good news that Christians are trying to offer. How are we to balance the 'yes' and the 'no' of the gospel?

One Christian response to Isaiah's message might be that 'in [Christ] every one of God's promises is a yes' (2 Corinthians 1.20). That needs to provide the context for whatever negative observation we might be offering. For whatever social or personal ill we face Christ offers a more attractive alternative – a yes. Communicating the truth is often a matter of tone and style more than anything else. May we speak today with the graciousness of Christ.

C O L L E C T	Almighty Father, whose will is to restore all things in your beloved Son, the King of all: govern the hearts and minds of those in authority, and bring the families of the nations, divided and torn apart by the ravages of sin, to be subject to his just and gentle rule; who is alive and reigns with you, in the unity of the Holy Spirit, one God, now and for ever.

| *Reflection by* **John Pritchard**

Psalms **21**, 24 *or* **5**, 6 (8)
Isaiah 5.25-end
Matthew 5.13-20

Tuesday 11 November

Isaiah 5.25-end

'... the light grows dark with clouds' (v.30)

The vivid language of this passage would have struck a chord with many peoples waiting in terror for an imminent invasion. From Britain in 1940 and Berlin in 1945 to Baghdad in 1993 and Ukraine in 2022, civilians have had to face the prospect of unknown and possibly untold suffering. The galling thing about Isaiah's prophecy, however, is that the one who has invited the enemy into their country is God himself, the One who was supposed to be their guide and guard. God seems to want the Assyrians to be his agents of judgement.

This way of seeing history has a long pedigree, but it assumes a particular way of seeing God's action in the world that needs some interpreting. God is indeed completely involved in the life of the world from the miracle of the molecule to the behaviour of humans, but to attribute wars and other disasters to God's direct ordering of events is to leave God facing a considerable charge-sheet. Perhaps it's more helpful to see God's actions as those of parents who engage constantly with their children through love, persuasion, encouragement and argument, but who know that ultimately, they have created free agents and that in the very act of creating those children they have limited their own freedom.

We bear the heavy responsibility of freedom to live in light or in darkness. What we do every day contributes to our success or failure in handling our God-given liberty.

God, our refuge and strength,
bring near the day when wars shall cease
and poverty and pain shall end,
that earth may know the peace of heaven
through Jesus Christ our Lord.

COLLECT

Reflection by **John Pritchard** | 305

Wednesday 12 November

Psalms **23**, 25 *or* **119.1-32**
Isaiah 6
Matthew 5.21-37

Isaiah 6

'Whom shall I send ...?' (v.8)

Isaiah's overwhelming experience of encountering God's holiness shapes his whole future ministry. Only Moses, Isaiah and Jeremiah in the Old Testament are entrusted with this level of intimacy with God and it leaves the prophet feeling utterly unworthy. Isaiah is then commissioned to take the hard message of catastrophic judgement to Jerusalem and Judah, with verse 13 being the only half-hint that there might be a way through. Strange that this is a common reading at an ordination service!

The point of convergence between this passage and ordination, of course, is the seminal nature of the experience both for prophet and ordinand. And not only those being ordained but many other Christians can point to seminal moments of conversion and call, times when everything fell into place and the future course of life was given significant shape.

Sometimes, however, it doesn't seem to work out and the seminal experience goes awry. In one of G.K. Chesterton's stories, Father Brown says, 'We have taken a wrong turning and come to a wrong place. Never mind. One can sometimes do good by being the right person in the wrong place.' Either way – gladly following a clear call or making good a wrong turning – the seraph can still bring a live coal from the altar and touch our lips, giving us the confidence that we are trusted as messengers. And the 'big picture' message we take out to others is one of love, not fear. Because only love transforms.

C	Almighty Father,
O	whose will is to restore all things
L	in your beloved Son, the King of all:
L	govern the hearts and minds of those in authority,
E	and bring the families of the nations,
C	divided and torn apart by the ravages of sin,
T	to be subject to his just and gentle rule;
	who is alive and reigns with you,
	in the unity of the Holy Spirit,
	one God, now and for ever.

| *Reflection by* **John Pritchard**

Psalms **26**, 27 *or* 14, **15**, 16
Isaiah 7.1-17
Matthew 5.38-end

Thursday 13 November

Isaiah 7.1-17

'... the young woman is with child and shall bear a son' (v.14)

The date is about 735 BC, and Ahaz is on the throne. When he refuses to join Syria and Israel in their alliance to resist the threat of Assyrian invasion, those two kingdoms attack Judah instead, and it's at this point that Isaiah goes to Ahaz with God's message that a young woman has already conceived and will bear a son with the significant name 'God with us.' Then, as usual, there's good news and bad news. The good news is that the threatening nations will soon have departed; the bad news is that the Assyrians will then sweep into Judah.

Kate Bowler was a young theologian with everything at her feet. She had her doctorate, tenure at her university, she had married and given birth to a small son. Then she found she had stage four cancer which is usually terminal. She wrote a remarkable book at that time: *Everything happens for a reason – and other lies I have loved.* In it she recognizes that she should have felt angry but she actually felt loved. And she concluded that the most important truths were these: 'God is here; we are loved; that is enough.'

That's a good statement to try on for size. It echoes the truth of Immanuel, God with us. It echoes the promise of Paul that nothing can separate us from God's love (Romans 8.39). It echoes the experience of countless Christians that whatever the situation 'God with us' is enough.

God, our refuge and strength,
bring near the day when wars shall cease
and poverty and pain shall end,
that earth may know the peace of heaven
through Jesus Christ our Lord.

COLLECT

Friday 14 November

Isaiah 8.1-15

'... the mighty flood waters ... will sweep on into Judah as a flood'
(vv.7, 8)

Ahaz has made a poor choice for Judah. Resisting the invitation of Syria and Israel to fight off the Assyrians, not only are those two small nations soon subdued but the Assyrians are about to sweep through Judah like a flood. The image is very vivid – the waters will reach up to the neck and fill the land.

It's hard to keep going indefinitely when disaster follows disaster. It's the tragic experience of many people and it makes you wonder how they survive. In his book *The Shape of Living*, the theologian David Ford writes of 'multiple overwhelmings', something that we may have felt in our own lives at times. Sometimes when you reach the end of your rope you just have to tie a knot and hang on. The image of water flooding your life, entering every crevice, can seem particularly apt: under great pressure, anxiety or pain, we can feel like we are drowning. A nun working in desperate times in Chile wrote a poem in which she spoke of water which had seemed like a friendly neighbour beginning to creep up, to shift silently across the sand, flowing like an open wound. Finally, she declares, there's no escape and you have to learn to breathe under water.

It's that breathing under water that can prove elusive but is often the finest religious response to suffering. There's no magic trick in faith that enables us to escape the pain of living. But there is an infinite resource in the presence and love of God, forever breathing life into our hearts, even under water.

COLLECT

Almighty Father,
whose will is to restore all things
in your beloved Son, the King of all:
govern the hearts and minds of those in authority,
and bring the families of the nations,
divided and torn apart by the ravages of sin,
to be subject to his just and gentle rule;
who is alive and reigns with you,
in the unity of the Holy Spirit,
one God, now and for ever.

| *Reflection by* **John Pritchard**

Psalms **33** *or* 20, 21, **23**
Isaiah 8.16 – 9.7
Matthew 6.19-end

Saturday 15 November

Isaiah 8.16 – 9.7

'The people who walked in darkness have seen a great light' (9.2)

The words echo forth across time from the eighth century BC to countless carol services in our day where puzzled congregants, uncertain of the meaning, nevertheless give in to the poetry of the occasion. As throughout Isaiah's prophecies, the images are powerful. 'Those who lived in a land of deep darkness (Israel, Judah, or your own city or neighbourhood), on them light has shined.' We are all included in the glorious possibilities laid out in this familiar passage. The coming Prince of Peace will bring justice, joy and freedom to all who want it.

Most of us have heard these promises so often that after Christmas they end up in a trunk of nostalgia kept in the attic along with the decorations. What matters is keeping hold of the words and bringing them into our daily lives and our present hopes. These are words to inhabit, not to pack away. But the inhabiting mustn't turn gold into lead. The sheer richness of poetic language is its strength. The poet Emily Dickinson said that the way she knew something was true poetry was because it made her feel physically that the top of her head had been blown off. Another poet, A.E. Housman spoke of a constriction of the throat and tears in the eyes.

The poetic nature of the language in passages like this is the way the truth stays alive in our hearts. The way to make the most of words like those in this passage is to say them every day and let them enlarge our imagination.

> God, our refuge and strength,
> bring near the day when wars shall cease
> and poverty and pain shall end,
> that earth may know the peace of heaven
> through Jesus Christ our Lord.

COLLECT

Reflection by **John Pritchard** | 309

Monday 17 November

Psalms 46, **47** *or* 27, **30**
Isaiah 9.8 – 10.4
Matthew 7.1-12

Isaiah 9.8 – 10.4

*'For all this, his anger has not turned away;
his hand is stretched out still' (10.4)*

Sometimes wickedness has to be named and called out. The refrain quoted here is repeated four times in today's reading from Isaiah. Hot on the heels of a familiar and wonderful prophecy at the beginning of chapter 9 come words of condemnation and judgement. They build up a picture of a regime that is the opposite of justice and righteousness, the qualities that will characterize the child who is born to be a wonderful counsellor and prince of peace. The people act out of pride and arrogance while their rulers lead them astray and their prophets speak lies.

It is difficult to talk about an angry God, but the imagery here suggests that evil brings its own reward as it burns like a fire, consuming everything in its path. When leaders make laws that are oppressive and unjust, such that the poor suffer, there are consequences as people turn on each other in their confusion and despair. What will it take to turn this bleak despair around? As we draw near to the season of Advent the cries of the suffering and the oppressed are with us still.

The great Advent themes around the coming of God, including the Four Last Things: heaven, hell, death and judgement, shake us out of our complacency about the way the world is. The longings of those in darkness know that only God can bring the change they yearn for. Pray for the victims of unjust laws in our society.

COLLECT | Heavenly Father,
whose blessed Son was revealed
   to destroy the works of the devil
and to make us the children of God and heirs of eternal life:
grant that we, having this hope,
may purify ourselves even as he is pure;
that when he shall appear in power and great glory
we may be made like him in his eternal and glorious kingdom;
where he is alive and reigns with you,
in the unity of the Holy Spirit,
one God, now and for ever.

| *Reflection by* **Liz Hoare**

Psalms 48, **52** *or* 32, **36**
Isaiah 10.5-19
Matthew 7.13-end

Isaiah 10.5-19

'Shall the axe vaunt itself over the one who wields it, or the saw magnify itself against the one who handles it?' (v.15)

There are very good reasons for the health and safety laws surrounding the use of dangerous machinery. Today, power saws and huge mechanized cutters have replaced the tools from the time of the prophet Isaiah, but even today's tools can be deadly if not handled wisely.

Today's reading offers a brief study in power used without accountability. It is full of vivid imagery: a rampaging bull, a nest full of abandoned eggs, tools that wield themselves and a burning fire. The backstory to all this is the making of iniquitous laws and oppressive statutes that prevent the needy from getting justice – especially the widows and orphans, always regarded as the most vulnerable members of society (10.1,2). The people responsible for this situation have abandoned all sense of accountability or the need for just laws that protect the weakest in society. Their actions render them no better than the enemy that is destroying them.

All of us have power to a greater or lesser degree and in Christ, Christians are shown the good way to use it: blessing the poor, walking the path of humility, and acknowledging that all power belongs to God. Over and over, Isaiah is called on to proclaim oracles condemning indiscriminate use of power together with the inevitable consequences that follow in its wake. Regularly meditating on how we use whatever power we have and placing ourselves before God with humble hearts is the only safe way to proceed.

Heavenly Lord,
you long for the world's salvation:
stir us from apathy,
restrain us from excess
and revive in us new hope
that all creation will one day be healed
in Jesus Christ our Lord.

COLLECT

Reflection by **Liz Hoare**

Wednesday 19 November

Isaiah 10.20-32

'A remnant will return, the remnant of Jacob, to the mighty God' (v.21)

It's surprising what can be done with a remnant. For years I had a piece of carpet in my small hallway, bought for a song, that welcomed visitors with its cheerful warming colour. With today's trend for recycling and upcycling, stunning things can be made out of left-over materials. In many of our shrinking congregations, it can feel as though only a remnant remains to keep things going. When everyone else has departed, it's hard for those who are left to stay positive and hopeful.

It's tempting to look back to the glory days, to wring our hands over what might have gone wrong, or to give in to the insidious whispers that it's no use trying and that we too, should give up. Where should we look for encouragement? In today's reading there is destruction all around: nowhere seems safe from the tempest that is raging. There is plenty more destruction to come in the book of Isaiah the prophet, but there are also persistent glimpses of hope and new life. Small and infrequent they might be, but they are never drowned out, and it is out of these glimmers of life that God will bring about a new world.

Isaiah's remnant had learned the importance of leaning on God rather than on the transient forces at work. This would have required courage and patience, but above all trust in the God of the impossible. Allow your imagination to catch a vision of new life and hope that sees with God's eyes.

COLLECT

Heavenly Father,
whose blessed Son was revealed
    to destroy the works of the devil
and to make us the children of God and heirs of eternal life:
grant that we, having this hope,
may purify ourselves even as he is pure;
that when he shall appear in power and great glory
we may be made like him in his eternal and glorious kingdom;
where he is alive and reigns with you,
in the unity of the Holy Spirit,
one God, now and for ever.

| *Reflection by* **Liz Hoare**

Thursday 20 November

Isaiah 10.33 – 11.9

'He shall not judge by what his eyes see, or decide by what his ears hear' (v.3)

From the remnant, now a rootstock, will emerge a new kind of leader on whom the Spirit of God rests. Here is life coming from an unexpected place, perhaps from a tree cut down in its prime. Learning to lean on God the source of life will bring about a new beginning, symbolized by a fresh green shoot.

In our world, where we often judge by appearances, it is startling to read that this leader will not rely on what his eyes tell him. We are also bombarded by soundbites and noisy rhetoric, but again, this person will not be swayed by loud, competing voices. Instead, the Spirit of the Lord will be the touchstone of sound judgement, for it is the spirit of wisdom and understanding, of counsel and might, of knowledge and the fear of the Lord.

We know instinctively that this kind of leader is rare. The pressure is on quick results, visible success and projecting the right image. It takes courage and determination to go against the spirit of the age. Wisdom takes time and experience to learn, understanding is more complex than following a few instructions and getting it right first time. It demands slow and steady discernment exercised with a deepening over time. Standing for what is right and fair is not the path to world power and influence, but this leader delights in the fear of the Lord who hears the cries of the poor and needy and cares.

Heavenly Lord,
you long for the world's salvation:
stir us from apathy,
restrain us from excess
and revive in us new hope
that all creation will one day be healed
in Jesus Christ our Lord.

COLLECT

Friday 21 November

Psalms **63**, 65 *or* 31
Isaiah 11.10 – end of 12
Matthew 8.23-end

Isaiah 11.10 – end of 12

'With joy you will draw water from the wells of salvation' (12.3)

In 1984 the liberation theologian Gustavo Gutiérrez published a book entitled *We Drink From Our Own Wells*. In it, he wrote of the joy that comes from the conviction that suffering born out of injustice will be overcome because God is a God of life.

Imagine a community that has little in the way of this world's goods and is denied a voice among those who wield power over them. Yet it is a community that knows goodness and kindness and experiences joy in daily life. Perhaps the prophet was visualizing such a community coming together to draw the daily supply of water from its communal well. It is a safe place where children play and women laugh together as they work. Their song is the words of the previous verse: 'Surely God is my salvation; I will trust and not be afraid, for the Lord God is my strength and might; he has become my salvation.' Their perspective on life is completely different from the rampaging armies vying for top position among the ranks of the powerful. They do not need to be forever looking over their shoulder in case they are next to be toppled from their place in the pecking order.

In God's kingdom all have a place, all are welcome. Their songs of praise resound all around them. Give thanks for those who today bear witness to the resources to be found in God's wells of salvation, regardless of their material circumstances, and pray for them – and that we might learn from them.

COLLECT | Heavenly Father,
whose blessed Son was revealed
   to destroy the works of the devil
and to make us the children of God and heirs of eternal life:
grant that we, having this hope,
may purify ourselves even as he is pure;
that when he shall appear in power and great glory
we may be made like him in his eternal and glorious kingdom;
where he is alive and reigns with you,
in the unity of the Holy Spirit,
one God, now and for ever.

Reflection by **Liz Hoare**

Psalms **78.1-39** *or* 41, **42**, 43
Isaiah 13.1-13
Matthew 9.1-17

Saturday 22 November

Isaiah 13.1-13

'The oracle concerning Babylon that Isaiah son of Amoz saw' (v.1)

Reading the bleaker parts of the book of Isaiah, it's easy to forget that this is a collection of prophecies given to human beings to be proclaimed to other human beings. Vast armies strut across its pages, there are terrifying scenes of bloodshed, upheavals in the earth itself and a pervading atmosphere of panic, confusion and noise.

Chapter 13 opens with a reminder that Isaiah, son of Amoz, received an oracle from the Lord about one of Israel's enemies and was tasked with making it known. We don't know a huge amount about Isaiah, what he was like, what kind of lifestyle he lived. Scholars argue as to how many individual prophets contributed to the book that bears his name and how best to date the various sections of the book. What we can be sure of is that they spoke from the conviction that God had revealed his purposes in oracles and visions.

They didn't undertake their calling lightly or for popularity. It was easy enough to pour down wrath upon the surrounding nations, but Israel and Judah did not escape condemnation for the evil they perpetrated. What was it like to tell their own people that judgement was on them? We might wish to consider today's prophets of doom and ponder their predictions before we dismiss them as gloomy pessimists who should be ignored. As we have seen with the way climate scientists were once dismissed, we would do well to weigh their words carefully first.

Heavenly Lord,
you long for the world's salvation:
stir us from apathy,
restrain us from excess
and revive in us new hope
that all creation will one day be healed
in Jesus Christ our Lord.

COLLECT

Reflection by **Liz Hoare** | 315

Monday 24 November

Isaiah 14.3-20

*'The whole earth is at rest and quiet;
they break forth into singing' (v.7)*

The Little Book of Calm was a best-selling self-help book in the 1990s, advertised as an antidote to a global stress epidemic. It contains such nuggets of advice as focusing on the present or sipping peppermint tea when feeling anxious, and they doubtless offered varying degrees of effectiveness.

Verse 7 of our reading represents a small oasis of peace amidst a vigorous taunt against the enemy Babylon. It is not, however, a moment of self-induced calm generated through willpower alone. It comes rather from acknowledging God's sovereignty and resting in God's promise to restore his people. What follows makes for uncomfortable reading for Christians taught that it is wrong to relish the downfall of others – even our enemies – for it is a lengthy diatribe mocking the once proud and mighty king of Babylon. We can almost hear the triumphant sneers of the people who had once been so cruelly treated, now that the tables are turned: 'You too have become as weak as we are! You have become like us!' (v.10).

It is spiteful in an almost juvenile way. This is perhaps not a model for our prayers, though its mood is echoed in some of the psalms used daily in the Church's liturgies. A better model might be to focus on the rest and quiet gifted to the earth – and listen for the voice of the God of peace. As Isaiah affirms elsewhere, 'In returning and rest you shall be saved; in quietness and trust shall be your strength' (30.15).

COLLECT

Eternal Father,
whose Son Jesus Christ ascended to the throne of heaven
    that he might rule over all things as Lord and King:
keep the Church in the unity of the Spirit
and in the bond of peace,
and bring the whole created order to worship at his feet;
who is alive and reigns with you,
in the unity of the Holy Spirit,
one God, now and for ever.

| *Reflection by* **Liz Hoare**

Psalms **97**, 98, 100 *or* **48**, 52
Isaiah 17
Matthew 9.35 – 10.15

Tuesday 25 November

Isaiah 17

'You have forgotten the God of your salvation' (v.10)

The history of God's people is a tragic seesaw of repentance, renewed trust and forgetfulness. They demonstrate the all-too-human tendency to drift from the centre and lose the way. Here, the people have fashioned idols that do not deliver (v.8) and have planted quick-growing 'pleasant plants' which blossom almost at once, but do not produce a harvest of any worth (v.11).

Despite more failure and bitter experience recounted here, however, there are small signs of hope amid the bleakness. The prophet sees a day of repentance and a turning back to the one who saves. The people will abandon the idols that have commanded their care and attention and look again to their Saviour and their rock of refuge. The nations round about roar and create turmoil, but they will become like chaff before the wind (v.13).

In our own time, we too are prone to being distracted by the idols of achievement, the quick fixes that lack deep roots: we are pulled this way and that by the noisy clamour of conflicting voices demanding our attention. Like God's people throughout the Hebrew Scriptures, we need reminders of where our true centre lies. The psalms describe the ups and downs of the journey of faith with searing honesty, portraying a faithful God throughout – one who is likened to a rock.

What memories does the 'rock of salvation' stir in you and what situations need a turning towards that rock and the renewal of hope?

God the Father,
help us to hear the call of Christ the King
and to follow in his service,
whose kingdom has no end;
for he reigns with you and the Holy Spirit,
one God, one glory.

COLLECT

Wednesday 26 November

Psalms 110, 111, **112**
or **119.57-80**
Isaiah 19
Matthew 10.16-33

Isaiah 19

'Blessed be Egypt my people, and Assyria the work of my hands, and Israel my heritage' (v.25)

Can this be the same collection of prophecies as the earlier chapters recorded in Isaiah? Assyria has been blasted from the face of the earth, condemned outright and judged for its arrogance and violent behaviour. Egypt, Israel's bitter enemy, has, in this very same oracle, been flayed to the extent that their hearts melted within them (v.1).

It is a reminder that we cannot contemplate Isaiah's God in one dimension only. God's justice and mercy are inextricably intertwined, and we must not separate them. There is a great deal of judgement pronounced in Isaiah, but it is trumped by mercy. The claim made here is astonishing by any account. Egypt was the tyrannical overlord that had enslaved the people of Israel, causing God to call Moses to lead them out through the wilderness to the promised land. Their relationship was that of bitter enemies from that time on. Yet here, Egypt has become 'my people' too, alongside Israel and Judah. And Assyria, 'rod of my anger' just a while ago, is now 'the work of my hands'.

These epithets are intimate ones, that imply God's loving care and reconciliation. Egypt and Assyria thus take their place alongside the original chosen people of God to stand in the place of blessing rather than curse. They suggest a level of mercy and forgiveness that spreads out over the earth beyond our wildest hopes. May we never give up praying and working for reconciliation that looks like this.

C O L L E C T	Eternal Father,
	whose Son Jesus Christ ascended to the throne of heaven
	that he might rule over all things as Lord and King:
	keep the Church in the unity of the Spirit
	and in the bond of peace,
	and bring the whole created order to worship at his feet;
	who is alive and reigns with you,
	in the unity of the Holy Spirit,
	one God, now and for ever.

Psalms **125**, 126, 127, 128
or 56, **57** (63*)
Isaiah 21.1-12
Matthew 10.34 – 11.1

Thursday 27 November

Isaiah 21.1-12

*'Upon a watchtower I stand, O Lord, continually by day,
and at my post I am stationed throughout the night' (v.8)*

The prophet in today's passage has received a 'stern' vision, a translation that does not do justice to the full extent of its horrific nature, where the betrayer betrays and the destroyer destroys (v.2). The recipient of the oracle is appalled by what he sees and hears and recounts vividly how deeply it affects him. He describes it as being in great physical pain, likening it to giving birth, so that he can no longer see nor hear and his mind is reeling. It made me pause to reflect how inured I have become to horror depicted on news screens and in television drama.

But then God commands a lookout to be posted in order to announce what he sees (v.6) whether or not it is good news for the hearers. Alas, the signs are news of further destruction. Nevertheless, the cry goes up: 'What of the night?' meaning how much of the night is left, how much more of this must we endure? Back comes the enigmatic reply: 'Morning's coming. But for now, it is still night. If you ask me again, I'll give the same answer' (*The Message*).

The approaching season of Advent calls the followers of Christ to be watchful as we wait for God's coming and God's kingdom. There are many situations in the world where we might respond similarly: we cling to hope of a new dawn, but right now, things remain dark and difficult. We are all to be watchers and sentinels. How should we read the signs of the times with realism and hope?

God the Father,
help us to hear the call of Christ the King
and to follow in his service,
whose kingdom has no end;
for he reigns with you and the Holy Spirit,
one God, one glory.

COLLECT

Reflection by **Liz Hoare** | 319

Friday 28 November

Psalm **139** *or* **51**, 54
Isaiah 22.1-14
Matthew 11.2-19

Isaiah 22.1-14

*'... do not try to comfort me for the destruction of
my beloved people' (v.4)*

'I feel your pain' has become something of a cliché, yet empathy is a vital aspect of what it means to be human. The ability to step into someone else's shoes and enter their world imaginatively is crucial for the connections we seek in relationships. It is never helpful to say to someone that we know exactly what they are going through, for we can never know fully what it is like to be someone else, or be in a situation that we ourselves have not experienced. Nevertheless, drawing alongside another in their trauma and refusing to shy away from strong emotions is vital, because grief and pain lead the sufferer to a terrible place of isolation and hopelessness. But what if our comfort is not wanted?

There are situations in individual lives and in the world so dreadful that nothing can be said to bring comfort. The destruction of the speaker's beloved people here is simply too much to bear. The prophet refuses all efforts to provide comfort and wishes to be left alone as he pours out his torrent of grief. Is it possible to hear within the prophet's anguish God's own grief embedded there also? The oracle goes on to say that despite the evidence that disaster was unfolding, still the people did not turn to God or have regard for God's ways (v.11).

We follow a God who is no stranger to rejection and whose experience on the cross showed him both receiving and giving comfort to others. Today we pray for all who are in despair.

C O L L E C T	Eternal Father, whose Son Jesus Christ ascended to the throne of heaven that he might rule over all things as Lord and King: keep the Church in the unity of the Spirit and in the bond of peace, and bring the whole created order to worship at his feet; who is alive and reigns with you, in the unity of the Holy Spirit, one God, now and for ever.

| *Reflection by* **Liz Hoare**

Saturday 29 November

Isaiah 24

'As it shall be, as with the people, so with the priest' (v.2)

We are well aware that both warfare and natural disasters cause indiscriminate suffering. Despite technology that claims to pinpoint targets, homes, schools and hospitals continue to be destroyed by bombs, while earthquakes and tsunamis flatten whole communities in minutes. Why God allows this scale of undeserved suffering is one of the age-old questions that human beings ask, a question which those with faith in a God of love find almost impossible to answer.

Isaiah makes it even harder to offer a response by apparently portraying God as not just allowing suffering, but being its cause. Our reading begins with the bald statement that the Lord is about to lay waste the earth and make it desolate (v.1). It goes on to say that the earth will be utterly despoiled, 'for the Lord has spoken this word'. Most Christians, having tied themselves in knots trying to answer the unanswerable, find themselves alongside Job who realizes the God is God and they are not; God's ways will always be a mystery. Nevertheless, Job chooses to trust in this God who is ultimately on the side of life and hope, not death and destruction.

Even as we read this difficult chapter, we are told that there are signs of life as a remnant remains (v.6) who still have reason to offer praise and glorify God. While the oracle quickly turns back to the mood of terror, it seems that God's everlasting covenant can never be destroyed and in that we find our hope.

God the Father,
help us to hear the call of Christ the King
and to follow in his service,
whose kingdom has no end;
for he reigns with you and the Holy Spirit,
one God, one glory.

COLLECT

Reflection by **Liz Hoare** | 321

Seasonal Prayers of Thanksgiving

Advent

Blessed are you, Sovereign God of all,
to you be praise and glory for ever.
In your tender compassion
the dawn from on high is breaking upon us
to dispel the lingering shadows of night.
As we look for your coming among us this day,
open our eyes to behold your presence
and strengthen our hands to do your will,
that the world may rejoice and give you praise.
Blessed be God, Father, Son and Holy Spirit.
Blessed be God for ever.

Christmas Season

Blessed are you, Sovereign God,
creator of heaven and earth,
to you be praise and glory for ever.
As your living Word, eternal in heaven,
assumed the frailty of our mortal flesh,
may the light of your love be born in us
to fill our hearts with joy as we sing:
Blessed be God, Father, Son and Holy Spirit.
Blessed be God for ever.

Epiphany

Blessed are you, Sovereign God,
king of the nations,
to you be praise and glory for ever.
From the rising of the sun to its setting
your name is proclaimed in all the world.
As the Sun of Righteousness dawns in our hearts
anoint our lips with the seal of your Spirit
that we may witness to your gospel
and sing your praise in all the earth.
Blessed be God, Father, Son and Holy Spirit.
Blessed be God for ever.

Blessed are you, Lord God of our salvation,
to you be glory and praise for ever.
In the darkness of our sin you have shone in our hearts
to give the light of the knowledge of the glory of God
in the face of Jesus Christ.
Open our eyes to acknowledge your presence,
that freed from the misery of sin and shame
we may grow into your likeness from glory to glory.
Blessed be God, Father, Son and Holy Spirit.
Blessed be God for ever.

Passiontide

Blessed are you, Lord God of our salvation,
to you be praise and glory for ever.
As a man of sorrows and acquainted with grief
your only Son was lifted up
that he might draw the whole world to himself.
May we walk this day in the way of the cross
and always be ready to share its weight,
declaring your love for all the world.
Blessed be God, Father, Son and Holy Spirit.
Blessed be God for ever.

Easter Season

Blessed are you, Sovereign Lord,
the God and Father of our Lord Jesus Christ,
to you be glory and praise for ever.
From the deep waters of death
you brought your people to new birth
by raising your Son to life in triumph.
Through him dark death has been destroyed
and radiant life is everywhere restored.
As you call us out of darkness into his marvellous light
may our lives reflect his glory
and our lips repeat the endless song.
Blessed be God, Father, Son and Holy Spirit.
Blessed be God for ever.

Blessed are you, Lord of heaven and earth,
to you be glory and praise for ever.
From the darkness of death you have raised your Christ
to the right hand of your majesty on high.
The pioneer of our faith, his passion accomplished,
has opened for us the way to heaven
and sends on us the promised Spirit.
May we be ready to follow the Way
and so be brought to the glory of his presence
where songs of triumph for ever sound:
Blessed be God, Father, Son and Holy Spirit.
Blessed be God for ever.

---

*From the day after Ascension Day
until the Day of Pentecost*

Blessed are you, creator God,
to you be praise and glory for ever.
As your Spirit moved over the face of the waters
bringing light and life to your creation,
pour out your Spirit on us today
that we may walk as children of light
and by your grace reveal your presence.
Blessed be God, Father, Son and Holy Spirit.
Blessed be God for ever.

---

*From All Saints until the day before
the First Sunday of Advent*

Blessed are you, Sovereign God,
ruler and judge of all,
to you be praise and glory for ever.
In the darkness of this age that is passing away
may the light of your presence which the saints enjoy
surround our steps as we journey on.
May we reflect your glory this day
and so be made ready to see your face
in the heavenly city where night shall be no more.
Blessed be God, Father, Son and Holy Spirit.
Blessed be God for ever.

The Lord's Prayer and The Grace

Our Father in heaven,
hallowed be your name,
your kingdom come,
your will be done,
on earth as in heaven.
Give us today our daily bread.
Forgive us our sins
as we forgive those who sin against us.
Lead us not into temptation
but deliver us from evil.
For the kingdom, the power,
and the glory are yours
now and for ever.
Amen.

(or)

Our Father, who art in heaven,
hallowed be thy name;
thy kingdom come;
thy will be done;
on earth as it is in heaven.
Give us this day our daily bread.
And forgive us our trespasses,
as we forgive those who trespass against us.
And lead us not into temptation;
but deliver us from evil.
For thine is the kingdom,
the power and the glory,
for ever and ever.
Amen.

The grace of our Lord Jesus Christ,
and the love of God,
and the fellowship of the Holy Spirit,
be with us all evermore.
Amen.

An Order for Night Prayer (Compline)

The Lord almighty grant us a quiet night and a perfect end.
Amen.

Our help is in the name of the Lord
who made heaven and earth.

A period of silence for reflection on the past day may follow.

The following or other suitable words of penitence may be used

**Most merciful God,
we confess to you,
before the whole company of heaven and one another,
that we have sinned in thought, word and deed
and in what we have failed to do.
Forgive us our sins,
heal us by your Spirit
and raise us to new life in Christ. Amen.**

O God, make speed to save us.
O Lord, make haste to help us.

**Glory to the Father and to the Son
and to the Holy Spirit;
as it was in the beginning is now
and shall be for ever. Amen.
Alleluia.**

The following or another suitable hymn may be sung

Before the ending of the day,
Creator of the world, we pray
That you, with steadfast love, would keep
Your watch around us while we sleep.

From evil dreams defend our sight,
From fears and terrors of the night;
Tread underfoot our deadly foe
That we no sinful thought may know.

O Father, that we ask be done
Through Jesus Christ, your only Son;
And Holy Spirit, by whose breath
Our souls are raised to life from death.

The Word of God

Psalmody

One or more of Psalms 4, 91 or 134 may be used.

Psalm 134

1   Come, bless the Lord, all you servants of the Lord, ◆
    you that by night stand in the house of the Lord.

2   Lift up your hands towards the sanctuary ◆
    and bless the Lord.

3   The Lord who made heaven and earth ◆
    give you blessing out of Zion.

**Glory to the Father and to the Son
and to the Holy Spirit;
as it was in the beginning is now
and shall be for ever. Amen.**

Scripture Reading

*One of the following short lessons or another suitable
passage is read*

You, O Lord, are in the midst of us and we are called by
your name; leave us not, O Lord our God.

Jeremiah 14.9

(or)

Be sober, be vigilant, because your adversary the devil is
prowling round like a roaring lion, seeking for someone
to devour. Resist him, strong in the faith.

1 Peter 5.8,9

(or)

The servants of the Lamb shall see the face of God, whose
name will be on their foreheads. There will be no more night:
they will not need the light of a lamp or the light of the sun,
for God will be their light, and they will reign for ever and
ever.

Revelation 22.4,5

The following responsory may be said

Into your hands, O Lord, I commend my spirit.
Into your hands, O Lord, I commend my spirit.
For you have redeemed me, Lord God of truth.
I commend my spirit.
Glory to the Father and to the Son
and to the Holy Spirit.
Into your hands, O Lord, I commend my spirit.

Or, in Easter

Into your hands, O Lord, I commend my spirit.
    Alleluia, alleluia.
Into your hands, O Lord, I commend my spirit.
    Alleluia, alleluia.
For you have redeemed me, Lord God of truth.
Alleluia, alleluia.
Glory to the Father and to the Son
and to the Holy Spirit.
Into your hands, O Lord, I commend my spirit.
    Alleluia, alleluia.

Keep me as the apple of your eye.
Hide me under the shadow of your wings.

Gospel Canticle

Nunc Dimittis (The Song of Simeon)

Save us, O Lord, while waking,
and guard us while sleeping,
that awake we may watch with Christ
and asleep may rest in peace.

1 Now, Lord, you let your servant go in peace:
   your word has been fulfilled.

2 My own eyes have seen the salvation
   which you have prepared in the sight of every people;

3 A light to reveal you to the nations
   and the glory of your people Israel.

Luke 2.29-32

**Glory to the Father and to the Son
and to the Holy Spirit;
as it was in the beginning is now
and shall be for ever. Amen.**

**Save us, O Lord, while waking,
and guard us while sleeping,
that awake we may watch with Christ
and asleep may rest in peace.**

Prayers

Intercessions and thanksgivings may be offered here.

The Collect

Visit this place, O Lord, we pray,
and drive far from it the snares of the enemy;
may your holy angels dwell with us and guard us in peace,
and may your blessing be always upon us;
through Jesus Christ our Lord.
Amen.

The Lord's Prayer (see p. 325) may be said.

The Conclusion

In peace we will lie down and sleep;
for you alone, Lord, make us dwell in safety.

Abide with us, Lord Jesus,
for the night is at hand and the day is now past.

As the night watch looks for the morning,
so do we look for you, O Christ.

[Come with the dawning of the day
and make yourself known in the breaking of the bread.]

The Lord bless us and watch over us;
the Lord make his face shine upon us and be gracious to us;
the Lord look kindly on us and give us peace.
Amen.

Index of readings

REFLECTIONS FOR DAILY PRAYER
App

Make Bible study and reflection a part of your routine wherever you go with the Reflections for Daily Prayer App for Apple and Android devices.

Download the app for free from the App Store (Apple devices) or Google Play (Android devices) and receive a week's worth of reflections free. Then purchase a monthly, three-monthly or annual subscription to receive up-to-date content.

Easter Season

Thursday 18 April 2024

Psalm **136** or **37***
Exodus 25.1-22
Luke 1.57-end

Luke 1.57-end

'... to give light to those who sit in darkness and in the shadow of death' (v.79)

Here we listen to another song of praise - this time from the mouth of Zechariah, who is also filled with the Holy Spirit. He praises God for what he is about to do both in Jesus and in John; he roots it in the ancient promises of Israel, he tells of God's merciful memory and power, and swings the lens round to the present and the future, for through the ministry of John and Jesus, the people will know and experience God's freedom, forgiveness, salvation and peace.

It is a song about life and light, sung in the wake of the birth of a treasured baby boy. It is music amidst great wonder and expectation. And yet, it is a song that does not forget those in darkness and those who are dying. Those who are sitting in darkness and in the shadow of death are not ignored in this scene of celebration and

available at
amazon appstore

REFLECTIONS FOR SUNDAYS (YEAR C)

Reflections for Sundays offers over 250 reflections on the Principal Readings for every Sunday and major Holy Day in Year C, from the same experienced team of writers that have made *Reflections for Daily Prayer* so successful. For each Sunday and major Holy Day, they provide:

- full lectionary details for the Principal Service
- a reflection on each Old Testament reading (both Continuous and Related)
- a reflection on the Epistle
- a reflection on the Gospel.

This book also contains a substantial introduction to the Gospel of Luke, written by Paula Gooder.

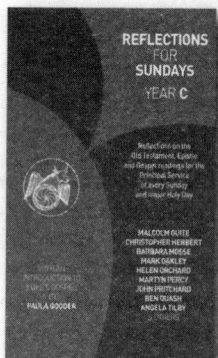

288 pages
ISBN 978 1 78140 039 5

Also available in Kindle and epub formats

REFLECTIONS ON THE PSALMS

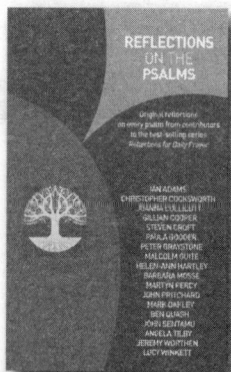

192 pages
ISBN 978 0 7151 4490 9

Reflections on the Psalms provides original and insightful meditations on each of the Bible's 150 Psalms.

Each reflection is accompanied by its corresponding Psalm refrain and prayer from the *Common Worship Psalter*, making this a valuable resource for personal or devotional use.

Specially written introductions by Paula Gooder and Steven Croft explore the Psalms and the Bible and the Psalms in the life of the Church.

REFLECTIONS FOR LENT 2025

Wednesday 5 March –
Saturday 19 April 2025

This shortened edition of *Reflections* is
ideal for group or church use during
Lent, or for anyone seeking a daily
devotional guide to this most holy
season of the Christian year.

It is also an ideal taster for those
wanting to begin a regular pattern of
prayer and reading.

Authors: Justine Allain Chapman,
David Ford, Malcolm Guite and John Perumbalath

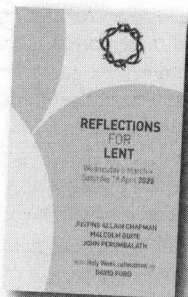

64 pages
ISBN 978 1 78140 484 3
Available November 2024

**Please note this book
reproduces the material
for Lent and Holy Week
found in the volume you are
now holding.**

RESOURCES FOR DAILY PRAYER

Common Worship: Daily Prayer

The official daily office of the Church of England,
Common Worship: Daily Prayer is a rich collection of
devotional material that will enable those
wanting to enrich their quiet times to develop
a regular pattern of prayer. It includes:

* Prayer During the Day
* Forms of Penitence
* Morning and Evening Prayer
* Night Prayer (Compline)
* Collects and Refrains
* Canticles
* Complete Psalter

896 pages • with 6 ribbons • 202 x 125mm
Hardback   978 0 7151 2199 3
Soft cased   978 0 7151 2178 8
Bonded leather   978 0 7151 2277 8